Communications in Computer and Information Science 3002

Series Editors

Rationale

The CCIS series is devoted to the publication of proceedings of computer science conferences. Its aim is to efficiently disseminate original research results in informatics in printed and electronic form. While the focus is on publication of peer-reviewed full papers presenting mature work, inclusion of reviewed short papers reporting on work in progress is welcome, too. Besides globally relevant meetings with internationally representative program committees guaranteeing a strict peer-reviewing and paper selection process, conferences run by societies or of high regional or national relevance are also considered for publication.

Topics

The topical scope of CCIS spans the entire spectrum of informatics ranging from foundational topics in the theory of computing to information and communications science and technology and a broad variety of interdisciplinary application fields.

Information for Volume Editors and Authors

Publication in CCIS is free of charge. No royalties are paid, however, we offer registered conference participants temporary free access to the online version of the conference proceedings on SpringerLink (http://link.springer.com) by means of an http referrer from the conference website and/or a number of complimentary printed copies, as specified in the official acceptance email of the event.

CCIS proceedings can be published in time for distribution at conferences or as post-proceedings, and delivered in the form of printed books and/or electronically as USBs and/or e-content licenses for accessing proceedings at SpringerLink. Furthermore, CCIS proceedings are included in the CCIS electronic book series hosted in the SpringerLink digital library at http://link.springer.com/bookseries/7899. Conferences publishing in CCIS are allowed to use our online conference service (Meteor) for managing the whole proceedings lifecycle (from submission and reviewing to preparing for publication) free of charge.

Publication process

The language of publication is exclusively English. Authors publishing in CCIS have to sign the Springer CCIS copyright transfer form, however, they are free to use their material published in CCIS for substantially changed, more elaborate subsequent publications elsewhere. For the preparation of the camera-ready papers/files, authors have to strictly adhere to the Springer CCIS Authors' Instructions and are strongly encouraged to use the CCIS LaTeX style files or templates.

Abstracting/Indexing

CCIS is abstracted/indexed in DBLP, Google Scholar, EI-Compendex, Mathematical Reviews, SCImago, Scopus. CCIS volumes are also submitted for the inclusion in ISI Proceedings.

How to start

To start the evaluation of your proposal for inclusion in the CCIS series, please send an e-mail to ccis@springer.com

Daniel Loebenberger · Marc Stöttinger
Editors

Migration and Agility in Cryptographic Systems

First International Workshop, MAgiCS 2026
Rome, Italy, May 10, 2026
Proceedings

Springer

Editors
Daniel Loebenberger
Fraunhofer AISEC / Amberg-Weiden
University of Applied Sciences
Amberg-Weiden, Germany

Marc Stöttinger
Hochschule RheinMain University
of Applied Sciences and Arts
Wiesbaden, Germany

ISSN 1865-0929 ISSN 1865-0937 (electronic)
Communications in Computer and Information Science
ISBN 978-3-032-28945-2 ISBN 978-3-032-28946-9 (eBook)
https://doi.org/10.1007/978-3-032-28946-9

This Springer imprint is published by the registered company Springer Nature Switzerland AG
The registered company address is: Gewerbestrasse 11, 6330 Cham, Switzerland

Preface

Cryptographic migration, specifically in the post-quantum setting, is a challenging and, in practice, mainly unsolved task. The problem sits at the intersection of applied IT and cryptographic engineering and addresses two fundamentally different audiences: practitioners who actually work in data centers and cryptographic engineers who design and implement cryptographic systems.

Despite advances in cryptographic technologies, the process of migrating existing systems and IT infrastructures to new standards presents significant challenges. Rapid transition appears to require a strong incentive to adopt new technology. The issue of migration is particularly prominent in the current transition towards post-quantum cryptography, which aims to protect data against future quantum computing threats. Due to its practical relevance, at least for high-security applications, there are numerous practical post-quantum migrations going on worldwide. Despite these worldwide activities, there is comparatively little research on the general structure of migration projects and how to suitably model cryptographic migration. In fact, many people consider migrating software and hardware components as a best-practice task.

So, people legitimately ask "Where Is the Research on Cryptographic Transition and Agility?" as David Ott did at IACR's Real World Crypto Symposium 2022 (RWC). Over recent years, the question of cryptographic transition and agility evolved from a perceived research gap into a more clearly emerging research area. While the practical transition to post-quantum cryptography gained momentum through standardization activities, migration handbooks, and governmental guidance, the scientific understanding of cryptographic migration as a structured problem was still comparatively limited in 2022, as highlighted by David Ott's question at RWC. In the following years, this began to change: migration and agility were increasingly recognized not merely as matters of best practice, but as topics requiring formal models, systematic methodologies, architectural support, and careful analysis of dependencies, complexity, and operational constraints. Against this backdrop, MAgiCS 2026 was established as the first Eurocrypt co-located workshop dedicated specifically to Migration and Agility in Cryptographic Systems, providing an international forum for consolidating and advancing this growing line of research.

For the workshop, we received 19 submissions, of which we selected 10 for presentation in Rome and one particularly practice-oriented contribution for a poster. The workshop contributions cover a coherent spectrum of challenges surrounding cryptographic migration and agility, ranging from conceptual foundations to system-level implementations and empirical evaluations.

A first cluster of works addresses Cryptography Bills of Materials (CBOMs) and system modeling, including standardization efforts based on CycloneDX, architecture-driven CBOM derivation, and the use of digital twins to analyze and support migration processes in complex IT infrastructures. Complementing these system-oriented perspectives, several papers investigate cryptographic migration itself, including comparative studies of existing PQC migration frameworks and formal approaches that aim to capture the inherent difficulty of migration through lower-bound intuitions.

A second thematic block focuses on benchmarking and performance evaluation of post-quantum schemes, highlighting both concrete resource-scaling behavior of signature schemes and methodological pitfalls in benchmarking approaches, particularly in the context of ML-DSA.

The proceedings also feature contributions on cryptographic agility, addressing policy externalization in large-scale infrastructures such as 5G PKIs, principled API design and assessment frameworks for agile applications, and the integration of agility considerations into emerging domains such as post-quantum blockchain systems. Together, these contributions give a multi-layered view on the transition to post-quantum cryptography, spanning formal theory, tooling and infrastructure, evaluation methodologies, and system design.

May 2026

Daniel Loebenberger
Marc Stöttinger

PQ SHIELD
genua. G+D XITASO

Organization

Program Chairs

Daniel Loebenberger	Fraunhofer AISEC / Amberg-Weiden University of Applied Sciences, Germany
Marc Stöttinger	Hochschule RheinMain University of Applied Sciences and Arts, Germany

Program Committee

Thomas Attema	TNO, Netherlands
Shivam Bhasin	Nanyang Technological University, Singapore
Fabrizio De Santis	Siemens AG, Germany
Silvio Dragone	IBM Research Europe - Zürich, Switzerland
Stephan Ehlen	Bundesamt für Sicherheit in der Informationstechnik, Germany
Stefan-Lukas Gazdag	genua, Germany
Michael Hutter	University of the Bundeswehr Munich, Germany; PQShield, UK
Michael Kasper	Fraunhofer Singapore, Singapore
Stefan Katzenbeisser	University of Passau, Germany
Juliane Krämer	University of Regensburg, Germany
Volker Krummel	Utimaco, Germany
Manfred Lochter	Bundesamt für Sicherheit in der Informationstechnik, Germany
Daniel Loebenberger	Fraunhofer AISEC / Amberg-Weiden University of Applied Sciences, Germany
Frank Morgner	Bundesdruckerei, Germany
Chris Müller	DB Systel GmbH, Germany
Ludovic Perret	EPITA; Sorbonne University, France
Hao Qin	National University of Singapore, Singapore
Melissa Rossi	CryptoExperts, France
Marc Stöttinger	Hochschule RheinMain University of Applied Sciences and Arts, Germany
Alexander Wiesmaier	Darmstadt University of Applied Sciences, Germany

Additional Reviewers

Thomas Aulbach
Jan Brinkmann
Michèle Feltz
François Gerard
Christian Holler
Stavros Kousidis
Carlos Lara-Nino
Eunisse Nzetchuen
Jong-Yeon Park
Maximiliane Weishäupl
Elif Yesilbek

Invited Contribution

Designing a Post-quantum Root of Trust: The Hardest Migration Problem You're Not Aware Of

Axel Y. Poschmann

PQShield Ltd

Abstract. The transition to post-quantum cryptography (PQC) is rapidly evolving from a theoretical concern into a regulatory and engineering imperative. Governments and standardization bodies—most prominently within Europe—are increasingly mandating or strongly recommending hybrid cryptographic approaches that combine classical and post-quantum primitives to ensure both near-term security and long-term resilience. While these developments provide necessary direction, they also expose a fundamental gap between high-level migration guidance and the realities of deploying secure systems in practice.

This talk argues that the primary bottleneck in post-quantum migration is not the selection or standardization of algorithms, but the redesign of the Root of Trust (RoT), and in particular secure boot mechanisms. As the immutable anchor of system integrity, the RoT is inherently resistant to change, yet it is precisely this component that must enforce and validate any transition to new cryptographic schemes. This creates a structural tension between the need for cryptographic agility and the constraints of long-lived hardware, certification regimes, and tightly coupled hardware–software architectures.

Focusing on PQ/T hybrid cryptography as currently advocated in European policy and industry practice, we analyze the challenges of integrating hybrid verification into secure boot chains. These include the design of dual-algorithm key hierarchies, and the management of increased computational and memory overhead. We further highlight practical constraints arising from silicon lifecycles, firmware update mechanisms, and certification processes, which collectively limit the achievable degree of agility in deployed systems.

Drawing on system-level perspectives and ongoing work in the FORTRESS project [1], this talk outlines emerging design patterns for hybrid Roots of Trust and identifies critical gaps in current research.

By grounding the discussion in secure boot and hardware-based trust anchors, this talk aims to shift the focus of post-quantum migration research toward the components where change is hardest but most consequential. Without rethinking the design of the Root of Trust, cryptographic migration strategies risk remaining theoretically sound but practically undeployable.

Keywords: Post-quantum cryptography · Root of Trust · Secure boot · Hybrid cryptography · Cryptographic agility

Reference

1. FORTRESS Project: Post-quantum Cryptography for Embedded Systems. https://pq-fortress.eu/

Contents

Poster Abstract

The Anatomy of Cryptography Bills of Materials: Standardization and Practice in CycloneDX

Basil Hess(✉)

IBM Research Europe,Zurich, Switzerland
bhe@zurich.ibm.com

Abstract. The migration to post-quantum cryptography (PQC) and increasing regulatory requirements such as the EU Cyber Resilience Act and DORA, increase the demand for comprehensive visibility into cryptographic assets across software systems. A Cryptography Bill of Materials (CBOM) provides a standardized inventory of cryptographic algorithms, protocols, certificates, and related material used within software components and services. This paper presents the anatomy of CBOMs as standardized in OWASP CycloneDX (ECMA-424), examining the object model for cryptographic assets, dependency relationships, and evidence capture. We analyze how CBOMs integrate with the broader xBOM ecosystem, including Software (SBOM), Operations (OBOM), Hardware (HBOM), and SaaS BOMs, to provide full-stack cryptographic transparency. Through practical use cases, we demonstrate how CBOMs enable policy-based compliance evaluation, support hybrid PQC migration strategies, and facilitate cryptographic agility. We discuss challenges in CBOM generation including naming ambiguities, configuration-driven cryptography, and the distinction between provision of cryptography and consumption. Finally, we outline evolution toward future CBOM revisions.

Keywords: Cryptography Bill of Materials · CBOM · CycloneDX · Post-Quantum Cryptography · Software Supply Chain · Bill of Materials · Cryptographic Inventory · PQC Migration

1 Introduction

Cryptography is pervasive in modern computing systems, embedded in source code, configuration files, certificates, hardware security modules, and cloud services. Organizations face increasing urgency to migrate to post-quantum cryptography (PQC) before cryptographically relevant quantum computers (CRQCs) become viable. Regulatory mandates reinforce this urgency. The EU Cyber Resilience Act (CRA) [7] strengthens requirements around secure software and associated technical documentation and SBOMs. The Digital Operational Resilience Act (DORA) [6] requires financial entities to manage ICT third-party

D. Loebenberger and M. Stöttinger (Eds.): MAgiCS 2026, CCIS 3002, pp. 1–19, 2026.
https://doi.org/10.1007/978-3-032-28946-9_1

risk, including security-relevant dependencies. The NIS2 Directive [5] mandates policies and procedures for the use of cryptography. The EU Roadmap for the Transition to Post-Quantum Cryptography [4] explicitly recommends machine-readable cryptographic inventories such as CBOM. In the United States, CNSA 2.0 [14] requires exclusive use of quantum-resistant cryptography for National Security Systems by 2033, with support mandated as early as 2025.

A Cryptography Bill of Materials (CBOM) addresses these requirements by providing a standardized, machine-processable object model to describe cryptographic assets and their dependencies. Unlike traditional software bills of materials (SBOMs) that enumerate software components and libraries, CBOMs capture the cryptographic dimensions: which algorithms are instantiated with what parameters, how they are configured at runtime, what protocols protect data in transit and at rest, and how certificates and keys are managed. An SBOM may reveal that an application depends on OpenSSL, but only a CBOM shows whether the application uses ECDH-secp256r1 for key exchange (vulnerable to quantum attacks) or ML-KEM-768 (quantum-resistant).

Creating actionable CBOMs presents several challenges. First, cryptographic algorithms suffer from naming ambiguities, the same algorithm might be known under different names (e.g., DESede, 3DES, TripleDES), and unique identifiers aren't globally available. Second, cryptographic behavior is often configuration-driven rather than hardcoded, making static code analysis insufficient. Runtime configurations, environment variables, and policies can alter which algorithms are negotiated. Third, modern systems employ hybrid cryptographic schemes combining classical and post-quantum algorithms (e.g., X25519-ML-KEM-768), requiring dependency modeling to capture both the hybrid construction and its constituents. Finally, cryptography extends beyond software to include hardware security modules (HSMs), trusted platform modules (TPMs), key management systems (KMS), cloud services, and operational configurations.

This paper presents a comprehensive analysis of CBOM standardization in OWASP CycloneDX, which has been ratified as the international standard ECMA-424. Our contributions include:

- An examination of the CycloneDX cryptographic asset model, covering algorithms, protocols, certificates, and related cryptographic material, and their dependencies
- Integration patterns with the broader xBOM ecosystem including OBOM, HBOM, SaaSBOM, and MBOM
- Practical use cases for policy-based compliance evaluation, CI/CD integration, and certificate lifecycle monitoring
- A real-world evaluation of actionable findings from CBOMs generated for source code (Keycloak) and a container image (nginx)
- Discussion of challenges and future directions for CBOM standardization

The remainder of this paper is organized as follows: Sect. 2 provides background on software supply chain transparency and the evolution of CycloneDX. Section 3 presents the anatomy of a CBOM with coverage of the cryptographic asset schema. Section 4 describes integration with other BOM types. Section 5 demonstrates practical applications. Section 6 evaluates CBOM generation on two real-world examples. Section 7 discusses challenges in the field and future work directions.

2 Background and Related Work

2.1 Software Bill of Materials

The concept of a Bill of Materials (BOM) originates from manufacturing, where it describes the components, parts, and materials required to build a product. In software, a Software Bill of Materials (SBOM) provides a formal, machine-readable inventory of components, libraries, and dependencies that comprise a software artifact. SBOMs gained significant attention following high-profile supply-chain incidents, notably the SolarWinds compromise [18] and Log4Shell (CVE-2021-44228) [11]. Two primary SBOM formats have emerged: SPDX (Software Package Data Exchange) [10], developed under the Linux Foundation, and CycloneDX [17], developed under OWASP. While SPDX originated from license compliance use cases, CycloneDX was designed from the outset for security and supply chain risk management. Both formats support expressing software components, their relationships, and associated metadata such as licenses, vulnerabilities, and provenance. CycloneDX was standardized as ECMA-424 [3] in 2024. Cryptographic support originated as fork by researchers that introduced cryptographic asset types in a v1.4 extension (2022), initially conceived as a reporting format for the cryptographic assets found in software projects. The scope has since broadened to integrate with the full feature set of CycloneDX. These extensions were integrated into the official specification through the CycloneDX Cryptography Working Group in v1.6 (2024), which added the `cryptographic-asset` type along with enhanced dependency semantics; v1.7 (2025) introduced comprehensive algorithm family definitions, naming patterns, and key lifecycle states per NIST SP 800-57 [1].

2.2 Related Work on Cryptographic Inventories

Prior to CBOM standardization, no well-defined reporting and exchangability format for cryptographic assets was available. Organizations rely on manual audits, static code analysis tools, or vendor-specific discovery solutions. NIST SP 1800-38 [12], currently in Initial Preliminary Draft, addresses this gap through two workstreams: cryptographic discovery (inventorying deployed cryptographic assets using automated tools) and interoperability testing (validating PQC algorithm interoperability across implementations). The project involves a consortium of industry participants and positions cryptographic inventory as a prerequisite for migration planning.

Research on cryptographic agility [15] has emphasized the importance of abstracting cryptographic implementations to enable seamless algorithm transitions. CBOMs support this goal by providing the visibility layer necessary to identify where cryptographic changes are needed and track migration progress.

The PKI Consortium [19], through its PQC Working Group and the PQC Capabilities Matrix (PQCCM), tracks vendor readiness for post-quantum algorithms and maintains a PQC Maturity Model (PQCMM) for evaluating organizational adoption. The Post-Quantum Cryptography Alliance (PQCA) [9], hosted by the Linux Foundation, develops open-source tooling including CBOMkit [20] for CBOM generation and compliance checking. Both organizations advocate cryptographic inventories as the foundation for migration governance.

3 Anatomy of a CBOM

A CycloneDX CBOM extends the standard BOM structure with cryptographic-specific components. At its core, a cryptographic asset is a `component` whose `type` is `cryptographic-asset`. The `cryptoProperties` object captures asset-specific attributes. Figure 1 illustrates the high-level structure. The specified CycloneDX schema is expressed as JSON, XML and Protobuf.

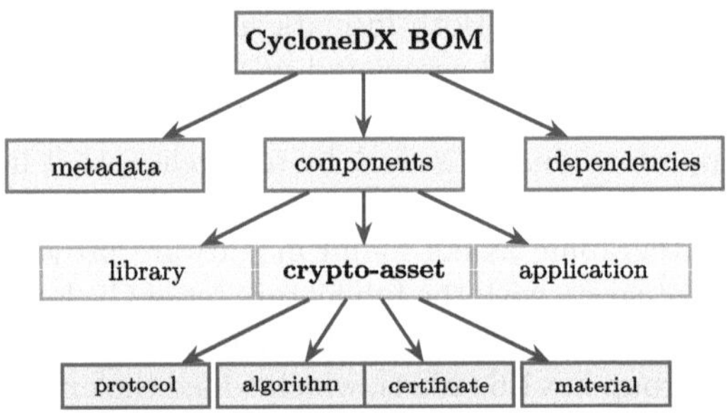

Fig. 1. CycloneDX BOM structure with cryptographic asset types. A CBOM uses components of type `cryptographic-asset` with subtypes for algorithms, protocols, certificates, and related cryptographic material.

3.1 Cryptographic Asset Types

CycloneDX defines four primary cryptographic asset types, each with specialized properties that capture the cryptography-relevant attributes necessary for compliance evaluation and migration planning.

Algorithms. Cryptographic algorithms represent the mechanisms used for cryptographic primitives, such as encryption, authentication, key exchange, and digital signatures and others. The `algorithmProperties` object, shown schematically in Fig. 2, captures:

- **Primitive**: The cryptographic building block (e.g., block cipher, stream cipher, hash, MAC, signature, public-key encryption, key encapsulation mechanism (KEM), key derivation function (KDF), key agreement, authenticated encryption, or combiner for hybrid schemes)
- **Algorithm Family**: A standardized identifier such as `AES`, `RSA`, `ML-KEM`, or `SLH-DSA`
- **Algorithm Name**: A name following a standardized naming pattern identifying the algorithm variant (e.g., `RSA-PKCS1-1.5-SHA-256-2048`)
- **Parameter Set Identifier**: Key lengths, digest sizes, or parameter set names (e.g., `256` for AES-256, `SHA2-128s` for SLH-DSA-SHA2-128s)
- **Elliptic Curve**: For ECC, the curve (e.g., secp256r1, curve25519)
- **Mode**: Block cipher mode of operation (`cbc`, `gcm`, `ctr`, etc.)
- **Padding**: Padding scheme (`pkcs7`, `oaep`, etc.)
- **Security Properties**: Specifies the formal guarantees about an algorithm's resistance to specific adversarial capabilities (e.g., IND-CPA, IND-CCA and IND-CCA2 security for KEMs)
- **Crypto Functions**: The functions available or implemented for the algorithm (e.g., keygen, encrypt, decrypt, tag)

```
"algorithmProperties": {
  "primitive": "kem",
  "algorithmFamily": "ML-KEM",
  "parameterSetIdentifier": "768",
  "executionEnvironment":
    "software-plain-ram",
  "implementationPlatform":
    "x86_64",
  "certificationLevel":
    ["fips140-3-l1"],
  "cryptoFunctions":
    ["keygen","encapsulate",
     "decapsulate"],
  "nistQuantumSecurityLevel": 3
}
```

```
"protocolProperties": {
  "type": "tls",
  "version": "1.3",
  "cipherSuites": [{
    "name":
     "TLS_AES_256_GCM_SHA384",
    "algorithms": [
      "aes-256-gcm",
      "sha-384"
    ],
    "identifiers":
      ["0x13,0x02"]
  }]
}
```

Fig. 2. Example `algorithmProperties` (left, ML-KEM-768) and `protocolProperties` (right, TLS 1.3 cipher suite) in CycloneDX 1.7.

Additionally, algorithms specify execution environment (software, hardware, TEE), implementation platform, and the certification level (e.g., FIPS 140-3 Level 1, CC EAL1). The `nistQuantumSecurityLevel` field tracks post-quantum security strength per NIST criteria [13], and `classicalSecurityLevel` specifies the classical security level in bits.

Protocols. Protocol assets describe cryptographic protocols that orchestrate multiple algorithms. The `protocolProperties` object supports:

- **Type**: Protocol family: `tls`, `ssh`, `ipsec`, `ike`, `quic`, etc.
- **Version**: Protocol version (e.g., TLS 1.3)
- **Cipher Suites**: For TLS, the supported cipher suites with their constituent algorithms
- **IKEv2 Transforms**: For IPsec, encryption (ENCR), pseudorandom functions (PRF), integrity (INTEG), and key exchange (KE) transforms

Since protocols relate to a set of cryptographic algorithms, their unique identifier within the BOM (bom-ref) can be referenced with an array `relatedCryptographicAssets`.

Certificates. Certificate assets represent X.509 certificates and other formats. The `certificateProperties` object includes:

- Subject and issuer distinguished names
- Validity period (`notValidBefore`, `notValidAfter`)
- Serial number and fingerprint
- Certificate format (e.g., X.509, CVC)
- Lifecycle state (`pre-activation`, `active`, `suspended`, `revoked`, `destroyed`)
- Standard certificate extensions and custom certificate extensions (key usage, extended key usage, subject alternative names, etc.)
- Related cryptographic assets (signature algorithm, subject public key)

Related Cryptographic Material. This category includes keys, tokens, and secrets. The `relatedCryptoMaterialProperties` object captures their metadata:

- **Type**: Key types include `private-key`, `public-key`, `secret-key`, `token`, `password`, `nonce`, `salt`, etc.
- **State**: Key lifecycle state per NIST SP 800-57 [1] (e.g., `active`, `suspended`, `deactivated`, `compromised`, `destroyed`)
- **Size**: Key length in bits
- **Format**: Key encoding format (PEM, DER, P8, etc.)
- **Secured By**: Protection mechanism (HSM, TPM, software)
- **Lifecycle dates**: (creation, activation, expiration)
- **Fingerprint**
- **Usage**: Defines the permitted usage for a key (e.g., encrypt, decrypt)

Related cryptographic material can be linked to other cryptographic assets to represent, for example, that the security of a key depends on the security of another key (e.g., used for securing the boot process).

Figure 3 shows examples of certificate and key material assets following the CycloneDX schema.

```
"certificateProperties": {
  "subjectName":
    "CN=api.example.com",
  "issuerName":
    "CN=Let's Encrypt R4",
  "notValidBefore":
    "2025-01-15T00:00:00Z",
  "notValidAfter":
    "2025-04-15T00:00:00Z",
  "certificateFormat": "X.509",
  "certificateExtensions": [{
    "name": "KeyUsage",
    "value": "digitalSignature"
  }],
  "lifecycleState": "active"
}
```

```
"relatedCryptoMaterialProperties":{
  "type": "private-key",
  "state": "active",
  "size": 256,
  "format": "PEM",
  "securedBy": {
    "mechanism": "hsm",
    "algorithmRef": "aes-256-kw"
  },
  "activationDate":
    "2025-01-15T00:00:00Z",
  "usage": ["sign"]
}
```

Fig. 3. Example `certificateProperties` (left, TLS server certificate) and `relatedCryptoMaterialProperties` (right, HSM-backed private key).

3.2 Resolving Naming Ambiguities

A significant challenge in cryptographic inventories is the proliferation of names for identical algorithms. For example, the NIST P-256 curve is variously known as `prime256v1` (OpenSSL), `secp256r1` (SECG) and `P-256` (NIST). Similarly, RSA might indicate different primitives: signature, key exchange, or key encapsulation; with several modes, paddings and other parameters possible. Identifying the exact variant and establishing a unified naming pattern is essential.

CycloneDX 1.7 addresses this through algorithm family definitions and naming patterns that captures the known parameter sets. The specification defines canonical algorithm families, enabling tools to normalize discovered algorithm names to a common identifier. The definitions are maintained in a separate schema file that acts as an algorithm registry. The methodology to identify this list was twofold: Prominent cryptographic protocols were selected: TLS (all versions), IPsec, SSH, 3GPP and PKCS#11. The standards defining these protocols were processed to extract each cryptographic algorithm used. Further, the algorithms available in popular libraries (OpenSSL, BouncyCastle) were included. This algorithm registry is maintained by CycloneDX, versioned separately from the core specification, and extensible through community contributions.

3.3 Dependency Modeling

Cryptographic assets rarely exist in isolation. CycloneDX models dependencies through two complementary relationships:

dependsOn. This relationship indicates that a component requires another component. For cryptographic assets, this models:

- **Constructions**: HMAC-SHA-1 `dependsOn` SHA-1; allowing to capture the context of the existence of SHA-1
- **Protocol-Algorithm**: TLS 1.3 `dependsOn` its negotiated cipher suite algorithms
- **Certificate-Algorithm**: A certificate `dependsOn` its signature algorithm and subject public key algorithm
- **Hybrid PQC Schemes**: Post-quantum migration often uses hybrid approaches combining classical and quantum-resistant algorithms. For example, hybrid key encapsulation may combine X25519 with ML-KEM-768. In a CBOM, this is modeled as a `combiner` algorithm with `dependsOn` relationships to both constituents. Figure 4 shows this structure for TLS with hybrid KEM and a classical signature.
- **Application-Credential**: An application `dependsOn` the certificates and keys it uses for authentication and encryption.
- **Certificate/Key-Key**: The security of a key might depend on the security of another key. For example, a key might be wrapped by a key-encryption key, or the security of a certificate in the OS trust store might ultimately depend on a key used during secure boot.

provides. This relationship indicates that a component implements or provides capabilities. Examples include:

- A cryptographic library (e.g., OpenSSL) `provides` multiple algorithms
- A hardware security module `provides` key storage and cryptographic operations

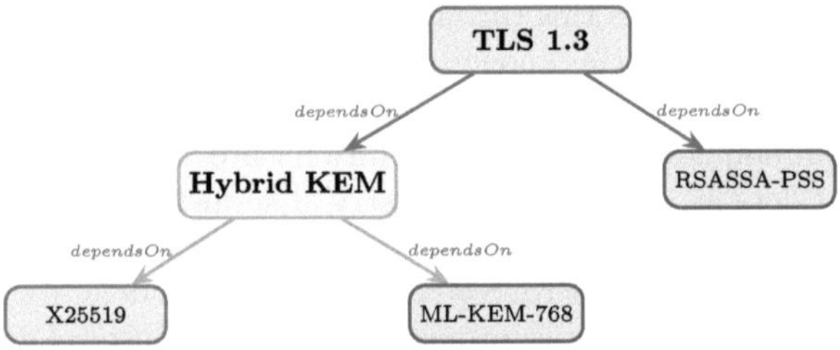

Fig. 4. Dependency graph for a hybrid post-quantum TLS 1.3 handshake. The protocol depends on a hybrid KEM combiner (combining X25519 and ML-KEM-768) and a signature algorithm (RSASSA-PSS). This structure enables policy evaluation to verify quantum resistance.

3.4 Evidence and Occurrences

CBOMs can include evidence of where and how cryptographic assets were discovered. The `evidence` object supports:

- **Occurrences**: File path, line number, offset, and symbol name where the cryptographic asset was detected, along with account info, system owner and job information that detected the asset
- **Additional Context**: Code snippets or configuration fragments
- **Confidence**: A value from 0 to 1 indicating detection confidence
- **Methods**: The technique used for detection (source code analysis, binary analysis, manifest analysis, etc.)

This evidence supports traceability, enabling developers to locate and modify cryptographic usage during migration efforts.

4 The xBOM Playbook

CycloneDX provides a unified specification for multiple BOM types, enabling organizations to compose comprehensive views of their systems. This means that CBOM inherits the features of all other BOM types. CBOMs integrate with other xBOM types to capture cryptographic assets across the full technology stack. Figure 5 illustrates how CBOM integrates with the broader xBOM ecosystem.

In practice, linking and aggregating related BOMs is supported by the CycloneDX BOM-Link mechanism [16], a formally registered IANA URN namespace. BOM-Link allows any BOM to reference another BOM by its serial number and version, enabling, for example, to reference the software capabilities in an SBOM as well as the run-time configuration in an OBOM, or a Product CBOM to link to the HBOM of its underlying hardware. This allows composing multiple specialized BOMs into a coherent view without requiring a monolithic "unified" BOM.

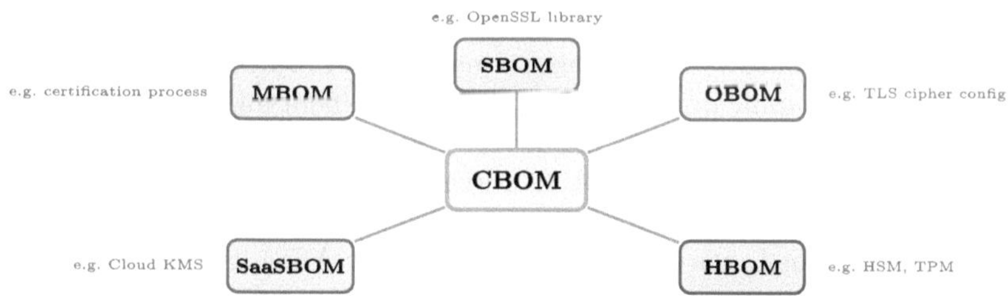

Fig. 5. CBOM integration within the CycloneDX xBOM ecosystem. Cryptographic assets intersect with software components (SBOM), operational configurations (OBOM), hardware (HBOM), services (SaaSBOM), and manufacturing processes (MBOM).

4.1 Operations BOM (OBOM)

Cryptographic behavior is frequently determined by configuration rather than code. An Operations BOM (OBOM) captures runtime configurations and their cryptographic implications. The OBOM lifecycle phase in CycloneDX represents "inventory that is running and operational," encompassing testing, staging and production environments.

For cryptographic agility, OBOM is essential. Consider OpenSSL's configuration file, which can enable or disable algorithms, configure cipher suite preferences, and specify provider modules. A code-level SBOM might show that an application links against OpenSSL, but only an OBOM reveals which algorithms are actually enabled at runtime.

Key OBOM patterns for cryptography include (1) TLS cipher suite configurations in web servers, (2) SSH key exchange and encryption algorithm preferences, (3) Database connection encryption settings.

By linking OBOM configuration data to CBOM cryptographic assets, organizations can answer questions such as: "Which production systems still allow TLS 1.0?" or "Where is RSA-2048 configured for authentication?"

Figure 6 illustrates this pattern with a shortened CBOM fragments. The OBOM excerpt shows how an OpenSSL configuration file (`DEFAULT_GROUPS`) governs the negotiated key exchange groups; the `dependencies` section links each activated algorithm back to this configuration, enabling drift detection when settings change.

4.2 Hardware BOM (HBOM)

Hardware often provides cryptographic capabilities through dedicated processors, accelerators, and secure enclaves. A Hardware BOM (HBOM) describes physical components including cryptographic coprocessors, HSMs, and TPMs.

In CycloneDX, hardware components use the `device` component type with associated cryptographic properties. An HSM component might provide multiple algorithms with execution environment set to `hardware` and appropriate certification level (e.g., FIPS 140-3 Level 3). Integrating HBOM and CBOM enables organizations to inventory hardware-backed key storage, identify cryptographic accelerators (e.g., for Lattice-based cryptography or AES), track HSM firmware versions with their supported algorithms, and map keys to physical protection boundaries. The HBOM excerpt in Fig. 6 shows a PQC-enabled HSM whose coprocessor `provides` ML-DSA-87, SLH-DSA-SHA2-256 s, and AES-256-Wrap-PAD with FIPS 140-3 Level 3 certification.

4.3 SaaS BOM (SaaSBOM)

Modern applications increasingly rely on external services for cryptographic operations. A SaaS BOM captures service dependencies including cloud key management services, certificate authorities, and cryptographic APIs.

OBOM – OpenSSL configuration

```
{"components": [
 {"name": "ML-KEM-768",
  "type": "cryptographic-asset",
  "cryptoProperties": {
   "assetType": "algorithm",
   "algorithmProperties": {
    "primitive": "kem",
    "nistQuantumSecurityLevel": 3
 }}},
 {"name": "x25519",
  "type": "cryptographic-asset",
  "cryptoProperties": {
   "assetType": "algorithm",
   "algorithmProperties": {
    "primitive": "key-agree"
 }}},
 {"name": "openssl-config",
  "type": "data",
  "data": {"type": "configuration",
   "contents": {"attachment":
    {"content": "DEFAULT_GROUPS=
     x25519:SecP256r1MLKEM768"
 }}}}],
"dependencies": [
 {"ref": "ML-KEM-768",
  "dependsOn": ["openssl-config"]},
 {"ref": "x25519",
  "dependsOn": ["openssl-config"]}
]}
```

HBOM – PQC-enabled HSM

```
{"components": [
  {"type": "device",
   "name": "cryptoprocessor",
   "bom-ref": "coproc-001",
   "properties": [
    {"name": "cdx:device:function",
     "value": "coprocessor"},
    {"name": "cdx:device:location",
     "value": "mainboard"}
  ]},
  {"name": "ML-DSA-87",
   "type": "cryptographic-asset",
   "cryptoProperties": {
    "assetType": "algorithm",
    "algorithmProperties": {
     "primitive": "signature",
     "executionEnvironment":
       "hardware",
     "certificationLevel":
       ["fips140-3-l3"],
     "nistQuantumSecurityLevel": 5
 }}},
  {"name": "AES-256-Wrap-PAD",
   "type": "cryptographic-asset",
   "cryptoProperties": {
    "algorithmProperties": {
     "primitive": "key-wrap",
     "executionEnvironment":
       "hardware"
  }}}],
 "dependencies": [
  {"ref": "coproc-001",
   "provides": ["ML-DSA-87",
     "AES-256-Wrap-PAD"]}
]}
```

Fig. 6. CycloneDX fragments for OBOM (left) and HBOM (right). The OBOM links cryptographic assets to an OpenSSL configuration via `dependsOn`; the HBOM uses `provides` to declare the algorithms implemented by a hardware coprocessor.

CycloneDX services specify endpoints, data flows with classification, authentication requirements, and trust zone boundaries. For cryptography, SaaSBOM use cases are cloud KMS, certificate authorities (public and private), code signing services, and HSM-as-a-Service providers. Linking SaaSBOM services to CBOM cryptographic assets enables verification that cryptographic assets managed by external services meet organizational security requirements.

4.4 Manufacturing BOM (MBOM)

The Manufacturing BOM captures formulation: how components were created, assembled, tested, and certified. For cryptographic assets, MBOM use cases are:

- Key generation procedures and ceremonies
- Certificate issuance workflows
- Cryptographic module testing and certification (FIPS 140 validation)
- Algorithm implementation verification

CycloneDX formulation supports workflows, tasks, and steps with inputs and outputs, documenting procedures such as HSM initialization, key generation, and key share distribution.

5 Use Cases and Practical Applications

5.1 Policy-Based Compliance Evaluation

CBOMs enable automated compliance checking against organizational or regulatory policies, by using the Common Expression Language (CEL) [8] for policy specification.

Figure 7 shows three example policies expressed in CEL. Policy evaluation produces compliance reports indicating which components pass or fail, with references to the evidence (file locations, line numbers) for remediation. While these examples target component-level attributes, CEL can equally operate on the *evidence* and *occurrences* arrays, enabling policies that reason about physical file locations, detection confidence, or detection method. For instance, this helps excluding occurrences in test directories from compliance checks.

(a) Prohibited Algorithm Detection

```
components.all(c,
  c.cryptoProperties.assetType
    == "algorithm"
  && c.name == "SHA-1"
  ? components.exists(cert,
      cert.cryptoProperties.assetType
        == "certificate"
      && cert.cryptoProperties
           .certificateProperties
           .subjectName
         == cert.cryptoProperties
              .certificateProperties
              .issuerName
      && cert.cryptoProperties
           .certificateProperties
           .certificateExtensions
           .exists(ext,
             ext.commonExtensionName
               == "basicConstraints"
             && ext.commonExtensionValue
                  .contains("CA:TRUE"))
      && cert.cryptoProperties
           .certificateProperties
           .relatedCryptographicAssets
           .exists(a,
             a.ref == c["bom-ref"]))
  : true)
```

(b) Minimum Key Sizes

```
components.all(c,
  c.cryptoProperties.assetType
    == "algorithm"
  && c.cryptoProperties
       .algorithmProperties
       .algorithmFamily == "RSA"
  ? int(c.cryptoProperties
          .algorithmProperties
          .parameterSetIdentifier)
      >= 2048
  : true)
```

(c) PQC Readiness Assessment (Authentication)

```
components.exists(c,
  c.cryptoProperties
    .algorithmProperties
    .algorithmFamily
    in ["ML-DSA", "SLH-DSA"])
```

Fig. 7. CEL policy examples for CBOM compliance evaluation. (a) SHA-1 is allowed only when referenced by a self-signed root CA certificate. (b) RSA keys must be at least 2048 bits. (c) At least one PQC signature algorithm must be present.

5.2 CI/CD Integration

CBOMs can be integrated into continuous integration and deployment pipelines to enforce cryptographic policies as part of the software development lifecycle.

Build-Time Generation. CBOM generation tools such as CBOMkit-hyperion [20] can scan source code repositories during the build phase, producing CBOMs as build artifacts.

Gate Enforcement. Policy evaluation can serve as a pipeline gate, failing builds that introduce prohibited cryptographic algorithms or configurations. This prevents cryptographic regressions before deployment.

Drift Detection. Comparing CBOMs across builds enables detection of cryptographic changes—new algorithms introduced, existing algorithms removed, or configuration modifications.

Dependency Updates. When updating cryptographic libraries, CBOM comparison reveals changes in provided algorithms. A library update might add PQC support or deprecate weak algorithms, and a CBOM history brings visibility to these changes.

5.3 Certificate Lifecycle Monitoring

CycloneDX 1.7's certificate lifecycle support enables certificate management. By maintaining CBOMs of deployed certificates, organizations can:

- **Monitoring Expiration**: Query CBOMs for certificates expiring within a defined window (e.g., 30 d)
- **Monitor TLS certificate lifespan**: Monitor certificates to comply with the 47-day lifespan introduced by the CA/Browser Forum [2], phased in from March 2026 through March 2029
- **Algorithm Deprecation**: Identify certificates using deprecated signature algorithms (e.g., RSA with SHA-1) for replacement
- **CA Trust Changes**: When a certificate authority is distrusted, query CBOMs to identify affected certificates
- **Key Compromise Response**: If a key is compromised, use CBOM relationships to identify all certificates and systems affected

The certificate lifecycle states (`active`, `suspended`, `deactivated`, `revoked`, `destroyed`) enable CBOMs to reflect real-time state of certificates. Figure 8 illustrates the key lifecycle state machine defined by NIST SP 800-57 [1].

Fig. 8. Key and certificate lifecycle states per NIST SP 800-57. CycloneDX 1.7 captures the current state in `relatedCryptoMaterialProperties.state` and `certificateProperties.lifecycleState`.

Table 1. Cryptographic inventory and dependency summary. For nginx, raw counts before deduplication are shown in parentheses.

Target	Analysis	Assets	Algo	Proto	Cert	Keys	Deps
Keycloak	source code	56	27	1	0	28	37
nginx	container	314 (8 104)	14 (5 400)	0	149 (1 350)	151 (1 354)	2 700

5.4 Post-quantum Migration Planning

CBOMs are particularly valuable for planning and tracking PQC migration. Organizations can inventory all classical cryptographic assets vulnerable to quantum attacks, identify dependencies between applications and cryptographic libraries, prioritize migration based on business criticality, data sensitivity and protection requirements, track hybrid deployment progress, and validate that migration is complete before decommissioning classical algorithms.

By linking CBOMs to risk assessments, organizations can prioritize migration of systems protecting long-lived secrets or sensitive data with extended confidentiality requirements.

6 Evaluation

We evaluate CBOMs on two real-world targets using CBOMkit [20] to demonstrate practical expressiveness, use for compliance, and the ability to surface actionable findings.

6.1 Targets and Method

We selected two targets exercising complementary lifecycle phases: (1) The source code of Keycloak[1]—an open-source identity and access management software, analyzed with CBOMkit-hyperion for source code scanning; and (2) The Docker container image of nginx[2], analyzed with CBOMkit-theia for file-system and certificate discovery. Algorithm names are normalized to CycloneDX 1.7 families. Container tools emit one component per file occurrence; we deduplicate by keying on (name, serialized `algorithmProperties`, OID) for algorithms, (subject, issuer, validity dates) for certificates, and (name, key value) for crypto material, merging all evidence locations into a single representative component.

[1] Java source code, https://github.com/keycloak/keycloak, tag `26.5.1`.

[2] `nginx:1.29.5` container image, https://hub.docker.com/_/nginx.

6.2 Results

Table 1 summarizes the deduplicated inventory and dependency graph for each target.

Keycloak. Static analysis identified 27 algorithms across 9 primitives and 49 files, plus 28 key assets and one protocol reference, spanning modern schemes (`ECDH`, `EdDSA`, `AES128-GCM`) alongside legacy ones (`MD5`, `SHA1`). The 37 dependency edges comprise 28 key→algorithm and 9 algorithm→algorithm links for compound schemes (e.g., `SHA512withRSA` → `SHA512`).

The single protocol asset is TLS, detected through 12 occurrences of the Java API `javax.net.ssl.SSLContext.getInstance()`. Regarding tool coverage, CBOMkit-hyperion performs well for standard crypto frameworks such as Java JCA and BouncyCastle, which account for the vast majority of Java crypto usage. However, it may miss cryptography accessed through less common or homegrown implementations. Static analysis can identify that the application instantiates a TLS context, but cannot determine the negotiated cipher suites or protocol version, which depend on runtime configuration, peer capabilities, and the underlying JSSE provider. Capturing the actually negotiated algorithms requires either configuration-level analysis (OBOM, see Sect. 4) or runtime instrumentation. This distinction between *capability* (what an application can negotiate) and *actual usage* (what is negotiated at runtime) is a fundamental limitation of static CBOM generation and motivates complementing SBOMs with OBOMs.

nginx. Container analysis yielded 8 104 raw components from 609 files under `/etc./ssl/certs/`, reducing to 314 unique assets: 14 algorithms, 149 certificates, 151 keys (107 RSA, 43 EC). Trust stores replicate CA certificates across individual `.pem` files and the bundled `ca-certificates.crt`, explaining the high raw count. All 2 700 dependency edges decompose signature algorithms into hash and asymmetric primitives.

6.3 Compliance Findings

Applying a standard policy set revealed four categories of actionable results.

1. Expired certificates: One expired root CA in the nginx trust store (Baltimore CyberTrust Root, expired 2025-05-13), traced via the CBOM `evidence` field.
2. Certificates with long validity spans: Periods of up to 35 years (Certum Trusted Network CA 2 (RSA), 2011–2046) raise the question of revocation if CRQCs become available within this period.
3. Small RSA exponents: DER-encoded SPKI parsing identified 3 of 107 RSA keys with $e < 65\,537$, which doesn't comply with FIPS 186-5.
4. Usage of legacy algorithms (MD5, SHA-1): In Keycloak, `MD5` and `SHA1` were flagged; the dependency graph links `SHA1withRSA` to its constituents, and evidence fields trace usage to specific source files.

These findings confirm that typed assets, dependency graphs, and file-level evidence enable automated policy evaluation without manual audit.

7 Discussion and Future Work

7.1 Comparison with SPDX

While this paper focuses on CycloneDX, SPDX [10] also targets software composition transparency. SPDX 3.0 introduced modular profiles that could support cryptographic extensions, though there is currently no native cryptographic support. Adopting a similar model will be important for cross-standard interoperability.

7.2 CBOM Generation Challenges

Practical CBOM generation encounters several fundamental challenges that impact completeness and accuracy:

Detection Accuracy. Static analysis tools may produce false positives (e.g., detecting test cases as actual usage) or false negatives (missing dynamically loaded libraries or unknown cryptographic implementations). Binary analysis is challenging for stripped binaries or obfuscated code. CBOMkit addresses this through multi-modal detection combining AST analysis, regular expressions, and language- and framework-specific extractors. False positives from test files can be mitigated through evidence-based filtering: since each detected asset carries an `evidence.occurrences` record with file paths, post-processing or CEL policies can exclude occurrences under test directories (e.g., `src/test/`) from compliance evaluation.

API Abstractions. Cryptographic operations behind service abstractions, such as cloud KMS providers or internal key management APIs, are opaque to static analysis. The algorithms used server-side are not visible in client code. This is addressed by modeling the service dependency in a SaaSBOM and having the service provider supply its own CBOM; the two can be linked via BOM-Link. Until vendors routinely publish CBOMs, such dependencies represent a blind spot in the inventory.

Transitive Dependencies. Modern applications often have hundreds of direct and transitive dependencies. A useful CBOM must capture cryptographic assets across this entire tree, not just direct usage. This requires recursive analysis and potentially runtime instrumentation to identify which dependency paths are exercised.

Scale and Governance. Large organizations with thousands of applications, hundreds of teams, and multi-cloud deployments require automated CBOM generation, aggregation, and governance workflows. Scalable tooling, centralized CBOM repositories, versioning strategies, and access control are essential for enterprise adoption. CBOMs must be updated regularly to remain accurate: a stale inventory may give false confidence in cryptographic compliance.

7.3 Future Directions

CycloneDX 2.0 and Behavioral Modeling. The next major version of CycloneDX plans to introduce Blueprints and Bill of Behaviors (BOB). For cryptography, behavioral modeling enables capturing not just *which* algorithms are present, but *how* they are used and *for what purpose*. For example, SHA-3 is a state-of-the-art hash function, but inappropriate for password hashing, for which specialized "slow" password hashing algorithms such as Argon2 or scrypt are preferred. Behavioral annotations will capture this distinction.

Risk Modeling. Future CBOM extensions may incorporate explicit risk quantification to prioritize migration. CBOMs could express not only current state but also target state and migration roadmaps.

Implementation Assurance. The security of cryptography ultimately depends on its implementation. A future version of CBOM will aim at capturing relevant properties such as side-channel resistance (e.g., against simple timing analysis or differential power analysis), memory safety guarantees, and formal methods employed to prove these properties.

Enhanced support for crypto agility. A key dimension of PQC migration is the effort needed to replace algorithms in deployed systems. While an OBOM can already express the data used to configure cryptographic assets, CBOMs should capture additional agility attributes for each cryptographic asset: whether the algorithm is *hardcoded* in source, *configurable* via runtime parameters, replaceable through *firmware updates*, capable of *hot-swap* without service interruption, or *vendor-locked* to a proprietary implementation. Combining agility metadata with security properties enables organizations to assess not just what cryptography is deployed, but how readily it can be migrated.

Registry of Protocols. Interaction with cryptography is predominantly through protocols such as TLS, SSH or IPsec. While CycloneDX already supports protocol assets in the CBOM structure, a protocol registry—analogous to the algorithm registry in v1.7—would catalog each protocol version with its associated cryptographic assets. Such a registry would enable automated mapping from protocol to their constituent algorithms, enabling the assessment of quantum readiness of the protocol.

Towards a Product CBOM. Consumers of products need visibility into the cryptographic posture of what they procure. Vendors can supply Product CBOMs to convey this information. A way to express a Product CBOM on an interface-based model across four logical planes: the *data plane* (e.g., data-in-transit protection via TLS), the *control plane* (e.g., internal key management via KMS), the *management plane* (e.g., administrative access via SSH), and the *security plane* (e.g., secure boot, trusted time synchronization). For each interface, the Product CBOM would capture identity and risk attributes, connectivity parameters, implementation details, and a PQC migration roadmap.

8 Conclusion

Cryptography Bills of Materials enable a shift from ad-hoc reports of cryptographic inventories to machine-readable governance. Regulatory mandates such as CRA, DORA, and NIS2 demand cryptographic transparency that only structured inventories can provide. This paper presented the anatomy of CBOMs as standardized in OWASP CycloneDX (ECMA-424), covering the cryptographic asset model, dependency relationships. integration with the xBOM ecosystem, and practical use cases including policy-based compliance, CI/CD pipeline gates, and certificate lifecycle monitoring. We have demonstrated the expressiveness of CBOMs with two practical examples of a source code project and a container image.

Several directions will expand CBOM utility: Product CBOMs for procurement visibility, crypto agility metadata capturing replaceability attributes, a protocol registry decomposing configurations into constituent primitives, and implementation assurance evidence linking deployed algorithms to formal verification and side-channel resistance. A successful post-quantum transition requires visibility into what cryptography is deployed, agility to swap algorithms when needed, and automation to enforce policies at scale. CBOMs fit this view as providing a standardized and interoperable visibility layer across the industry.

Acknowledgements. The author thanks Steve Springett, Nicklas Körtge, Matt Rutkowski, Martin Schmatz, Ian Deakin, Thibaud Ecarot, Marc Stöttinger and Mike Osborne for their contributions to the development of CBOM and the CycloneDX Cryptography Working Group.

References

1. Barker, E.: NIST special publication 800-57 part 1 rev. 5: Recommendation for key management. Tech. rep., National Institute of Standards and Technology (2020). https://doi.org/10.6028/NIST.SP.800-57pt1r5
2. CA/Browser Forum: Ballot SC-081 v3: Introducing schedule of reducing validity and data reuse periods (2025). https://cabforum.org/
3. Ecma International: ECMA-424 – CycloneDX bill of materials specification. Tech. rep., Ecma International (2025). https://ecma-international.org/publications-and-standards/standards/ecma-424/
4. European Commission: Recommendation on a coordinated implementation roadmap for the transition to post-quantum cryptography. Tech. Rep. C(2024) 2393 final, European Commission, Brussels (2024)
5. European Parliament and Council: Directive (EU) 2022/2555 on measures for a high common level of cybersecurity across the Union (NIS2) (2022). https://eur-lex.europa.eu/eli/dir/2022/2555
6. European Parliament and Council: Regulation (EU) 2022/2554 on digital operational resilience for the financial sector (DORA) (2022). https://eur-lex.europa.eu/eli/reg/2022/2554

7. European Parliament and Council: Regulation (EU) 2024/2847 on horizontal cybersecurity requirements for products with digital elements (Cyber Resilience Act) (2024). https://eur-lex.europa.eu/eli/reg/2024/2847/oj
8. Google: Common expression language (CEL) (2025). https://github.com/google/cel-spec
9. Linux Foundation: Post-quantum cryptography alliance (PQCA) (2024). https://pqca.org
10. Linux Foundation: SPDX specification (2024). https://spdx.dev/specifications/
11. MITRE: CVE-2021-44228: Apache Log4j2 remote code execution vulnerability (2021). https://cve.mitre.org/cgi-bin/cvename.cgi?name=CVE-2021-44228
12. National Cybersecurity Center of Excellence: NIST special publication 1800-38: Migration to post-quantum cryptography (initial preliminary draft). Tech. rep., National Institute of Standards and Technology (2023). https://csrc.nist.gov/pubs/sp/1800/38/iprd-(1)
13. National Institute of Standards and Technology: Post-quantum cryptography standardization (2024). https://csrc.nist.gov/projects/post-quantum-cryptography
14. National Security Agency: Commercial national security algorithm suite 2.0 (CNSA 2.0) cybersecurity advisory. Tech. rep., NSA, Fort Meade, MD (2022). https://media.defense.gov/2022/Sep/07/2003071834/-1/-1/0/CSA_CNSA_2.0_ALGORITHMS_.PDF
15. Ott, D., Peikert, C.: Identifying research challenges in post quantum cryptography migration and cryptographic agility (2019). arXiv:1909.07353 arXiv preprint
16. OWASP Foundation: CycloneDX BOM-Link (2024). https://cyclonedx.org/capabilities/bomlink/, iANA-registered URN namespace
17. OWASP Foundation: CycloneDX software bill of materials standard (2024). https://cyclonedx.org
18. Peisert, S., et al.: Perspectives on the SolarWinds incident. IEEE Secur. Privacy **19**(2), 7–13 (2021). https://doi.org/10.1109/MSEC.2021.3051235
19. PKI Consortium: Post-quantum cryptography working group (2024). https://pkic.org/wg/pqc/charter/
20. Post-Quantum Cryptography Alliance: CBOMkit – open-source toolset for cryptography bill of materials (2024). https://github.com/PQCA/cbomkit

Architecture-Derived CBOMs for Cryptographic Migration: A Security-Aware Architecture Tradeoff Method

Eduard Hirsch[1(✉)] and Kristina Raab[2]

[1] University of Applied Sciences Amberg-Weiden, 92224 Amberg, Germany
e.hirsch@oth-aw.de
[2] Fraunhofer AISEC, 85748 Garching, Germany
kristina.raab@aisec.fraunhofer.de

Abstract. Cryptographic migration driven by algorithm deprecation, regulatory change, and post-quantum readiness requires more than an inventory of cryptographic assets. Existing Cryptographic Bills of Materials (CBOMs) are typically tool- or inventory-derived. They lack architectural intent, rationale, and security context, limiting their usefulness for migration planning. This paper introduces Security-Aware Architecture Tradeoff Analysis Method (SATAM), a security-aware adaptation of scenario-based architecture evaluation that derives an architecture-grounded, context-sensitive CBOM. SATAM integrates established approaches: ATAM, arc42, STRIDE, ADR, and CARAF. These Generated artifacts are used to annotate CBOM entries with architectural context, security intent, and migration-critical metadata using CycloneDX-compatible extensions. Following a Design Science Research approach, the paper presents the method design, a conceptual traceability model, and an illustrative application. The results demonstrate that architecture-derived CBOMs capture migration-relevant context that is typically absent from inventory-based approaches. Thereby, SATAM improves availability of information required for informed cryptographic migration planning and long-term cryptographic agility.

Keywords: Cryptographic Migration · Architecture Tradeoff Analysis · Cryptographic Bill of Materials · Security-Aware Architecture · Post-Quantum Cryptography

1 Introduction

Cryptographic systems are subject to continuous change driven by algorithm deprecation, emerging vulnerabilities, regulatory requirements, and the anticipated transition to post-quantum cryptography [1]. As a result, software systems increasingly face the need for systematic cryptographic migration rather than

D. Loebenberger and M. Stöttinger (Eds.): MAgiCS 2026, CCIS 3002, pp. 20–39, 2026.
https://doi.org/10.1007/978-3-032-28946-9_2

one-time cryptographic upgrades [15]. However, cryptography is deeply embedded in software architectures, often implicitly and without explicit documentation of its security intent, architectural role, or underlying design rationale. This lack of architectural transparency significantly complicates migration planning and increases the risk of unintended security regressions [6,24].

Recent efforts to improve cryptographic transparency, such as Cryptographic Bill of Materials(CBOM), aim to enumerate cryptographic algorithms, libraries, and key parameters used within a system. While such inventories are a necessary first step, they are typically derived from tooling or static analysis. They remain largely disconnected from the underlying architecture, following inventory first approaches [16,19]. As a consequence, existing CBOMs rarely explain why cryptography is used, which threats components address, or what tradeoffs were considered. Nevertheless, this information is essential for informed decisions [16]. Without this contextual information, cryptographic migrations are significantly limited, as it becomes difficult to assess the security impact, feasibility, and risk of replacing cryptographic mechanisms. Similarly, established security practices such as threat modeling focus on identifying potential attacks but do not systematically capture architectural decisions or their implications for cryptographic agility.

The *central problem* addressed in this paper is that existing CBOMs provide limited support for migration-critical architectural questions. In particular, they do not clearly indicate in what sense cryptographic mechanisms are security-relevant or which architectural decisions constrain change. They also fail to show how cryptographic replacements affect system-level security properties and risk assessment.

The *objective of this work* is to design and evaluate a security-aware architecture evaluation method that enables the construction of an architecture-derived CBOM. During the generation process it is getting enriched with security intent, architectural rationale, and migration-critical metadata like risk assessment. To this end, we introduce (SATAM), an approach that adapts scenario-based architecture evaluation to explicitly address cryptographic decisions and their role in mitigating security threats. SATAM integrates threat modeling, security quality attribute scenarios, and architectural decision analysis to make cryptographic assumptions explicit and traceable. The resulting CBOM is not merely an inventory, but an artifact of the architectural design process that underlies cryptographic migration and long-term agility in complex interdependent systems.

Following a Design Science Research approach, we address the following *design evaluation question*:

Design Question: Does the proposed design artifact SATAM enable the construction of an architecture-grounded, context-sensitive CBOM by making cryptographic decisions and their security rationale explicit and traceable? To address this design question, this paper makes the following *contributions*:

(i) SATAM, a security-aware adaptation of scenario-based architecture evaluation that explicitly captures cryptographic decisions and enables the derivation of architecture-grounded, context-sensitive CBOM; (ii) a traceability model linking architectural elements, security threats, design decisions, and cryptographic assets; and (iii) an illustrative integration of (CARAF) to demonstrate how architecture-derived artifacts can provide structured input for cryptographic risk assessment.

The method and artifacts are evaluated analytically and through a proof-of-concept, demonstrating how architecture-derived CBOMs increase transparency and provide structured information to support informed cryptographic migration planning.

2 Background and Related Work

2.1 Architecture Evaluation Method

Architecture evaluation methods assess whether a software architecture satisfies quality requirements by analyzing architectural structures and design decisions. A prominent example is the (ATAM), a scenario-based approach that evaluates stakeholder-defined quality attribute scenarios against architectural approaches to identify risks, tradeoffs, and design rationale [4,13].

While ATAM is widely applied to performance and modifiability concerns, its treatment of security is typically high-level and does not explicitly address cryptographic mechanisms or migration concerns. Nevertheless, its structured scenario-based reasoning provides a suitable foundation for security-oriented extensions that require architectural context and traceability.

ATAM is independent of specific documentation frameworks but is often combined in practice with arc42 [23], which structures architectural views, quality requirements, and architectural decisions. In this work, arc42 serves as the baseline architectural description used to identify security-relevant decision points and cryptographic assets.

2.2 Security Architecture and Threat Modeling

Security architecture analysis evaluates whether architectural structures and decisions adequately mitigate relevant threats, which are typically defined through explicit threat models. Threat modeling provides a systematic means to identify how architectural elements may be misused or attacked and serves as a key input to security-focused architecture evaluation [12].

In this work, STRIDE is applied to architectural elements such as components, data flows, and trust boundaries to structure security concerns and ensure systematic threat coverage. STRIDE threats are then transformed into (Security QAS) [4,7], which describe required system behavior in response to security-relevant stimuli under defined conditions. Security QAS follow the established scenario structure used in architecture evaluation methods and enable systematic analysis of how architectural decisions and cryptographic mechanisms contribute to security properties.

2.3 Cryptographic Transparency and Decision Rationale

Cryptographic transparency has gained increasing attention through the introduction of (SBOMs)and, more recently, CBOMs [3,8]. While SBOMs focus on software components and dependencies, CBOMs aim to enumerate cryptographic algorithms, libraries, protocols, and key parameters used within a system. Such inventories are valuable for compliance and vulnerability management but are typically derived from tooling or static analysis and remain disconnected from architectural context.

Architecture Decision Records (ADRs) [18] further provide a lightweight and established means to document architectural decisions, including their context, rationale, and consequences. In the context of cryptographic systems, ADRs can capture the reasoning behind cryptographic choices, such as algorithm selection, key management approaches, or protocol usage. However, ADRs are typically maintained separately from CBOMs and are not systematically linked to cryptographic inventories.

CARAF [14] is a proactive approach for analyzing risks arising from limited cryptographic agility, particularly in the context of future threats such as post-quantum cryptography. In this work, CARAF is used to illustrate how architecture-derived artifacts can provide structured input for cryptographic risk assessment.

2.4 Related Work

Prior work on architecture evaluation has demonstrated that scenario-based methods such as ATAM can be extended to incorporate security concerns, for example by integrating threat modeling techniques such as STRIDE [12]. These approaches focus primarily on identifying architectural security risks and trade-offs rather than producing reusable artifacts for cryptographic transparency or migration planning.

Recent work on Cryptographic Bills of Materials emphasizes the need for systematic cryptographic discovery as a prerequisite for cryptographic migration, particularly in the context of post-quantum cryptography [5,17]. CBOM concepts and data models have been proposed and standardized within initiatives such as OWASP CycloneDX [19,20]. These efforts define the scope of cryptographic inventories and highlight the importance of capturing algorithms, protocols, and key material. Nevertheless, current CBOM approaches are predominantly tool- or inventory-driven and capture cryptographic usage largely in isolation from architectural context and decision rationale [8].

Research has shown that tool-generated SBOMs often suffer from incompleteness, semantic ambiguity, and limited downstream utility for security decision-making [25,26]. Studies on stakeholder usage indicate that the absence of contextual and semantic information significantly reduces the practical value of Bill of Materials (BOM) in complex decision-making scenarios [21]. Although these studies focus on SBOMs, their findings are directly applicable to CBOMs and suggest that inventory-level representations alone are insufficient for supporting cryptographic migration.

Taken together, existing work provides mature methods for scenario-based architecture evaluation, systematic threat identification, and cryptographic inventorying, as well as mechanisms to document architectural decisions and assess cryptographic agility risks. However, these approaches are typically applied in isolation and do not provide a unified method to derive migration-relevant CBOMs, grounded in architectural analysis and security reasoning. This gap motivates the integration of architecture evaluation, threat modeling, decision documentation, and cryptographic inventorying in a single, security-aware evaluation method. Section 4 introduces SATAM, which builds on the concepts outlined in this section and combines them into a coherent process for deriving architecture-grounded, migration-relevant CBOMs.

3 Design Science Research Approach

This work follows a Design Science Research (DSR) approach [9], which is well suited for designing and validating artifacts that address practical problems. The primary artifact of this work is SATAM, a security-aware architecture evaluation method for deriving context-sensitive CBOMs.

Within the DSR framework, the problem was identified as the lack of a systematic way to derive migration-relevant CBOMs from architectural analysis. Existing CBOM approaches focus on cryptographic discovery but provide limited architectural context and decision rationale, while established architecture evaluation methods offer limited support for cryptographic migration concerns.

Rather than introducing a new inventory format or cryptographic analysis technique, this work focuses on adapting scenario-based architecture evaluation to make cryptographic decisions explicit, analyzable, and traceable. This problem framing directly guided the design of SATAM as a security-aware extension of existing architecture evaluation practice.

3.1 Artifact Design

Following DSR principles, the artifact was designed by adapting and integrating established concepts from software architecture evaluation and security engineering. SATAM is a method-level artifact that extends scenario-based architecture evaluation with structured threat modeling, security quality attribute scenarios, cryptography-specific analysis, and explicit documentation of architectural decisions.

The design emphasizes traceability between architectural elements, security concerns, cryptographic decisions, and cryptographic assets. This ensures that the resulting CBOM captures not only which cryptographic mechanisms are used, but also the architectural rationale for their use and the implications for future migration.

In addition, the design allows architecture-derived CBOM artifacts to provide structured input for a hybrid qualitative and quantitative cryptographic risk assessment, illustrated in this work through the integration of the CARAF.

3.2 Evaluation Strategy

The artifact is evaluated using a combination of analytical and illustrative methods, which is appropriate for an early-stage DSR contribution. Analytical evaluation is used to assess internal consistency, traceability, and conceptual completeness of the method, as well as its alignment with established architecture evaluation practices. In addition, an illustrative example is used to demonstrate the applicability of SATAM and to show how architectural analysis results are transformed into an annotated CBOM.

An empirical evaluation in an industrial setting is outside the scope of this paper and is identified as future work.

4 Security-Aware Architecture Tradeoff Analysis Method (SATAM) Towards CBOM

This section introduces SATAM as a method-level artifact that extends scenario-based architecture evaluation to derive migration-relevant CBOMs. SATAM builds on ATAM and preserves its overall structure, while introducing explicit security analysis steps and cryptographic decision artifacts. Its objective is not only to identify architectural risks and tradeoffs, but also to produce an annotated CBOM that captures cryptographic assets together with architectural context, security intent, and migration-relevant metadata.

SATAM emphasizes explicit traceability between architectural elements, security concerns, cryptographic decisions, and CBOM entries. This ensures migration-relevant reasoning across architectural artifacts.

SATAM follows the same high-level phases as ATAM but augments them with security-specific activities and artifacts. In particular, SATAM introduces explicit security stakeholders, treats security as a first-class quality concern, and requires cryptographic mechanisms and key management aspects to be visible in the architectural representation. These extensions ensure that cryptographic assumptions are surfaced early in the evaluation process.

During the evaluation phase, SATAM combines structured threat modeling with scenario-based analysis. STRIDE is applied to architectural elements, data flows, and trust boundaries to identify security-relevant threats, which are then transformed into QAS These scenarios form the basis for analyzing architectural approaches and associated cryptographic mechanisms.

Cryptographic decisions identified during the evaluation are treated as explicit architectural decision candidates and documented using ADRs. To assess their long-term suitability, SATAM uses CARAF as a risk analysis lens. CARAF provides a structured methodology for evaluating cryptographic

Table 1. SATAM extensions to ATAM and resulting artifacts (authoritative process overview)

ATAM step	SATAM activities and key artifacts
Preparation phase	
	Identify security/cryptography stakeholders; define security accountability; prepare arc42 architecture description as evaluation baseline **Output:** Security roles, CBOM ownership, security-focused arc42
Kickoff phase	
Presentation of	
Method	Position SATAM as ATAM with security annotation; define CBOM as primary outcome; clarify evaluation scope **Output:** Evaluation scope, CBOM schema
Objectives	Treat security explicitly as a business risk; introduce STRIDE as threat assessment input; explain the role of QAS and ADRs **Output:** Security drivers, initial QAS templates
Architecture	Present arc42 architecture in a security-readable form (trust boundaries, crypto termination points, key ownership) **Output:** Initial crypto inventory, ADR candidates
Evaluation phase	
Quality Tree	Derive the security branch of the quality tree; derive concrete security scenarios by applying STRIDE to architectural elements and flows. **Output:** STRIDE-tagged security scenarios
Analysis	Refine security scenarios into concrete Security QAS; analyze architectural and cryptographic approaches; apply CARAF to assess risks based on findings; finalize ADRs **Output:** Final QAS, ADRs, risks, tradeoffs, CARAF assessment
Results	
	Architecture baseline, security scenarios, ADRs, CARAF findings ⇒ integrated into crypto inventory **Output:** Annotated, context-sensitive CBOM

tradeoffs–specifically agility, transition costs, and quantum-readiness. This process yields a clear profile of identified risks and justified cryptographic decisions for a future-proof security posture.

A key distinction of SATAM is that evaluation results are consolidated into a machine-readable CBOM. Instead of treating the CBOM as a standalone inventory, SATAM derives entries directly from architectural analysis artifacts.

Table 1 summarizes the SATAM steps and highlights the extensions beyond standard ATAM. Table 2 shows how all CARAF inputs, except adversarial capability assumptions, are systematically derived from SATAM artifacts.

Table 2. Mapping of SATAM artifacts to CARAF inputs for cryptographic migration risk assessment

CARAF input	Provided by SATAM artifact	Explanation
Cryptographic asset	Architecture-derived CBOM entry	Cryptographic mechanisms derived from security-readable architecture; consolidated as CBOM entries for risk analysis.
Protected asset	arc42 architecture views;CBOM entry	Architectural elements and data flows; concrete system context of protected assets.
Threat rationale	STRIDE-tagged scenarios	Threat categories (e.g., tampering, disclosure, privilege escalation); motivation for cryptographic protection.
Security requirements	Security Quality Attribute Scenarios(Security QAS)	Measurable criteria (e.g., TLS 1.3 enforcement, downgrade resistance); long-term suitability constraints.
Cryptographic decision	Architecture Decision Records (ADRs)	Selected cryptographic approach; rationale; architectural consequences.
Migration time drivers (Y)	ADR consequences; deployment and operational notes	Rollout constraints; certificate life cycles; interoperability dependencies; operational coupling.
Data lifetime (X)	Security QAS assumptions; regulatory context	Required confidentiality and integrity durations; long-term protection needs.
Cryptographic horizon (Z)	External assumptions (e.g., PQC timelines)	Adversarial capability horizon; contextualized by CBOM assets and requirements.
Risk mitigation options	CARAF findings linked to ADRs	Actionable mitigation directions; direct reference to architectural decisions.

Essential Elements of SATAM. SATAM integrates established techniques such as arc42, STRIDE, Security QAS, ADRs, and CARAF. However, not all of these are methodologically mandatory. The essential contribution of SATAM lies in four minimal requirements:

1. A security-readable architecture baseline in which cryptographic assets can be located in architectural context.
2. Explicit identification of cryptographic assets and their protected elements or data flows.
3. A traceability chain linking threats or security scenarios to architectural elements, cryptographic mechanisms, and architectural decisions.
4. A machine-readable CBOM representation that preserves this traceability.

Specific techniques (e.g., STRIDE for threat modeling, arc42 as documentation template, or CARAF for risk estimation) are replaceable modules. The novelty of SATAM lies in consolidating architecture evaluation outputs into a traceability-preserving, migration-relevant CBOM rather than in the individual techniques themselves.

5 Conceptual Traceability Model for Architecture-Derived CBOMs

This section defines the conceptual traceability model that specifies the structure of architecture-derived CBOMs produced by SATAM. The model does not introduce additional analysis steps. Instead, it defines the mandatory relationships between architectural artifacts and CBOM entries required to ensure migration relevance.

The *traceability model defines* the following core relationships: (i) cryptographic assets are derived from and bound to architectural elements; (ii) security threats identified using STRIDE are associated with architectural elements and data flows; (iii) identified threats are refined into Security QAS; (iv) cryptographic design decisions are documented as ADRs in response to QAS; (v) ADRs are evaluated using CARAF to assess migration-relevant risk; and (vi) CBOM entries reference cryptographic assets together with their associated architectural elements, QAS, ADRs, and CARAF assessments.

The architecture description (arc42, see Sect. 2.1) forms the structural foundation of the traceability model. Architectural elements, including components, data flows, deployment nodes, and trust boundaries, act as anchors for all subsequent traceability links.

Security threats are collected by applying STRIDE to architectural elements and interactions. STRIDE threats represent potential violations of security properties but do not yet specify required system behavior. To enable architectural evaluation, identified threats are transformed into QAS. Security QAS describe the expected system response to security-relevant stimuli under defined conditions and provide measurable criteria for assessing architectural suitability.

Architectural responses to Security QAS often involve explicit cryptographic choices, such as algorithm selection, protocol usage, or key management strategies. These choices are captured as ADRs, which document decision context, rationale, and consequences. Within SATAM, ADRs act as the primary carriers of cryptographic design intent and form a critical link between security requirements and concrete architectural solutions.

Within the traceability model, CARAF provides qualitative and quantitative assessments of cryptographic decisions documented in ADRs. These assessments capture migration-relevant risk considerations and constraints that influence the feasibility and timing of cryptographic change.

The CBOM is derived by consolidating these traceability relationships. The CBOM entry corresponds to a cryptographic asset identified in the architecture. Each is annotated with references to the architectural elements it protects and the QAS it supports. Additionally, it includes the STRIDE threats it mitigates, the ADRs justifying its selection, and the CARAF findings that characterize its migration impact. Through this integration, the CBOM becomes an architectural artifact that reflects both the technical composition and the security rationale of cryptographic usage.

By making these relationships explicit, the traceability model enables validation of CBOM completeness and consistency. The resulting CBOM is not a static inventory, but an architectural artifact reflecting security intent and migration constraints.

Maintenance and Lifecycle. SATAM is designed as a continuous process rather than a one-time evaluation activity. All artifacts are anchored in the architecture baseline and evolve together with it. Changes in architectural elements propagate along traceability links and identify affected QAS, ADRs, and cryptographic assets. The CBOM is treated as a derived artifact and is regenerated from the underlying model. This approach reduces manual maintenance effort and ensures consistency by construction.

Re-evaluation Triggers. SATAM supports incremental re-evaluation based on defined triggers. *Architecture-driven triggers* include changes in components, interfaces, data flows, or trust boundaries. *Threat-driven triggers* arise from updated threat models or new attack vectors. *Cryptography-driven triggers* include algorithm deprecation and regulatory changes. *Operational triggers* include changes in deployment, certificate lifecycle, or key management. These triggers enable targeted updates while preserving overall consistency.

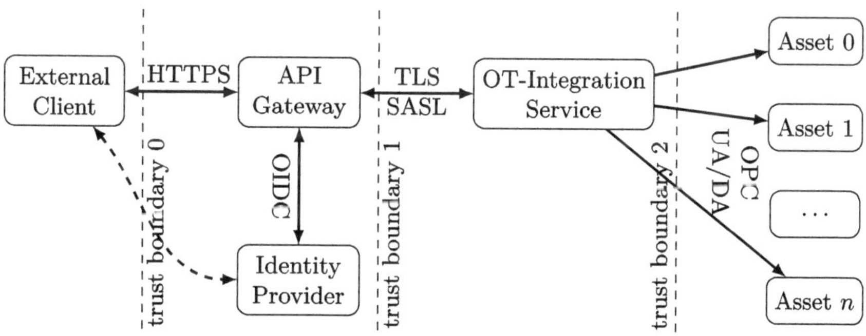

Fig. 1. Security-readable architecture baseline used as SATAM input.

6 Proof of Concept

6.1 Example Arc42 Architecture Baseline

We consider a simplified industrial architecture where an external client interacts with an OT environment via an API gateway and an OT integration service.

The integration service communicates with industrial assets using OPC UA. This design follows established OPC UA-based industrial data architectures [10], where OPC UA is used for both control interaction and data acquisition across heterogeneous devices.

Figure 1 shows the security-readable architecture baseline. It makes trust boundaries and cryptographic termination points explicit. This view corresponds to a building block view based on an arc42 documentation [22,23].

6.2 STRIDE Threat Collection and How It Drives Security QAS

SATAM applies STRIDE to architectural elements and flows. This yields threats that are specific to the architecture, not generic checklists. Figure 2 illustrates threat collection on two flows: the public client-to-gateway (edge) and internal service-to-assets flow (svc-assets).

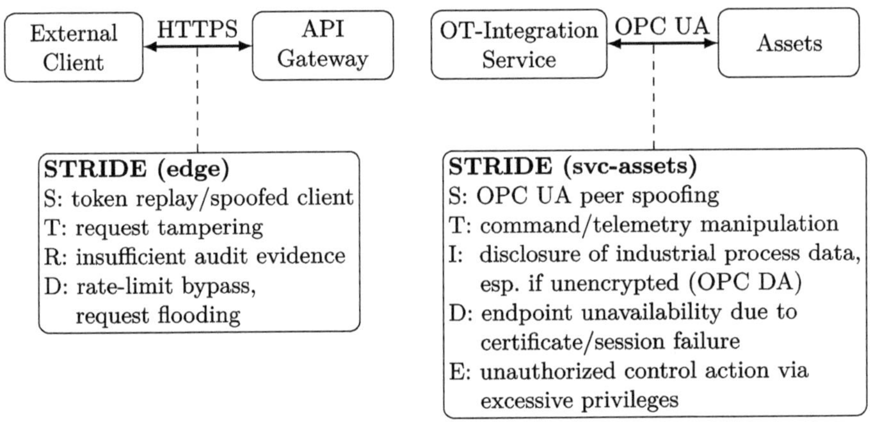

Fig. 2. STRIDE threats identified in architecture flows.

STRIDE threats are then converted into QAS. This conversion makes the analysis actionable, because QAS specify required system behavior and measurable acceptance criteria. For example, the STRIDE *tampering* threat on the service-to-assets flow yields a QAS primarily addressing integrity while also capturing timing and availability constraints (see Table 3).

6.3 Security QAS and How It Feeds CARAF

Tablen 3 shows the QAS derived from the STRIDE *tampering* threat (Fig. 2) identified for the service-to-assets flow. The response measures (RMs) are intentionally concrete, because they become an evaluation criteria during the CARAF-based analysis.

Table 3. Security QAS derived from STRIDE threats

QAS-OT-OPC-1: Secure and timely industrial communication	
Source	Attacker in IT or OT network
Stimulus	Injection, modification, or eavesdropping of OPC UA messages or unprotected OPC DA data (using `Sign` only)
Environment	OPC UA communication between OT Integration Service and PLC under normal operation and certificate rotation
Artifact	OPC UA and legacy OPC DA communication channels
Response	Authenticated and unmodified messages are enforced for secure channels, while risks from legacy communication are controlled to maintain stable operation
RMs	Auth failures rejected at handshake; integrity violations detected within one cycle; latency $\leq X$ ms; availability $\geq 99.9\%$ during certificate lifecycle events; OPC DA confined to high-risk trusted zones

This QAS drives the CARAF evaluation by defining measurable criteria for secure and timely OPC communication. It constrains architectural options across latency, availability, and compatibility dimensions but is also taking legacy constraints into account. In our example, enforcing authentication and integrity under timing constraints restricts the choice of OPC UA security modes. Further, it requires compensating controls for legacy communication, impacting cryptographic agility and operational effort.

6.4 ADRs and CARAF Evaluation

Figure 3 makes the SATAM evaluation chain explicit. STRIDE contributes the threat rationale, Security QAS provide measurable requirements, ADRs capture the chosen architectural response, and CARAF records migration-relevant findings.

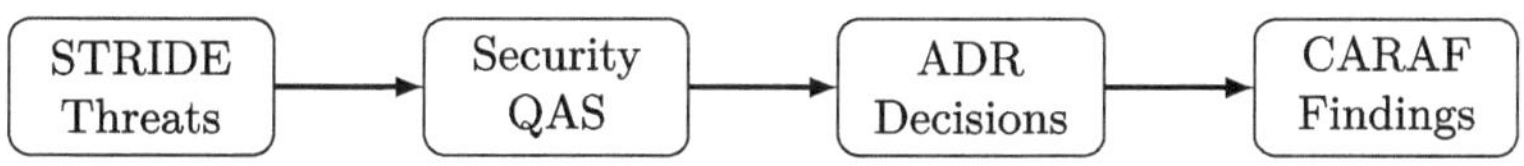

Example chain:
`T/I/S/E` on svc–assets → `QAS-OT-OPC-1` → `ADR-OT-OPC-1`
⇒ CARAF-OT-OPC-1 (action required, Risk 600,000 €)

Fig. 3. SATAM evaluation chain.

ADR Example. `ADR-OT-OPC-1` (in Table 4) documents the decision to enforce OPC UA `SignAndEncrypt` where supported and to isolate legacy OPC DA within trusted zones. It explicitly references the STRIDE threats (`T,I,S,E`) and the Security QAS `QAS-OT-OPC-1` as justification. The decision reflects a trade-off between confidentiality, integrity, and authentication on the one hand, and latency, availability, and legacy compatibility on the other.

CARAF Example. Table 5 shows an excerpt of CARAF findings derived from `ADR-OT-OPC-1` in the light of `QAS-OT-OPC-1` and the STRIDE rationale. The example focuses on migration-relevant aspects, including the effort of adopting secure OPC UA modes and handling legacy OPC DA. It is important to note that this excerpt is illustrative and demonstrates how architecture-derived artifacts populate the risk model, rather than providing a calibrated risk estimate.

Table 4. Condensed architecture decision record

ADR-OT-OPC-1: OPC communication security	
Status	Accepted
Context	OT-integration-to-PLC communication crosses trust boundary; legacy OPC DA included; STRIDE identified TISE-threats; QAS-OT-OPC-1: integrity and authentication under latency and availability constraints
Decision	Use OPC UA `SignAndEncrypt` for service-to-assets where supported; isolate/restrict OPC DA within trusted zones.
Rationale	Prioritizes confidentiality, integrity, and authentication (QAS-OT-OPC-1), trading higher latency and complexity for reduced exposure of process data and control commands; legacy and timing constraints handled via selective deployment and compensating controls.
Consequences	Confidentiality, integrity, and authentication for OPC UA where supported; increased latency and operational complexity; certificate management required; OPC DA remains unprotected and requires isolation and monitoring.
References	**STRIDE**: TISE(D); **QAS**: QAS-OT-OPC-1; **CARAF**: CARAF-OT-OPC-1

6.5 Deriving the Annotated CBOM

The SATAM evaluation chain produces a CBOM entry for each cryptographic asset annotated with stable references. The information can now be consolidated into a structured CBOM.

Listing 1 summarizes the identified cryptographic assets together with their architectural context and traceability links to STRIDE threats, Security QAS, ADRs as well as CARAF findings. These CARAF-derived enrichments are considerations such as agility, future-proofing, and key risks. Together, these represent a logical decomposition of the assessed information and are consolidated into a single CBOM artifact.

Table 5. Example risk record based on Mosca's Theorem used within CARAF

CARAF-OT-OPC-1: CARAF-OT-OPC-1 risk record	
Protected asset	Communication channel svc-assets and industrial process data (QAS-OT-OPC-1)
Mosca parameters	Determine Mosca parameters (X, Y, Z) based on data lifetime, migration time for OPC UA security modes and OPC DA replacement, and quantum horizon
Risk check	Exposure of sensitive process data and control commands, assumption of $X + Y > Z \Rightarrow$ **action required**
Drivers of Y	Derived from ADR-OT-OPC-1 consequences and operational constraints: certificate management for OPC UA, legacy OPC DA client replacement, compatibility constraints, phased rollout across OT assets
Risk [14]	Risk = $T_r \times$ Cost, cost model e.g., based on [2,11]
Mitigation direction	Reduce Y via crypto agility (standardized OPC UA security policies, automated certificate handling, asset inventory); plan migration from OPC DA to secure OPC UA; evaluate lightweight or phased encryption adoption
References	Assessment based on **STRIDE**: `TISE(D)`; **QAS**: QAS-OT-OPC-1; **ADR**: ADR-OT-OPC-1

The JSON in Listing 1 shows a simplified JSON example encoded according to the CycloneDX 1.7 specification. Each cryptographic asset is represented as a component and annotated using component properties to reference SATAM-specific metadata. These properties include architectural context, STRIDE threat categories, references to Security QAS, ADRs, and CARAF findings related to migration impact.

That representation preserves the traceability relationships shown in Listing 1 using CycloneDX-compatible properties. For example, the OPC UA `SignAndEncrypt` entry references the same identifiers as declared during the SATAM evaluation. These are identifiers applied for STRIDE threats, Security QAS, ADR, but also for CARAF notes on risk assessment. The corresponding OPC DA entry captures the absence of cryptographic protection and associated risks within the same framework. This ensures consistency between human-readable and machine-readable CBOM representations.

SATAM thus produces an artifact that supports both expert review and automated migration analysis. The resulting CBOM bridges architecture evaluation and cryptographic migration tooling while preserving architectural rationale. This proof of concept demonstrates that SATAM can be applied end-to-end to a realistic architecture, yielding an architecture-grounded CBOM with explicit traceability and migration-relevant annotations.

7 Evaluation

SATAM is evaluated analytically and through a proof-of-concept demonstration. As a methodological contribution, the evaluation focuses on internal consistency, traceability completeness, and feasibility rather than industrial-scale empirical validation.

7.1 Analytical Evaluation

The analytical evaluation assesses whether SATAM fulfills its intended objectives and addresses the identified design question. First, SATAM is internally consistent with established scenario-based architecture evaluation methods. It preserves the core ATAM phases while introducing security-specific extensions that are methodologically coherent and grounded in established practices (see Sects. 4and 5).

Listing 1. Minimal CBOM JSON excerpt of components highlighting the OPC UA versus OPC DA tradeoff

```
{
  "bom-ref": "CBOM-OT-OPCUA-1", "type": "cryptographic-asset",
  "name": "OPC~UA Security", "version": "SignAndEncrypt", "properties": [
    { "name": "satam.context.flow", "value": "svc-assets" },
    { "name": "satam.stride", "value": "S,T,I,D,E" },
    { "name": "satam.securityQasRefs", "value": "QAS-OT-OPC-1" },
    { "name": "satam.adrRefs", "value": "ADR-OT-OPC-1" },
    { "name": "satam.caraf.id", "value": "CARAF-OT-OPC-1" },
    { "name": "satam.caraf.risk", "value": "150000 Euro" },
    { "name": "satam.caraf.risk.detail",
      "value": "increased latency due to encryption" }
  ]
}, {
  "bom-ref": "CBOM-OT-OPCDA-1", "type": "cryptographic-asset",
  "name": "OPC~DA", "version": "legacy", "properties": [
    { "name": "satam.context.flow", "value": "svc-assets" },
    { "name": "satam.stride", "value": "S,T,I,E" },
    { "name": "satam.securityQasRefs", "value": "QAS-OT-OPC-1" },
    { "name": "satam.adrRefs", "value": "ADR-OT-OPC-1" },
    { "name": "satam.caraf.id", "value": "CARAF-OT-OPC-1" },
    { "name": "satam.caraf.risk", "value": "500000 Euro" },
    { "name": "satam.caraf.risk.detail",
      "value": "eavesdropping and manipulation of process data" }
  ]
}
```

Second, SATAM provides explicit traceability across architectural elements, security concerns, cryptographic decisions, and CBOM entries, as defined Sect. 5. This traceability directly addresses the limitations of inventory-based CBOMs and supports reasoning about cryptographic migration impact. In contrast to inventory-first CBOMs, SATAM-derived CBOMs do not merely enumerate cryptographic mechanisms, but make explicit why cryptography is used, which security properties it enforces, and how architectural decisions constrain change.

Third, the method is suitable for its intended purpose of supporting cryptographic migration. SATAM explicitly captures decision rationale and migration-relevant tradeoffs. This enables SATAM architectural reasoning about change impact, dependency constraints, and algorithm agility, as illustrated by the CARAF-based migration analysis in Sect. 6. As a result, SATAM-derived CBOMs expose migration-critical constraints, such as dependency coupling, roll-out effort, and key management life cycles, which are typically opaque in tool-generated inventories.

7.2 Illustrative Evaluation

The proof of concept in Sect. 6 demonstrates the applicability of SATAM on a realistic, yet manageable, system. The example shows the process of deriving STRIDE threats from the architecture and transforming them into Security QAS. It further illustrates how cryptographic decisions are documented as ADRs and how CARAF is applied to assess migration-relevant properties. The resulting CBOM excerpt and JSON representation confirm that the method produces a coherent, machine-readable artifact that preserves architectural rationale.

While the example does not provide empirical evidence of effectiveness in practice, it demonstrates feasibility and clarity of the approach. This level of evaluation is appropriate for an early-stage DSR contribution and provides a foundation for future empirical studies.

Limitations and Validity. The evaluation is limited to a proof-of-concept instantiation on a compact reference architecture and relies on analytical reasoning rather than empirical measurement. The effort required to apply SATAM and the scalability of the approach for large, evolving systems have not been empirically assessed. Additionally, CARAF inputs and cost parameters in the example are illustrative and context-dependent. Future work includes empirical validation in industrial settings and longitudinal studies of cryptographic migration decisions. SATAM partially supports automation, as CBOM generation, traceability linking, and consistency checks can be derived from the underlying architectural artifacts. Security scenario definition and architectural decision-making remain expert-driven.

7.3 Task-Based Migration Comparison

To illustrate practical impact, we compare an inventory-derived CBOM and a SATAM-derived CBOM using representative migration tasks (Table 6).

The comparison does not claim quantitative performance improvement. It illustrates that SATAMreduces information reconstruction effort by preserving architectural intent and security rationale within the CBOM artifact itself.

Table 6. Task-based comparison of migration support in the OT example

Migration task	Inventory-derived CBOM	SATAM-derived CBOM
Replace legacy OPC DA with secure OPC UA	Identifies protocol presence only. Trust boundaries, affected flows, and security consequences must be reconstructed manually.	Identifies the affected OT flow, linked STRIDE threats, referenced Security QAS, and ADR rationale. Migration scope, residual exposure, and required compensating controls get visible.
Strengthen OPC UA from `Sign` to `SignAndEncrypt`	Lists OPC UA usage only. Performance, compatibility, and deployment implications assessed externally.	Links the change to the relevant OT communication flow, Security QAS constraints, and ADR tradeoff. Migration impact on latency, certificate handling, and rollout complexity is directly visible.
OT security prioritization (availability-constrained)	Requires separate risk estimation. Legacy exposure and migration effort are not traceable from the inventory alone.	Provides traceability to security scenarios and CARAF-based migration risks, supporting prioritization that accounts for security benefit, operational effort, and legacy constraints.
Upgrade HTTPS to PQC-safe TLS	Identifies HTTPS usage only. Affected endpoints and migration dependencies must be reconstructed manually.	Identifies the client-to-gateway flow, linked STRIDE threats, and Security QAS/ADR context. Supports assessment of PQC readiness, rollout scope, and impact on interoperability.

8 Conclusion

This paper presented the Security-Aware Architecture Tradeoff Analysis Method for deriving architecture-grounded, migration-relevant CBOMs. In contrast to existing inventory-driven approaches, SATAM treats cryptographic transparency as an architectural concern and derives CBOM entries directly from scenario-based architecture evaluation. SATAM links cryptographic assets to architectural elements, security threats, security quality attribute scenarios, and architectural decisions. This results into CBOMs embedding security rationale and design intent that are essential for informed cryptographic migration.

The central contribution of this work is the consolidation of architectural evaluation outcomes into a structured CBOM artifact. Unlike tool- or inventory-derived CBOMs, the architecture-derived CBOM produced by SATAM makes cryptographic usage understandable in its architectural and security context and exposes constraints that influence the feasibility of change. This positions the CBOM not only as a compliance or discovery artifact, but as a practical input for cryptographic migration planning and long-term cryptographic agility.

Limitations and Future Work. The evaluation is limited to an analytical assessment and a proof-of-concept instantiation, and no industrial case study has yet been conducted. As a result, the practical effort, scalability, and cost-benefit characteristics of SATAM in real-world environments remain to be validated. In addition, the current presentation assumes familiarity with architecture documentation and evaluation practices, which may limit applicability in organizations without established architectural governance.

Future research will empirically evaluate SATAM in industrial contexts through comparative studies with automated CBOM generation tools. Key priorities include developing tool support to automate the SATAM workflow, refining CBOM profiles for emerging requirements such as post-quantum cryptography, and integrating the approach into secure development pipelines for continuous architecture evaluation. While SATAM introduces upfront analysis effort, it can reduce repeated manual effort by preserving architectural context and enabling partial automation of artifact generation and consistency checking.

The results indicate that, SATAM enables the construction of architecture-grounded, migration-relevant CBOMs by making cryptographic decisions and their security rationale explicit and traceable.

References

1. Alagic, G., et al.: Status Report on the Fourth Round of the NIST Post-Quantum Cryptography Standardization Process. Tech. Rep. NISTIR 8545, National Institute of Standards and Technology (2025). https://doi.org/10.6028/nist.ir.8545
2. Algarni, A.M., Thayananthan, V., Malaiya, Y.K.: Quantitative assessment of cybersecurity risks for mitigating data breaches in business systems. Appl. Sci. **11**(8), 3678 (2021). https://doi.org/10.3390/app11083678, defines the mathematical ALE (Annual Loss Expectancy) model used to convertpotential breach costs into a yearly financial risk value
3. Arora, A., Wright, V., Garman, C.: Strengthening the security of operational technology: understanding contemporary bill of materials. J. Critical Infrastruct. Policy **3**, 111–135 (2022). https://doi.org/10.18278/jcip.3.1.8
4. Bass, L., Clements, P., Kazman, R.: Software Architecture in Practice. Addison-Wesley Professional, 4th edn. (2021)
5. Bundesamt für Sicherheit in der Informationstechnik (BSI): Migration to Post Quantum Cryptography. Tech. rep., BSI (May 2021). https://www.bsi.bund.de/SharedDocs/Downloads/EN/BSI/Crypto/Migration_to_Post_Quantum_Cryptography.pdf
6. Dang, Q., Kelsey, J., McKay, K., Bassham, L., Chang, S.J.: Considerations for Cryptographic Agility and Migration. Tech. Rep. NISTIR 8259, National Institute of Standards and Technology (2019). https://doi.org/10.6028/NIST.IR.8259
7. Hassouna, A.B.: Atraf-driven imrad methodology: Tradeoff and risk analysis of software architectures across abstraction levels (2025). https://doi.org/10.48550/arxiv.2505.03624. arXiv
8. Hess, B., Körtge, N.: Standardization of Cryptography Bill of Materials in OWASP CycloneDX. Poster, ETSI/IQC QSC 2024 (2024). https://research.ibm.com/publications/standardization-of-cryptography-bill-of-materials-in-owasp-cyclonedx

9. Hevner, A.R., March, S.T., Park, J., Ram, S.: Design science in information systems research. MIS Q. **28**(1), 75–105 (2004)
10. Hirsch, E., Hoher, S., Huber, S.: An OPC UA-based industrial big data architecture. In: 2023 IEEE 21st International Conference on Industrial Informatics (INDIN), pp. 1–7 (2023). https://doi.org/10.1109/INDIN51400.2023.10217899
11. IBM Security and Ponemon Institute: Cost of a data breach report 2025. Tech. rep., IBM Corporation (2025). https://www.ibm.com/reports/data-breach, provides the empirical basis for the 158 Euro per-record cost in the financial sector, accounting for detection, notification, and lost business
12. Ibnugraha, P.D., et al.: Evaluation of security in software architecture using combination of ATAM and STRIDE. J. Theor. Appl. Inform. Technol. (2015). https://www.jatit.org/volumes/Vol75No1/2Vol75No1.pdf
13. Kazman, R., Klein, M., Clements, P.: ATAM: Method for Architecture Evaluation. Tech. Rep. CMU/SEI-2000-TR-004, Software Engineering Institute, Carnegie Mellon University (Aug 2000). https://www.sei.cmu.edu/documents/629/2000_005_001_13706.pdf
14. Ma, C., Colon, L., Dera, J., Rashidi, B., Garg, V.: Caraf: Crypto agility risk assessment framework. J. Cybersecur. **7**(1), tyab013 (2021). https://doi.org/10.1093/cybsec/tyab013
15. Näther, C., Herzinger, D., Gazdag, S.L., Steghöfer, J.P., Daum, S., Loebenberger, D.: Migrating software systems towards post-quantum cryptography – a systematic literature review. IEEE Access 132107–132127 (2024). https://doi.org/10.1109/ACCESS.2024.3450306
16. National Telecommunications and Information Administration: Framing Software Component Transparency: Establishing a Common Software Bill of Materials (SBOM), Second Edition. Tech. rep., U.S. Department of Commerce (NTIA) (Oct 2021). https://www.ntia.gov/files/ntia/publications/ntia_sbom_framing_2nd_edition_20211021.pdf, defines an SBOM as a nested inventory (i.e., a list of ingredients)
17. Newhouse, W., et al.: NIST SP 1800-38B: Migration to Post-Quantum Cryptography: Cryptographic Discovery (Preliminary Draft). Tech. rep., NIST NCCoE (Dec 2023). https://www.nccoe.nist.gov/sites/default/files/2023-12/pqc-migration-nist-sp-1800-38b-preliminary-draft.pdf
18. Nygard, M.: Documenting Architecture Decisions. Blog post (November 2011). https://www.cognitect.com/blog/2011/11/15/documenting-architecture-decisions, the foundational article for Architecture Decision Records (ADRs)
19. OWASP CycloneDX Project: Authoritative guide to CBOM. Tech. rep., OWASP Foundation (Apr 2024). https://cyclonedx.org/guides/OWASP_CycloneDX-Authoritative-Guide-to-CBOM-en.pdf, describes CBOM as a structured, comprehensive inventory of cryptographic assets and their properties
20. OWASP CycloneDX Project: Cryptography bill of materials (CBOM). Web page (2024). https://cyclonedx.org/capabilities/cbom/
21. Stalnaker, T., et al.: BOMs away! inside the minds of stakeholders. In: International Conference on Software Engineering (ICSE) (2024). https://ojcchar.github.io/files/27-icse24-sboms.pdf
22. Starke, G., Hruschka, P.: arc42: The Template for Software Architecture Documentation and Communication. https://arc42.org (2024). Accessed 28 Jan 2026
23. Starke, G., Simons, M., Zörner, S., Müller, R.D., Lösch, H.: arc42 by Example: Real software architectures, documented with the arc42 template. Leanpub, 3rd edn. (2023). https://leanpub.com/arc42byexample

24. Tyree, J., Akerman, A.: Architecture decisions: demystifying architecture. IEEE Softw. **22**(2), 19–27 (2005). https://doi.org/10.1109/MS.2005.27
25. Xia, B., et al.: An Empirical Study on Software Bill of Materials. arXiv (2023). https://arxiv.org/pdf/2301.05362
26. Zhou, L., et al.: A Reality Check on SBOM-based Vulnerability Management: An Empirical Study and A Path Forward. arXiv (2025). https://arxiv.org/pdf/2511.20313

Supporting Cryptographic Migration with an IT Infrastructure Digital Twin

Daniel Herzinger[1(✉)], Christian Näther[2], and Stefan-Lukas Gazdag[1]

[1] genua GmbH, 85551 Kirchheim near Munich, Germany
{daniel_herzinger,stefan-lukas_gazdag}@genua.de
[2] Xitaso GmbH, 86153 Augsburg, Germany
christian.naether@xitaso.com

Abstract. Modern IT infrastructures are composed of heterogeneous services with complex dependencies and security configurations. During migration or modernization efforts, incomplete or outdated knowledge about communication relationships, protocol usage, and cryptographic dependencies represents a major source of risk.

This paper presents an approach for the automated construction of a graph-based digital twin of an IT infrastructure, developed using Design Science Research (DSR). It collects data in transit using a dedicated, extensible processing pipeline that extracts, parses, and transforms network-, protocol-, and cryptography-level information into a unified graph representation. The resulting digital twin is implemented using a graph database, enabling interactive exploration through graph queries and visualizations.

The graph-based model explicitly represents communication relationships, protocols, and associated cryptographic properties, allowing heterogeneous infrastructure information to be integrated into a coherent schema. Based on this representation, the digital twin is the first solution that supports the cataloging and analysis of cryptographic mechanisms including dependencies, providing a structured foundation for post-quantum cryptography (PQC) migration planning and improved cryptographic agility in complex IT environments.

Keywords: Post-Quantum Cryptography · PQC-Migration · Digital Twin · Graph-Based Modeling · IT Infrastructure · Cryptographic Agility

1 Introduction

Ellen Ullman poetically noted that "We build our computers the way we build our cities—over time, without a plan, on top of ruins" [32]. This quote highlights the complexity and consequent challenges of modern computer systems and, in particular, of historically grown IT infrastructures. Over time, they evolve into highly interconnected and heterogeneous environments that are nonetheless critical for the day-to-day operation of society.

D. Loebenberger and M. Stöttinger (Eds.): MAgiCS 2026, CCIS 3002, pp. 40–60, 2026.
https://doi.org/10.1007/978-3-032-28946-9_3

The upcoming migration from classical cryptography to quantum-safe algorithms further exacerbates this complexity. In light of the expected advances in quantum computing and migration deadlines often discussed around 2030 [6,10], organizations face significant urgency combined with substantial uncertainty. The security properties of Post-Quantum Cryptography (PQC) algorithms, their implementation, and their introduction into existing security protocols remain active research topics. As a result, infrastructures must be adapted under time pressure and with limited certainty about optimal migration strategies.

To navigate this difficult environment, a fundamental prerequisite for PQC migration is visibility into where and how cryptography is used. This need has led to the concept of cryptographic inventories [3,9], which aim to document cryptographic mechanisms and their deployment. Still, creating and maintaining such inventories requires dedicated processes and tooling [9] and often fails to capture dynamic aspects, such as cryptographic usage in transit or dependencies between communicating components. Beyond inventory creation, understanding dependencies between cryptographic instantiations and other infrastructure components is essential for migration planning [4,9]. Cryptographic mechanisms rarely operate in isolation. Instead, they are embedded within protocols and communication paths that span multiple systems. Consequently, dependency information must either be integrated into cryptographic inventories or represented through complementary artifacts. Given the scale and dynamism of modern infrastructures, gathering and maintaining this information must be highly automated and tool-assisted to remain feasible.

Existing approaches to post-quantum cryptography migration—including software analysis tools and Software Bills of Materials (SBOMs) [21,24,26], traditional asset inventories and Configuration Management Databases (CMDBs) [3,9], and network and device monitoring—provide fragmented views that are either static, manually maintained, or disconnected from infrastructure models. What is missing is an integrated representation that continuously links assets, communication paths, and in-transit cryptography at scale. To address this gap, we adopt *digital twins* as a unifying modeling paradigm for complex IT infrastructures. Originally established in engineering and cyber-physical systems, digital twins describe continuously synchronized digital representations of real-world systems that reflect both structural properties and observed behavior [12,31]. In the infrastructure domain, digital twins aim to capture dynamic relationships and operational context, as reflected in Wu et al.'s Digital Twin Networks concept [33] and Raza et al.'s Network Digital Twin survey [27]. While digital twins have been proposed for infrastructure management and security [25,34], current models do not treat cryptographic properties of network communication—such as protocols, algorithms, and trust relationships—as first-class, queryable elements. Applied to the context of PQC migration, a digital twin should integrate heterogeneous data sources—such as asset descriptions, network observations, and protocol-level interactions—into a coherent, queryable model that evolves alongside the underlying infrastructure. Such a model comprises information about the infrastructure's assets, network topology, and communication paths including the cryptography used in transit, enabling more accurate and actionable analysis for migration planning than static inventories or disconnected monitoring data alone.

We address this by proposing a graph-based digital twin of an IT infrastructure, together with a modular data pipeline that ingests heterogeneous infrastructure data and transforms it into the proposed representation. Our innovative design is modular and designed for integration, making it possible to adjust and extend it for the use in real-world infrastructures and future research. In detail, we make the following contributions:

- We present a communication-centric modeling approach for a digital twin that explicitly represents cryptographic dependencies emerging from network and protocol interactions.
- We introduce a graph-based digital twin implementation for IT infrastructures with an automated data pipeline that observes assets and topologies, as well as their communication behavior, protocol usage, and cryptographic properties in transit.
- We evaluate the resulting digital twin and pipeline and show how they enable analysis and prioritization tasks essential for PQC migration planning and cryptographic agility.

2 Related Work

In the following, we review existing approaches on identifying cryptographic usage for PQC migration and on modeling cryptographic dependencies in complex IT infrastructures to highlight remaining gaps.

A growing body of research addresses challenges related to the migration to PQC [22]. Several efforts focus on identifying and classifying cryptographic usage within software systems, for example by analyzing binaries or source code to detect quantum-vulnerable algorithms and libraries [26,29]. Related initiatives such as SBOMs and emerging Cryptography Bills of Materials (CBOMs) [23] aim to improve transparency by documenting software components and cryptographic implementations [16,21,24]. Together, these approaches enhance software supply chain visibility and provide valuable insight into individual artifacts. However, they primarily focus on static software views and provide limited awareness of communication paths, protocol interactions, and cross-system dependencies within operational infrastructures.

To complement this software-centric view, infrastructure-centric inventories aim to document the involved systems and their relationships. Traditional asset management and CMDBs offer partial support for documenting infrastructure components and relationships, leading to an increasing relevance in the face of the PQC transition [3,9]. However, they typically rely on manual processes and static representations which are a fitting solution for documentation but insufficient for capturing dynamic communication behavior and cryptographic usage in transit. To complement static inventories, more advanced techniques rely on dynamic analysis of network communication, for example through monitoring and traffic analysis tools. These approaches can observe protocols and connections to reveal cryptographic mechanisms used in practice, as shown by Schmitt et al. [30]. Yet, they only extract their findings without the context necessary for integrating it into models which would then assist cryptographic migration.

To reason about these dependencies at scale, graph-based dependency models have been suggested to analyze cryptographic dependencies and to prioritize migration steps across complex systems [13]. These approaches highlight the importance of dependency awareness, but they often assume that detailed and accurate infrastructure information is already available through inventories or documentation, which in practice is frequently incomplete, outdated, or fragmented. This motivates holistic infrastructure models that integrate heterogeneous data sources and can be maintained as the infrastructure evolves. Such integrated and evolvable representations naturally align with the digital twin paradigm, which has been explored in various areas of computer security and infrastructure management. In the security domain, Qureshi et al. survey security-enhancing digital twins and emphasize that a digital twin, by combining data with a system model, enables tasks such as monitoring, simulation, and automation [25]. Foundational work further characterizes digital twins through continuous and bidirectional integration between physical and virtual counterparts [11,20]. Building on these notions, Wu et al. describe their *Digital Twin Networks* as a co-evolution of physical and virtual spaces enabled by modeling and data processing technologies [33]. Also the IRTF NMRG discusses network-oriented digital twins and proposed a reference architecture and core elements such as data, models, mapping, interfaces, and logic [34]. ETSI provides complementary terminology and guidance, and Raza et al. survey Network Digital Twin architectures and their use for network analysis, emulation, and control [1,2,27]. Across these lines of work, digital twins are thus typically grounded in asset-centric representations and data-driven synchronization concepts, to enable simulation and performance-centric decision support for network operations.

To our knowledge, none of the surveyed models makes cryptographic properties of end-to-end network communication, such as negotiated protocol parameters, cryptographic algorithms, or certificate and trust relationships first-class and queryable elements of the infrastructure model. As a result, their applicability to cryptographic agility and PQC migration planning remains limited. This gap motivates digital twin models that are specifically designed to represent communication-centric dependencies and cryptographic characteristics in complex, evolving IT infrastructures.

3 Methodology

We follow the Design Science Research (DSR) methodology by Hevner et al. [15] in the development of our approach. It focuses on the purposeful design and evaluation of artifacts addressing relevant real-world problems. In our work, the

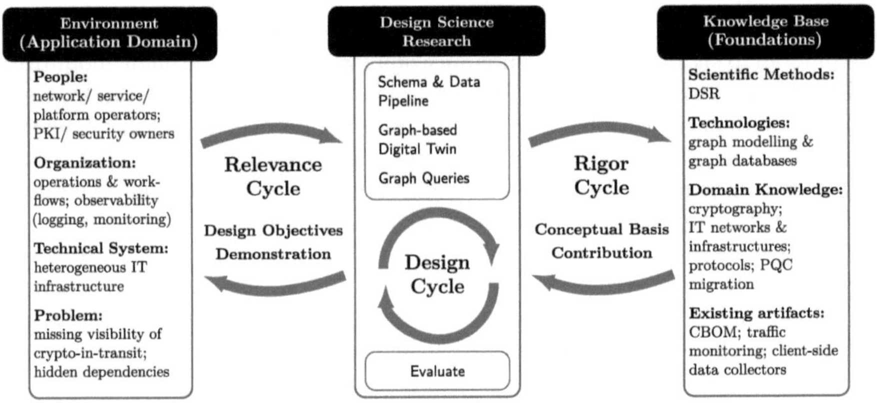

Fig. 1. Graph-based digital twin for PQC migration in a Design Science Research setting: mapping the application environment, design objectives and demonstration (relevance cycle), conceptual foundation and artifact contribution (rigor cycle), and iterative build-evaluate activities (design cycle). Adapted from Hevner's three-cycle view of design science research [14].

real-world problem is to support PQC migration by making cryptographic dependencies in IT infrastructures observable and analyzable. The primary outcome of this research is a graph-based digital twin of an IT infrastructure constituting the central artifact of the DSR process. The artifact represents infrastructure components, communication relationships, protocols, and associated cryptographic properties in a unified graph model. Beyond the conceptual model itself, it comprises the underlying graph schema and a data processing pipeline that collects, parses, and transforms heterogeneous infrastructure data into the proposed representation.

As illustrated by Fig. 1, we position our work within the *Design Science Research* activity, which connects the *environment* (application domain) and the *knowledge base* (foundations) through the relevance, rigor, and design cycles. Within this Design Science Research activity, we develop the artifact comprising the graph schema, the data pipeline, and the graph-based digital twin. We refine it through iterative build-evaluate cycles in the *design cycle*. These iterations are reflected in the pipeline design and implementation described in Sects. 4.2 and 4.3, and in the evaluation and analysis presented in Sect. 5.

For our initial implementation, we use a Graph DataBase (GDB) and implement a minimal end-to-end pipeline in Sect. 4.3 to validate feasibility and enable early demonstrations. We then refine the artifact by adding parser and transformer modules, extending protocol coverage, and improving the capture of cryptographic dependencies. To ensure practical relevance, we characterize the application domain in which the artifact will operate. Following Hevner et al. [15], we describe this domain through the *environment* along people, organizational aspects, technical systems, and problems.

Figure 1 provides illustrative examples based on our problem analysis and requirements elicitation in the PQC migration context, covering key stakeholders, organizational workflows and observability practices, and the heterogeneity of IT infrastructures that leads to missing visibility of cryptography in transit and dependencies. Building on this characterization of the environment, we connect the identified practical challenges to concrete artifact requirements through the *Relevance Cycle*. In the Relevance Cycle, we derive design objectives and validate them through demonstration and feedback. Concretely, we ground the artifact in the PQC migration problem described in Sect. 1, translate the resulting requirements into design objectives that are operationalized by RQ1 and RQ2, and use the containerized infrastructure scenario in Sect. 5.1 as a running example for demonstration and evaluation.

The *Knowledge Base* activity captures the scientific foundations and domain knowledge that inform our design. In particular, it includes design science research methods, graph modeling and graph database concepts, and foundational knowledge about cryptography, networks, protocols, and PQC migration. In the *rigor cycle*, we ground the artifact in the knowledge base by reviewing and comparing modeling techniques for representing an IT infrastructure digital twin.

From this review, we derive that a graph-based representation is well-suited to capture connectivity and dependency structures, motivating the graph-based modeling approach in Sect. 4. Based on these insights, we design the graph schema as the core artifact representation in Sect. 4.1, linking infrastructure entities, communication relationships, protocols, and cryptographic mechanisms. Concretely, concepts from graph databases inform our schema design and query patterns, while protocol and cryptography fundamentals guide how we represent negotiated parameters and trust relationships.

To operationalize the design objectives and structure the iterative build and evaluation of the artifact across the relevance, rigor, and design cycles, we formulate the following research questions:

RQ1: *Which data-based modeling and data processing approach enables the construction of a digital twin that represents communication relationships, protocols, and cryptographic properties of an IT infrastructure?*
This research question addresses the design and construction of the proposed artifact within the DSR design cycle. It focuses on how heterogeneous infrastructure data, such as network communication, protocol usage, and cryptographic properties, can be collected, processed, and structured using a graph-based modeling approach. The goal is to define suitable schema elements, relationships, and data processing steps that allow these diverse information sources to be integrated into a unified digital twin.

RQ2: *Which types of analysis and prioritization to support post-quantum cryptography migration can be conducted using an IT infrastructure digital twin?*
This research question investigates how the constructed digital twin can be used to analyze cryptographic dependencies within an IT infrastructure and thus corresponds to the demonstration and evaluation activities of the DSR

process. It examines how graph-based queries, visualizations, and filtering mechanisms enable the identification of protocol usage, cryptographic exposure, and migration-relevant components. Furthermore, it explores how the graph representation can support prioritization heuristics, for example based on connectivity or exposure, to inform decision-making in the context of cryptographic agility and PQC migration.

4 Graph-Based Infrastructure Modeling

To support IT infrastructure cryptographic migration, we adopt a graph-based modeling approach to construct a digital twin that captures communication behavior in operation. This aligns well with emerging graph models for infrastructural migration (see, e.g., [13,17]). The model is designed to make communication relationships, protocol usage, and crypto mechanisms explicit, enabling systematic analysis of dependencies relevant to crypto-agility and PQC migration.

Infrastructure entities such as hosts, containers, interfaces, and services, as well as connections and crypto algorithms are represented as nodes. The network topology, compositions, and usage relationships between the entities are modeled as edges. This representation allows both structural properties (e.g., connectivity and reachability) and security-relevant properties (e.g., protocol usage and cryptographic protection) to be expressed within a unified model.

The abstraction deliberately focuses on network- and protocol-level interactions rather than individual software artifacts. This design choice reflects the observation that cryptographic dependencies relevant for migration planning often emerge from communication paths and protocol usage in transit, rather than from isolated libraries or executables. By modeling how systems interact in practice, the digital twin captures dependencies that are difficult to identify using static, asset-centric representations. The transient nature of this data makes maintaining such a dynamic representation more challenging. Yet, by leveraging existing monitoring tools within a data pipeline we manage to keep the graph based digital twin close to the dynamic reality of real-world IT infrastructures.

Storing the infrastructure representation in a graph data model directly encodes structural relationships in the underlying data format. This enables flexible query-based exploration and visualization of communication paths and cryptographic dependencies without requiring transformations between multiple representations. The graph-based digital twin serves as the conceptual foundation for the schema definition, data acquisition, and evaluation steps.

4.1 Graph Schema and Digital Twin Representation

The core of the proposed digital twin is a graph schema that captures infrastructure entities, their communication relationships, and associated cryptographic

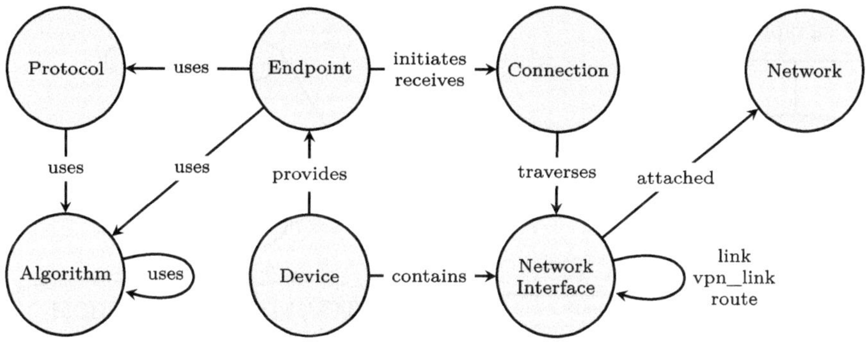

Fig. 2. Conceptual graph schema used for representing infrastructure components, communication relationships, and cryptographic properties in the digital twin. Devices can further be marked as gateways, segregating network security zones. Also, endpoints allow for further differentiation into client and server endpoints.

properties in a unified representation. Figure 2 illustrates the conceptual structure of the schema used to instantiate the digital twin and shows how different infrastructure layers and security-relevant aspects are connected.

Nodes represent the infrastructure's devices and their network interfaces. They allow different abstraction levels to be captured explicitly. In practice, these nodes connected by the link edges yield the layer two topology. The layer three topology is depicted by these and the network nodes they are attached to as well as their route edges. The communication between infrastructure entities is represented by the connection nodes that have edges to the devices' endpoints and to the interfaces they traversed in the network, as observed in transit.

The protocol and algorithm nodes align with the structure of CBOMs to ease integration into standard tooling and processes. The explicit modeling of crypto protocols better reflects the systems' secure communication in practice. The model shows cryptographic mechanisms used by a certain protocol or also by a given service endpoint. An important aspect for PQC migration are hybrid algorithms. In that case a combination, like "ML-KEM768+X25519", has additional "uses" edges to the specific algorithms it consists of, like "ML-KEM768" and "X25519".

The schema's layered structure allows analyses to focus on individual aspects of the infrastructure or to combine multiple layers when assessing cryptographic dependencies and migration impact. The schema is realized as a property graph within a GDB providing a concrete digital twin which directly reflects the conceptual model shown in Fig. 2.

4.2 Data Acquisition and Processing Pipeline

Populating the graph-based digital twin requires a data acquisition and processing pipeline that captures relevant infrastructure information as it occurs in operation and transforms it into our unified representation. The pipeline is

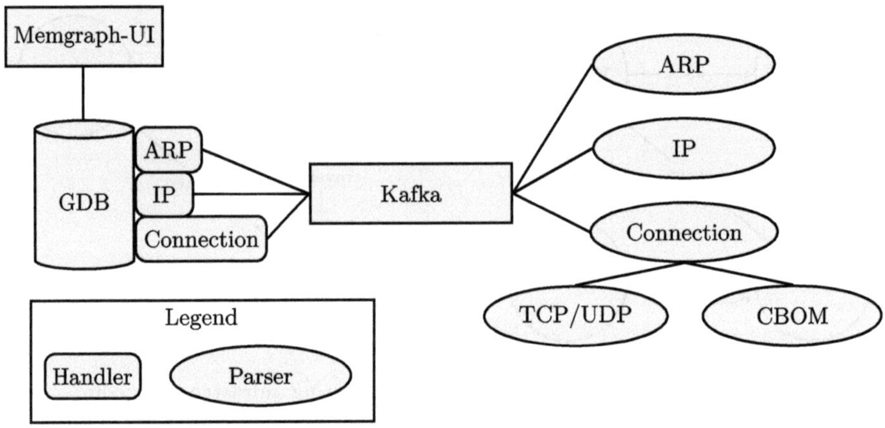

Fig. 3. The architecture of our pipeline including the sensor scripts on the clients and gateways, as well as the systems representing the Digital Twin itself. The edges represent system interactions.

designed to observe communication behavior and cryptographic usage in transit, thereby complementing static configuration artifacts with runtime-derived insights.

The pipeline follows a staged approach in which heterogeneous observations are incrementally refined and aligned with the graph schema. All stages run continuously and each piece of information runs through every phase to be finally implemented into the digital twin. In the first phase, sensors collect data from the infrastructure's system interfaces. The gateways scan the network traffic with Deep Packet Inspection (DPI) sensors. The yielded information covers connectivity, communication, protocol, and cryptography usage that may not be fully specified in static documentation or configuration.

In the subsequent processing stage, dedicated parsers extract the relevant information from the observed data. Network related observations, such as link-layer relationships or IP addresses, are interpreted and converted into dedicated formats. Cryptography-related information is handled using CBOMs, increasing compatibility by compliance with existing standards. Embedding both formats into a common structure preserves associations between communication endpoints, network path finding, protocols, and employed cryptographic mechanisms.

In the final stage of the pipeline, handler scripts on the database side compile the processed observations into the graph schema described in Sect. 4.1. This transformation step ensures that heterogeneous inputs are mapped consistently to nodes, relationships, and properties. As a result, observations originating from different sources and protocol layers become directly comparable and jointly analyzable within the digital twin.

4.3 Database and Data Pipeline Implementation

We now describe how the proposed graph-based digital twin is instantiated and populated with observed infrastructure data. Figure 3 depicts the overall data flow from infrastructure observations to the populated graph representation. The instantiation combines existing tooling with custom transformation logic mapping observed communication behavior, protocol usage, and cryptographic information to the graph schema introduced in Sect. 4.1, enabling their explicit representation and linkage within the digital twin.

As shown on the right side of Fig. 3, the pipeline begins with the collection of network- and protocol-level observations from the running infrastructure. These include connectivity information, active communication relationships, interface configurations, and protocol usage. Python and bash scripts inspect the devices' Address Resolution Protocol (ARP) tables, interface configurations, and routing information. On central network components, such as gateways, protocol- and cryptography-related information is additionally extracted using the proprietary DPI scanner Qosmos[1]. It provides detailed insights into protocols such as the cryptographic mechanisms offered within an SSH handshake. Also, the parsers normalize the information into JSON or even standardized CBOM formats.

The central part of Fig. 3 illustrates the Apache Kafka[2]-based streaming pipeline. It collects these JSON inputs from different producers, bundles and partitions them into dedicated topics, and queues them until consumption. This decouples data collection and transformation from persistence and enables the incremental population of the digital twin. Under heavy load the queueing protects the database from being overloaded. The pipeline uses common data formats like JSON and the built upon CBOM which facilitates interoperability, as new producers or consumers only need to support these shared representations.

As depicted on the left side of Fig. 3, the processed observations are finally persisted in a Memgraph[3] GDB by inserting them into *Cypher* queries which then create the schema introduced in Sect. 4.1. The GDB directly supports traversal-based queries and pattern matching required to analyze communication paths and cryptographic dependencies, making it the natural implementation choice. It does, however, lack in performance especially when met with large amounts of write queries in a short amount of time. Our graph model already inherently reduces the number of write queries by not including transient information like source ports. Thus, after having stored the "normality" of a given infrastructure, incoming information is mostly knwon already. Still, memgraph promises better performance than other GDBs, making it the best option for our implementation. While decisions in favor of certain tooling like Qosmos or Memgraph are based on relevant design considerations, similar tools may be integrated if they sufficiently provide the necessary feature set. Running different sensors in parallel is supported by the modular pipeline architecture.

---

[1] https://qosmos.net.
[2] https://kafka.apache.org.
[3] www.memgraph.com.

The resulting graph representation of the infrastructure forms the basis for the queries, visualizations, and analytical results presented in the next section. Those results, in turn, allow for well-informed decision-making and structured reasoning during PQC migration planning.

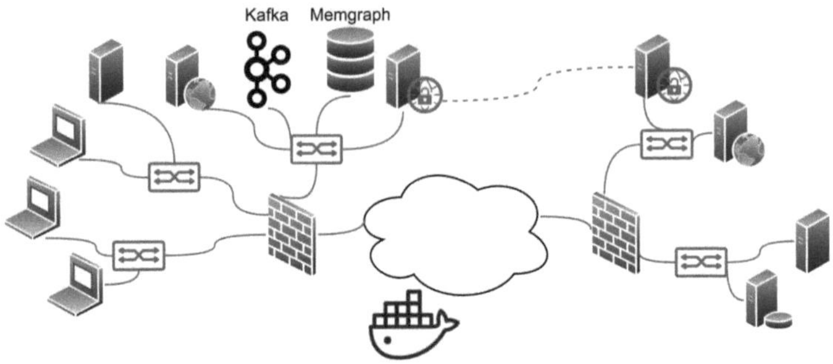

Fig. 4. Topology of the containerized infrastructure used to evaluate the graph-based digital twin. It combines different application-level services, separated network zones and VPNs which are depicted as a dashed line.

5 Evaluation

This section presents an exploratory evaluation of the proposed graph-based digital twin introduced in Sect. 4. We evaluate the implementation in the context of a containerized IT infrastructure and examine which insights we can derive for cryptographic migration. The evaluation focuses on how the graph-based digital twin enables visibility of cryptographic usage, communication dependencies, and infrastructure topology.

5.1 IT-Infrastructure Use Case

As a representative use case, we consider an exemplary IT infrastructure deployed using Docker, designed to expose characteristic communication patterns and crypto mechanisms found in real-world IT environments. It serves as a controlled yet realistic environment for evaluating the ability of the graph-based digital twin to model and analyze cryptographic dependencies across multiple layers.

Figure 4 illustrates the overall structure of the evaluation platform and its main components. The setup comprises several containers assuming distinct roles, including clients, application services, security gateways, and dedicated VPN components. These components are organized into zones separated by the security gateways, reflecting typical trust boundaries in enterprise infrastructures. Communication between components is protected using cryptographic mechanisms at both the application layer, e.g., SSH, and the network layer, e.g.,

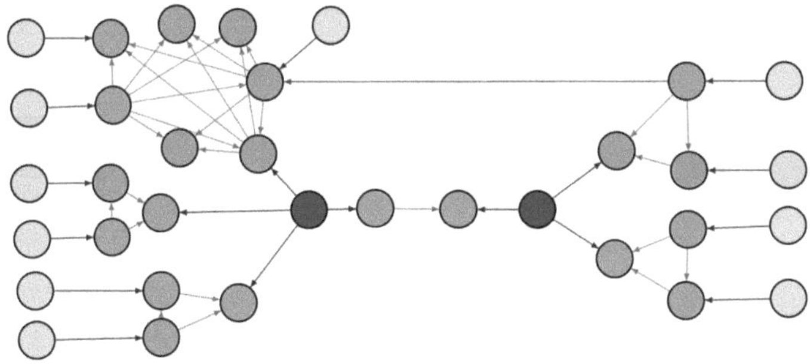

Fig. 5. Visual result of the infrastructure's layer two topology query. Red nodes represent firewalls, blue nodes network interfaces, and yellow nodes client or server systems. Link directions are a technical necessity for the GDB without further meaning; the red link indicates VPN connectivity. Interfaces without hosts were inferred from neighboring ARP entries. Additional attributes such as addresses and hostnames are stored as properties but omitted here for readability.

with a VPN. This provides a suitable basis for evaluating layered cryptographic dependencies.

Client containers are configured to initiate communication and generate network traffic within the environment. Application functionality is provided by service containers that expose endpoints accessed by the clients. In addition to application-level communication, clients access selected services via SSH, introducing protocol-level cryptographic protection. These connections' analysis results forms the basis for evaluating the analysis quality of the digital twin.

Beyond application-layer security, the infrastructure incorporates a dedicated VPN component. The VPN containers establish an IPsec-based encrypted overlay network using StrongSwan[4], providing cryptographic protection at the network layer for selected communication paths. This introduces an additional class of cryptographic dependencies that is independent of application protocols and highlights the coexistence of multiple cryptographic mechanisms within the same infrastructure. This forms the basis for evaluating whether the digital twin can recognize the different protection layers and adjust its prioritization.

Overall, the use case intentionally combines multiple communication paths, trust boundaries, and cryptographic protection mechanisms. These characteristics enable the evaluation of how the proposed digital twin captures communication behavior in transit, represents cryptographic dependencies across layers, and supports the analyses presented next.

5.2 Results

We now present the results obtained after instantiating the graph-based digital twin and its pipeline in the context described in Sects. 4.3 and 5.1. The results are

[4] https://strongswan.org.

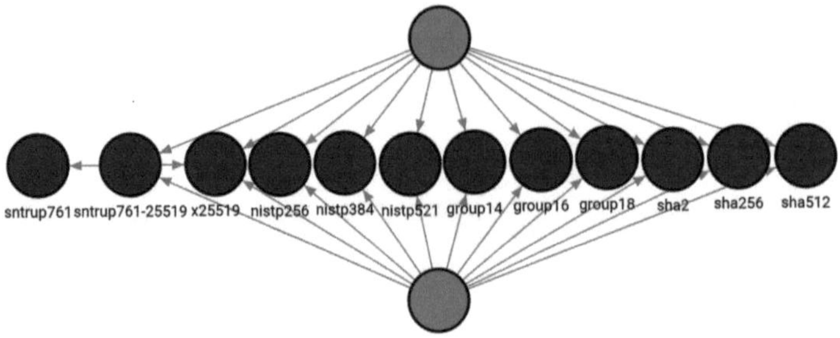

Fig. 6. Visual result of SSH endpoints (orange) and their configured cryptographic algorithms (purple). There, *group*prefers to a specific Diffie–Hellman group. Hybrid configurations are represented by additional algorithm nodes. (Color figure online)

structured along the OSI layers and describe the resulting graph representation at different levels of abstraction. They show which information is available after processing the observed infrastructure data. All results are presented descriptively; interpretation and discussion are deferred to Sect. 5.3.

After executing the data pipeline, the digital twin contains a graph-based representation of the OSI layer two topology derived from the observed infrastructure data. Nodes represent devices and their associated network interfaces, while relationships capture observed layer two connectivity. Figure 5 illustrates the resulting topology as represented in the digital twin.

The layer two topology is constructed by aggregating interface configurations and neighborhood information collected at runtime, including refreshed ARP tables. Interfaces without directly observable hosts are inferred from neighboring ARP entries, enabling the representation of intermediate network elements. Once all observation messages have been processed at least once, the digital twin contains a consistent view of layer two connectivity across the infrastructure.

The following *Cypher* query extracts the layer two topology from the digital twin and is used to generate the visualization shown in Fig. 5:

```
MATCH (device) -[con:contains]-> (nic:Network_Interface)
  -[link:link|:vpn_link]- (rnic:Network_Interface)
RETURN *
```

Once layer two is set, the digital twin is extended with information from OSI layer three. Interface configurations and routing tables parsed from the observed systems are integrated into the existing graph representation. This step enriches the digital twin with IP-level addressing and routing relationships by associating network interfaces with their configured addresses and routing entries.

This complements the previously described topology. Providing the addressing and routing context is required to relate network-level connectivity to higher-layer communication endpoints. This information forms the structural basis for the protocol-level and cryptography-related results presented in the following section.

In addition to the previously described network-level representation, we can also capture protocol-level communication and the associated cryptographic configurations observed in the infrastructure. Based on observations obtained from DPI scanners deployed at network gateways, the digital twin represents protocol-level connections and associates them with the cryptographic algorithms configured at the respective communication endpoints.

Figure 6 shows a subgraph for SSH communication. Nodes represent SSH endpoints and cryptographic algorithms, while relationships capture the usage of specific algorithms by individual endpoints. Hybrid configurations are represented by modeling the combination as its own algorithm then having usage relationships to the algorithms it is comprised of. This way we can observe that the two endpoints of Fig. 6 offer "sntrup761", a PQC algorithm, but only in conjunction with a classical elliptic curve, not on its own. Capturing the hybrid context is necessary to navigate the current regulatory landscape (s. [7]).

The following *Cypher* query extracts the SSH-related subgraph and retrieves the associated crypto algorithms and hybrid relationships shown in Fig. 6:

```
MATCH (endpoint) -[:uses]-> (:Protocol {name: "ssh"})
MATCH (endpoint) -[alg_use:uses]-> (alg:Algorithm)
OPTIONAL MATCH (alg) -[hybrid_use:uses]-> (alg2:Algorithm)
RETURN *
```

Modeling Communication, Protocols, and Cryptography (RQ1)

The results address RQ1 by showing how observed communication paths, protocol usage, and associated cryptographic configurations are explicitly represented within the graph-based digital twin. Across the described OSI layers, protocol-level connections are linked to their underlying network context and configured cryptographic mechanisms, making cryptographic dependencies observable in relation to concrete communication paths.

5.3 Result Utilization for Cryptographic Migration

With these results in place, we now illustrate how the digital twin can be utilized to support cryptographic migration tasks. We focus on the use of the graph representation to analyze communication relationships, identify cryptographic dependencies, and derive migration-relevant views of the infrastructure.

The utilization is demonstrated using query-based analyses that operate on the populated digital twin and prove its applicability. These analyses make use of the modeled network topology, protocol-level communication, and associated cryptographic configurations. The following examples build on these results by showing how increasingly specific queries combining several graph layers reduce large sets of observed communication relationships to those connections and systems that are most relevant for concrete migration goals.

One essential step is the semi-automatic prioritization of connections to be migrated. While the exact factors for risk estimation may vary from organization to organization, finding the connections with the biggest risk is the common starting point [13,18,22]. To do this, we manually mark security-relevant, central infrastructure components, such as gateways and firewalls, which define trust boundaries between network segments. After identifying these components, the digital twin can partition the layer two topology into segments that correspond to network security zones [5,19]. These zones represent areas of differing exposure and protection levels within the infrastructure and can be manually annotated with qualitative security levels to reflect their relative criticality. Usually, the organization operating such an infrastructure has to be compliant to regulation, e.g. [5], meaning they already have defined security zones which should match these results, easing the annotation process.

Based on this annotated topology, communication relationships can be analyzed with respect to the security zones they originate from, traverse, or terminate in. Connections that cross multiple zones or connect highly protected zones with less trusted networks can thus be identified explicitly. This provides a structured basis for automatically prioritizing cryptographic migration activities according to the exposure and relevance of individual communication paths.

To demonstrate the utilization in the infrastructure context, the digital twin is manually annotated with security zones, where a security level of *0* denotes public or untrusted zones and higher values indicate increasingly critical ones, with a maximum of *3*. Query-based analyses can then be applied to extract those communication relationships that traverse zones of differing security levels. E. g., this *Cypher* query retrieves connections that originate in a public zone and terminate in a highly protected zone or vice versa, and are thus most critical:

```
MATCH ({sec_lvl: 0}) <-[:traverses]- (connection:Connection)
  -[:traverses]-> ({sec_lvl: 3})
RETURN connection;
```

In large infrastructures, the resulting set is expectedly still large. Further refinement comes from filtering for non-PQC connections, leaving only the queries that still need to be migrated. This is possible by enhancing the previous query:

```
WITH connection
MATCH (connection) <-[]- (ep:Endpoint) <-[:uses]- (alg:Algorithm)
WHERE NOT EXISTS((connection) <-[:initiates|:receives]- (:Endpoint)
  -[:uses]-> (:Algorithm {pq_sec_lvl: 3})) AND
  NOT EXISTS((connection) <-[:initiates|:receives]- (:Endpoint)
  -[:uses]-> (:Algorithm {pqc_sec_lvl: 5}))
RETURN connection
```

To draft a migration plan, we not only need abstract information about connections, but which software on which device must be adjusted in the end. The digital twin can yield the devices and their specific endpoints. To obtain them, we can further enhance our previous query with the following subquery:

```
WITH connection
MATCH (connection) <-[has]- (ep:Endpoint) <-[provides]- (dev:Device)
RETURN *
```

Combining all those subqueries leaves us with a list of all highly critical, non-quantum-safe connections, including the software endpoints that initiate/receive them and their respective devices. Using the digital twin, we can further specify the queries to answer exactly those questions relevant for planning a given migration step. E.g., we can also yield only specific protocols, only servers or clients, or only devices in a given subnet or with networking hardware from a specific vendor (by filtering for their MAC address vendor prefix).

Utilizing Results for Cryptographic Migration (RQ2)

The presented utilization addresses RQ2 by illustrating how the graph-based digital twin supports cryptographic migration activities. Query-based analyses enable identification of communication paths and prioritization based on their network context and exposure.
By selecting and grouping migration-relevant communication relationships together with their associated protocols and cryptographic configurations, the digital twin supports concrete migration planning decisions and enables the verification of cryptographic configurations before and after migration.

6 Discussion and Future Work

The evaluation demonstrates how the proposed graph-based digital twin's automatically collected information enables a structured view of cryptographic usage and dependencies that emerge from communication behavior in operation. The digital twin explicitly visualizes which components communicate, which protocols are employed, and which cryptographic mechanisms protect these interactions. To prevent an information overload it further allows for specific querying, filtering for only the relevant information for a specific migration step. Beyond planning, the digital twin can verify migration steps and observe cryptographic configuration during operation, enabling continuous oversight across different migration phases.

The graph structure further supports exploratory analysis of migration impact. Traversing communication paths allows analysts to reason about how changes to cryptographic mechanisms at one point in the infrastructure may influence dependent components. In addition, structural properties of the graph, such as the degree of connectivity or the position of components within communication paths, can be used to identify components that are particularly exposed or central to infrastructure operation. Such components may warrant special attention during migration planning due to their potential impact on availability or security.

Rather than aiming for fully automated decision-making and prescribing a single prioritization metric, the digital twin enables the application of heuristics that combine cryptographic properties with structural and contextual information. For example, communication paths traversing multiple security zones or crossing trust boundaries may be considered more critical than isolated internal connections. Integrating these aspects within a unified representation supports exploratory analysis and well-informed, semi-automatic reasoning and prioritization about migration-relevant components according to individual policies. In this sense, the evaluation illustrates how the proposed approach can contribute to understanding cryptographic dependencies in complex infrastructures, even in the absence of complete or perfectly accurate data.

6.1 Limitations

The evaluation is based on a containerized infrastructure instantiated using a Docker network rather than a heterogeneous production environment. This setup does not capture all organizational and operational complexities nor the scale of real-world infrastructures, leaving a gap between our evaluation and real-world use. Yet, it reflects a deployment model that is increasingly prevalent in modern IT systems. Importantly, the containerized environment employs standard network protocols and cryptographic mechanisms that are representative of those used in non-containerized deployments. Yet, we did not systematically evaluate the performance of the graph construction and data processing under large scale load. While the Kafka pipeline is designed to exactly support such deployments, the GDB may, especially in the early phases of deployment, struggle with the amount of new incoming data.

The construction of the digital twin relies on the availability and quality of observable infrastructure data. We used sensor scripts based on python and bash to extract relevant information from the devices. On the gateways we have a DPI scanner installed which extracts information about the data in transit. In the real world, broadly deploying all the sensors and their dependencies, like a python interpreter, on a wide range of different systems may cause effort for already strained IT departments. The same issues could arise when deploying DPI scanners on various different proprietary security gateways.

To deal with these challenges, a good strategy is to use redundant sensors. E.g., additionally to the ARP cache of systems they could also sniff on ARP traffic off of the switches' management ports. Regarding redundant sensors addressing OSI layer three, other management systems, like DNS and DHCP, could be valuable data sources. Finally, we could attach to preexisting DPI tools of organizations instead of deploying new ones. The standard interfaces and data formats, i.e., Kafka and CBOM/JSON, ease the process of integrating new sensors. Also, those limitations do not prevent the digital twin from working. Instead, full coverage of all systems and networks in large infrastructures incurs a significant additional effort, sometimes leaving uncovered corner cases.

The limitation in terms of what the sensor network is able to process also extends to different quirks of real-world networks. Our implementation currently does not cover common technologies like Network Address Translation (NAT), IPv6, let alone legacy protocols. Some privacy enhancing technologies prevent analyzing the used cryptography, e.g., TLS1.3's encrypted client hello [28]. Yet, those are still uncommon ([28] is not final) and can be addressed by scanners opening the encrypted connections [8]. None of these limitations constitute insurmountable challenges. They do, however, increase the amount of labor for achieving an infrastructure's full coverage, leaving gray areas considering a realistic and cost-efficient implementation.

6.2 Future Work

One strategy to counteract the incomplete representation of real-world infrastructures is to increase the number of different technologies and corner cases the digital twin can process. Especially the integration of additional data sources is important. Those can, on the one hand, address other networking aspects, but can also come from other approaches, such as software-level analyses, complementing our network-centric perspective. Furthermore, combining our in-transit observations with existing static artifacts such as SBOMs/CBOMs created from software analysis or other inventories may further enhance the completeness of the cryptographic dependency analysis. The model already using those standard formats and its modular design built for integration ease these future processes. Still, adjusting it to represent the combined view on an infrastructure remains open research, which will lead to a more holistic understanding of PQC migration tooling. In addition to scaling the amount of different data sources, evaluating it in large-scale infrastructures is an important next step. Such an evaluation enables an even clearer understanding of its scalability and practical applicability in real-world PQC migration contexts.

For large scale deployment in the real-world, the digital twin also has to be able to "forget" information, as it right now only grows monotonely. Evaluating different mechanisms, like an end-of-life for each data point or partial rewrites for some kind of information, and implementing the most applicable ones also remains future work.

Finally, the proposed approach may benefit from further theoretical work on the applicability of graph theory on migration problems [13,17], possibly diving further e. g. into weighted graphs for prioritization and more.

7 Conclusion

This paper presented a graph-based digital twin for representing and analyzing cryptographic dependencies of IT infrastructures. Motivated by the increasing complexity of modern networks and the urgency of PQC migration, we applied a DSR approach to design, instantiate, and evaluate an artifact that visualizes communication relationships, protocol usage, and cryptographic properties.

We demonstrated how a data pipeline can automatically collect infrastructure data observed in transit and transform it into a unified graph representation, enabling interactive exploration and analysis. By modeling infrastructure components, communication paths, and crypto mechanisms within a graph schema, the digital twin provides a foundation for understanding (crypto) dependencies that are difficult to capture using only traditional inventory-based approaches.

The exploratory evaluation showed that the graph-based digital twin supports both the intuitive structural analysis of cryptographic dependencies and the prioritization of migration-relevant components, thereby directly addressing the research questions posed in this work. Query-based exploration and visualization allows stakeholders to focus on relevant points of interest and reason about their protocol usage, exposure, and potential migration impact, supporting informed decision-making in the context of PQC migration planning and improved cryptographic agility.

Overall, we show by providing an open and research-driven approach, that distributed sensors can gather the relevant network-related information, send it to our data pipeline, and store it in the analyzable graph representation. This architecture allows for easy extension with and integration of new sensors. So, instead of attempting a one-size-fits-all solution and thereby disregarding the complexity of modern IT infrastructures, we designed a blueprint for holistic migration tooling. This foundation can then be extended to either interact with or include software or asset focused tools and different scanning techniques to merge all the information into one clear, coherent picture. This supports practitioners with PQC migration and, in turn, cryptographic agility.

References

1. SmartM2M; Digital Twins: Functionalities and communication Reference Architecture. Technical Specification ETSI TS 103 846 V1.1.1, ETSI (Aug 2024). https://www.etsi.org/deliver/etsi_ts/103800_103899/103846/01.01.01_60/ts_103846v010101p.pdf
2. Zero-touch network and Service Management (ZSM); Network Digital Twin. Group Report ETSI GR ZSM 015 V1.1.1, ETSI (Feb 2024). https://www.etsi.org/deliver/etsi_gr/ZSM/001_099/015/01.01.01_60/gr_ZSM015v010101p.pdf
3. Alagic, G., et al.: Status report on the fourth round of the NIST post-quantum cryptography standardization process. NIST interagency/internal report (nistir 8545), National Institute of Standards and Technology (NIST) (March 2025). https://doi.org/10.6028/NIST.IR.8545
4. Bernstein, D., Lange, T., Levin, J., Yang, B.Y.: PQConnect: automated post-quantum end-to-end tunnels. In: Network and Distributed System Security Symposium (NDSS). Internet Society (December 2024). https://doi.org/10.14722/ndss.2025.241879
5. Bundesamt für Sicherheit in der Informationstechnik (BSI): IT-Grundschutz-Kompendium (2022), https://www.bsi.bund.de/DE/Themen/Unternehmen-und-Organisationen/Standards-und-Zertifizierung/IT-Grundschutz/IT-Grundschutz-Kompendium/it-grundschutz-kompendium_node.html, offizielle Webseite
6. Bundesamt für Sicherheit in der Informationstechnik (BSI): Securing Tomorrow, Today: Transitioning to PostQuantum Cryptography (11 2024). https://www.bsi.bund.de/SharedDocs/Downloads/EN/BSI/Crypto/PQC-joint-statement.pdf

7. Bundesamt für Sicherheit in der Informationstechnik (BSI): Cryptographic Mechanisms: Recommendations and Key Lengths. Tech. Rep. BSI TR-02102-1 (2025)
8. Danilchenko, V., Theobald, M., Cohen, D.: Bootstrapping security configuration for IoT devices on networks with TLS inspection. In: 2019 IEEE Globecom Workshops (GC Wkshps), pp. 1–7 (2019). https://doi.org/10.1109/GCWkshps45667.2019.9024325
9. ENISA: Post-Quantum Cryptography: Current State and Quantum Mitigation (2021). https://www.enisa.europa.eu/publications/post-quantum-cryptography-current-state-and-quantum-mitigation
10. European Commission: A Coordinated Implementation Roadmap for the Transition to Post-Quantum Cryptography (2025). https://digital-strategy.ec.europa.eu/en/library/coordinated-implementation-roadmap-transition-post-quantum-cryptography. Accessed on 04 Feb 2026
11. Fuller, A., Fan, Z., Day, C., Barlow, C.: Digital twin: enabling technologies, challenges and open research. IEEE Access **8**, 108952–108971 (2020). https://doi.org/10.1109/ACCESS.2020.2998358
12. Grieves, M.: Digital Twin: Manufacturing Excellence through Virtual Factory Replication. White Paper (2014)
13. Hasan, K., et al.: A framework for migrating to post-quantum cryptography: security dependency analysis and case studies. IEEE Access **12**, 23427–23450 (2024). https://doi.org/10.1109/ACCESS.2024.3360412
14. Hevner, A.R.: A three cycle view of design science research. Scand. J. Inf. Syst. **19**(2), 87–92 (2007)
15. Hevner, A.R., March, S.T., Park, J., Ram, S.: Design science in information systems research. In: MIS Quarterly, vol. 28, pp. 75–105 (2004)
16. Linux Foundation: SPDX 3.0 Specification (2023)
17. Loebenberger, D., Gazdag, S.L., Herzinger, D., Hirsch, E., Näther, C., Steghöfer, J.P.: On the Formalization of Cryptographic Migration. arXiv/abs/2408.05997 (2025). https://doi.org/10.48550/arXiv.2408.05997, preprint
18. Ma, C., Colon, L., Dera, J., Rashidi, B., Garg, V.: CARAF: Crypto Agility Risk Assessment Framework. J. Cybersec. **7**(1), tyab013 (05 2021). https://doi.org/10.1093/cybsec/tyab013
19. Malik, S.: Network security principles and practices (2003)
20. Minerva, R., Lee, G.M., Crespi, N.: Digital twin in the Iot context: a survey on technical features, scenarios, and architectural models. Proc. IEEE **108**(10), 1785–1824 (2020). https://doi.org/10.1109/JPROC.2020.2998530
21. NTIA: The Minimum Elements for a Software Bill of Materials (2021)
22. Näther, C., Herzinger, D., Gazdag, S.L., Steghöfer, J.P., Daum, S., Loebenberger, D.: Migrating software systems toward post-quantum cryptography-a systematic literature review. IEEE Access **12**, 132107–132126 (2024). https://doi.org/10.1109/ACCESS.2024.3450306
23. OWASP: Cryptography Bill of Materials (CBOM) (2026). https://cyclonedx.org/capabilities/cbom/. Accessed 04 Feb 2026
24. OWASP Foundation: CycloneDX Specification (2023)
25. Qureshi, A.R., Asensio, A., Imran, M., Garcia, J., Masip-Bruin, X.: A survey on security enhancing digital twins: Models, applications and tools. Comput. Commun. **238**, 108158 (2025). https://doi.org/10.1016/j.comcom.2025.108158, https://www.sciencedirect.com/science/article/pii/S014036642500115X
26. Rattanavipanon, N., Suaboot, J., Werapun, W.: A toolchain for assisting migration of software executables towards post-quantum cryptography. IEEE Access (2024). https://doi.org/10.1109/ACCESS.2024.3524309

27. Raza, S.M., Minerva, R., Crespi, N., Alvi, M., Herath, M., Dutta, H.: A comprehensive survey of network digital twin architecture, capabilities, challenges, and requirements for edge–cloud continuum. Comput. Commun. **236**, 108144 (2025). https://doi.org/10.1016/j.comcom.2025.108144, https://www.sciencedirect.com/science/article/pii/S014036642500101X
28. Rescorla, E., Oku, K., Sullivan, N., Wood, C.: TLS Encrypted Client Hello. Internet-Draft draft-ietf-tls-esni-25, Internet Engineering Task Force (Jun 2025), work in Progress
29. SCAN Open Source Solutions SL: Crypto Finder: Source-Level Cryptography Visibility. https://www.scanoss.com/post/crypto-finder-source-level-cryptography-visibility (2026). Accessed 10 Feb 2026
30. Schmitt, N., Henrich, J., Heinz, D., Alnahawi, N., Wiesmaier, A.: On criteria and tooling for cryptographic inventories. In: Sicherheit 2024, pp. 49–63. Gesellschaft für Informatik e.V., Bonn (2024). https://doi.org/10.18420/sicherheit2024_003
31. Tao, F., Zhang, M., Liu, Y., Nee, A.Y.C.: Digital twin in industry: state-of-the-art. IEEE Trans. Industr. Inf. **15**(4), 2405–2415 (2019). https://doi.org/10.1109/TII.2018.2873186
32. Ullman, E.: Life in Code: A Personal History of Technology. MCD, New York (2017), ISBN 978-0-374-53451-2
33. Wu, Y., Zhang, K., Zhang, Y.: Digital twin networks: a survey. IEEE Internet Things J. **8**(18), 13789–13804 (2021). https://doi.org/10.1109/JIOT.2021.3079510
34. Zhou, C., et al.: Network digital twin: concepts and reference architecture. Internet-Draft draft-irtf-nmrg-network-digital-twin-arch-11, Internet Engineering Task Force (Jul 2025). https://datatracker.ietf.org/doc/draft-irtf-nmrg-network-digital-twin-arch/11/, work in Progress

A Study of PQC Migration Frameworks

Eunisse Nzetchuen[1(✉)], Marc Stöttinger[1], Alexander Wiesmaier[2,3,4], and Elif Yeşilbek[2,3]

[1] Hochschule RheinMain–University of Applied Sciences and Arts, 65195 Wiesbaden, Germany
{eunisse.nzetchuen,marc.steottinger}@hs-rm.de
[2] Hochschule Darmstadt - University of Applied Sciences, 64295 Darmstadt, Germany
alexander.wiesmaier@h-da.de, elif.yesilbek@stud.h-da.de
[3] European University of Technology, European Union, Darmstadt, Germany
[4] National Research Center for Applied Cybersecurity ATHENE, 64295 Darmstadt, Germany

Abstract. Quantum-safe alternatives are expected to replace most of the asymmetric cryptography algorithms currently in use in the near future. The migration of numerous systems and infrastructures to PQC is guided by the timelines established by various bodies. Hence, the transition to PQC poses a significant challenge, as it involves the exchange of frequently used algorithms employed in numerous protocols and applications within the next five to ten years. Consequently, to facilitate a consolidated and organized transition, PQC migration frameworks are necessary. Therefore, in this paper we conduct a comprehensive literature review of proposed PQC migration frameworks. We investigate existing frameworks and evaluate them regarding their completeness and soundness of applied methods, such as crypto-agility posture.

Keywords: post-quantum cryptography (PQC) · crypto-agility · PQC migration

1 Introduction

Cryptography is an indispensable tool to secure our information systems and part of almost all the IT services we consume. Asymmetric cryptography, e.g., RSA or ECC, relies on certain mathematical problems that are considered to be difficult to solve in polynomial time. In 1994, Shor [31] published an algorithm that can solve the mathematical problems of prime factorization and the discrete logarithm problem. Most of the asymmetric cryptography algorithms are based on these problems. Furthermore, the quantum algorithm Grover presented in [15] reduces the security strength of symmetric cryptography algorithms, including hash functions.

Even though these algorithms were published almost three decades ago, their impact became more visible due to recent advancements in the field of quantum computing. NIST started a standardization process [11] for a new set of

D. Loebenberger and M. Stöttinger (Eds.): MAgiCS 2026, CCIS 3002, pp. 61–81, 2026.
https://doi.org/10.1007/978-3-032-28946-9_4

algorithms that are resilient against quantum computers running the aforementioned quantum algorithms. In 2025, three algorithms were standardized, one for key encapsulation and two for digital signatures. The process is still ongoing for more algorithms. Furthermore, NIST plans to deprecate the quantum-vulnerable algorithms by 2030 and will disallow them by 2035 due to the draft of the NIST document [23], while the EU also published timelines concerning 2030 and 2035 [12].

This transition may be intricate and challenging because there are numerous algorithms in this field that are implemented by numerous systems, and the alternative algorithms are relatively recent. Without an appropriate migration framework, the consequences would be substantial and would only intensify the transition efforts. Consequently, the objective of this paper is to evaluate and contrast the current academic literature regarding PQC migration frameworks. Furthermore, our objective is to offer supplementary insights by concentrating on specific aspects of the migration, including the identification of cryptography, dependency analysis, risk assessment, crypto-agility, and key management. Our contributions are an overview of the different methods utilized in the existing frameworks and a comparison of them regarding their maturity. Additionally, we discuss possible shortcomings regarding our perspective in terms of the methodologies and frameworks proposed for a consolidated PQC migration. This investigation has identified that the majority of frameworks focus solely on the identification of cryptographic assets and the prioritization, neglecting the methodologies for a coordinated transition and maintenance.

The paper is further structured as follows. Section 2 explains the related work, our methodology, and introduces our research questions. Section 3 evaluates the proposed methods for the transition. This evaluation is done based on the criteria of migration stages, identification of cryptography, dependency analysis, risk assessment, crypto-agility, and key management, as each is represented by a dedicated subsection. In Sect. 4 we provide answers to our research questions. In Sect. 5 we conclude with final remarks and indicate the future work.

2 Related Work and Methodology

Even before the new standardized PQC algorithms have been announced by the NIST, first publications encounter the issue of how to transition to PQC. Therefore, multiple survey papers have been published on this topic. Some are focusing in general on PQC and crypto agility [1,2,4,27]. While others are more focused on specific application domains [21,26,29].

The authors in [2] provide an overview of PQC and crypto-agility progress as a survey paper. As they take a look at the progress made on the PQC algorithms at the time, they also consider the performance impact and security of PQC algorithms. Conversely, Ott et al. in [27] offer a comprehensive selection of obstacles that must be resolved to implement PQC migration. The publication [21] is a survey paper evaluating the current situation of PQC transition in the automotive domain and existing research gaps in this domain. Another example of a domain-oriented paper that concentrates on PQC migration is [29], which has a particular emphasis on the health care sector. With a general emphasis on the migration of software systems to PQC, the most comprehensive survey on PQC migration with the most universal domain is presented in [26], since the authors focus on the migration of software systems in general.

Nevertheless, each of these surveys on PQC migration addresses the obstacles and potential solutions for transitioning existing systems to a quantum-safe solution that incorporates PQC. The individual methods of the frameworks applied for the transition procedure are not thoroughly examined or compared in any of these existing survey publications.

2.1 Methodology on the Literature Research

We also adhere to the methodology and survey structure of PRISMA for a structured literature review, as outlined in [28]. The PRIMSA framework describes how a structured and reproducible literature research should be conducted in a scientific environment. Our structured study starts with a review of existing survey publications addressing PQC guidelines and migration frameworks from domain-specific perspectives, cf. [2–4,21,22,27,29]. From these surveys, the cited publications were examined and incorporated into an initial pool of candidate works. In addition, a targeted literature search was conducted using Google Scholar with the search string "*(post-quantum) AND (migration) AND (framework)*", restricted to publications released between 2020 and 2026. This search yielded 3,760 publications, which were added to the pool. Of these, 51 publications were identified as explicitly addressing PQC migration frameworks or guidelines by a dedicated keyword search in the abstracts and titles of the beforehand identified publications. The resulting set comprised journal articles, workshop papers, peer-reviewed conference publications, arXiv preprints, white papers, standards, technical reports, and government guidelines. Formats that were entirely non-academic, including blogs, webpages, podcasts, webinars, and RSS feeds, were excluded.

A detailed review of the 51 publications led to the identification of 22 papers that propose comprehensive frameworks for PQC migration, as opposed to high-level guidance, abstract recommendations, timelines, or road maps. We also conducted a minor snowballing concept and also encountered interesting cross-references in the previously identified publications during this review process to add additional papers to the review pool by cross-checking the references within the previously selected publications under review.

2.2 Central Research Questions

The main objective of our study is to examine the robustness and technical maturity of the frameworks. Therefore, we investigated the frameworks under the perspective of what kind of process activities or stages the different frameworks propose to conduct the PQC migration. Within this, we put special emphasis on the diagnosis of the system to transform regarding the analysis section.

Especially in terms of how the different cryptographic assets (crypto primitives, protocols, keys, etc.) are identified and what relationship or dependency they have to each other. Also regarding how to prioritize them in terms of what asset needs to be migrated first. In addition, we are interested in the extent to which crypto agility and key management are taken into account in the frameworks. Those are very essential elements in our perspective when it comes to ensuring a long-term secure cryptographic transition framework. To this end, our research questions are:

RQ1: What methods within existing frameworks for PQC migration are used and are they suitable enough for the steps in the migration phases?
RQ2: Do existing frameworks for migration methods take cryptographic agility into account, and if so, to what extent in terms of their properties and a common definition?
RQ3: What migration stages consider key management and to what extent?

3 Analysis and Evaluation

Categorization of the selected literature is predicated on our literature review. This categorization corroborates the responses to our research questions. In the following, we explain these categories and our related findings in the literature.

3.1 Migration Stages

PQC migration can be viewed as a sequence of stages, each representing a discrete process step that is executed once the preceding phase has produced the required outcomes. In this work, the term stage is used to refer to such self-contained steps at an appropriate level of abstraction. The literature was analyzed with respect to the migration stages proposed by existing PQC migration frameworks, with the objective of identifying similarities, differences, and essential process steps. Across the reviewed contributions, the PQC migration process can generally be mapped to four high-level activities, namely *Identify*, *Plan*, *Execute*, and *Maintain* [26]. The stages defined in the individual frameworks were assigned to these activities to enable a systematic comparison of their granularity and emphasis. The analysis indicates that the frameworks differ in terms of the number of stages and the level of detail of the individual steps. Thereby, the mapping of the stages to the four general activities varies among the proposed frameworks.

All frameworks, as summarized in Table 1. It includes stages that can be assigned to the *Identify* activity, focusing on asset identification and the determination of migration scope. However, the frameworks differ considerably in the level of detail and in the methods used to identify and assess critical assets. Some contributions, such as [16] and [25], address only the *Identify* activity and do not explicitly cover the remaining migration activities. The framework proposed in [6] defines only two stages. Its *pre-migration phase* combines asset identification with the development of a migration strategy, thereby spanning both the *Identify* and *Plan* activities, as reflected in Table 1. Overall, most frameworks place a strong emphasis on asset identification and prioritization, reflecting a predominantly design- or architecture-oriented perspective on PQC migration. Among the 22 identified frameworks, only [4] assigns greater importance to the *Execute* and *Maintain* activities than to the initial phases. This framework focuses on steps closely aligned with operational security tasks and is derived from the NIST Cybersecurity Framework 2.0 [24], with emphasis on the operational aspects of the *Maintain* activity in the context of PQC migration.

Among the reviewed contributions, the framework proposed in [13] represents the most comprehensive and methodologically detailed approach, followed by the framework presented in [3]. The framework in [13] is explicitly designed for large and complex systems and adopts a multistage, iterative, and process-driven methodology. It requires comprehensive asset inventories, systematic dependency analyses at both intra- and inter-departmental levels, and structured vulnerability assessments based on the decomposition of organizations into subsystems to manage complexity. A defining characteristic of this approach is the extensive use of standardized questionnaires, which facilitate the consistent collection of data related to risks, migration requirements, dependencies, and vulnerabilities. Risk-based prioritization constitutes a core element of the framework and is derived from operational lifetimes, estimated migration effort, and projected quantum threat timelines, with explicit reference to Mosca's theorem.

In contrast, the migration process proposed by Roberts [29] is less formalized but strongly practice-oriented, with a specific focus on healthcare systems. The initial stages concentrate on governance and asset prioritization based on confidentiality and retention requirements, followed by low-risk hybrid deployments and pilot implementations that emphasize crypto-agility. Compared to [13], this approach favors domain-specific applicability and actionable guidance over methodological depth.

The PMMP framework presented in [33] is especially designed to be embedded into an (existing) IT security management system (ISMS), e.g., ISO 27001 [18], but can also be used standalone, although less effective in that case. It is also thought to serve as a template for processes for cryptographic migration apart from PQC migration. In addition, it is connected to CAMM [17] that provides a taxonomy to measure the level of crypto-agility of IT systems.

Overall, the comparison highlights a clear trade-off between methodological rigor and operational simplicity. The framework in [13] offers the most structured and comprehensive methodology and is therefore well suited to large enterprises requiring formalized migration processes. Although the framework in [3] is also quite detailed, it is more focused on governance during the migration in contrast to [3]. In contrast, [29] provides a pragmatic, sector-specific migration path, while [35] contributes historically informed, high-level guidance that complements more detailed technical frameworks. The approach of [33], for example, complements other approaches by being a relatively simple extension to be inte-

Table 1. Overview of the different stages of the various frameworks. The different migration stages are mapped to the four generic migration activities proposed in [26].

Frame-works	Dedicated stages within the activity			
	Identify	Plan	Execute	Maintain
[13]	– Identify enterprise architecture – Generate asset inventories – Dependency analysis – Vulnerability analysis – Cross-department analysis – Migration requirements analysis – Migration risk analysis	– Initial priority analysis – Generate migration plans	– Execute migration plans	– Prepare next iteration
[3]	– Inventory of cryptographic Assets – Inventory of data assets – Inventory of the suppliers of cryptographic assets – Risk assessment	– Migration plan	– Execute	
[4]	– Identify	– Protect		– Detect – Respond – Recover
[6]	– Pre-migration phase			– Post-migration phase
[16]	– Asset identification – Dependency analysis			
[22]	– Identify threats – Inventory of assets – Risk estimation	– Risk mitiga-tion – Orga-nization Roadmap		
[25]	– Quantum-readiness roadmap – Crypto inventory – Discuss suppliers roadmap – Determine supply chain Quantum-readiness			
[26]	– Asset identification – Crypto identification – Crypto assessment	– Planing	– Execu-tion	– Maintain
[33]	– Governance handling – Asset identification – Risk assessment	– Cluster and priotize		– Test and moni-tor
[34]	– Preparation – Discovery – Risk assessment	– Risk mitiga-tion	– Migra-tion to PQC	

grated into existing management processes, leveraging an organization's established processes and steering mechanisms for the migration.

3.2 Approach to Identifying Cryptography

Understanding the cryptographic algorithms employed in a system is one of the most critical steps of the migration process. A system cannot be migrated without the knowledge of the cryptography used, its location, and its specifics. The stage of cryptographic discovery is referenced in numerous proposed frameworks, as depicted in Table 1. The scope of this elaboration is contingent upon the methods employed and the type of data collected. In [30], a set of requirements and metrics for cryptographic inventories is presented. They introduce a prototype of semi-automated cryptography discovery tooling for creating cryptographic inventories containing structured Cryptographic Bill of Materials (CBOM), cf. [19].

Depending on the organization, the strategy towards identifying cryptography or, in general, the discovery approach could differ [3]. Some frameworks suggest a few preliminary works be done before identifying cryptography, such as determining the scope [22,33]. Cryptography policies are also regarded as a pre-processing step in certain frameworks to facilitate prioritization and identify assets [3]. In addition, White et al. [34] elaborate on what type of cryptographic data they capture. The inventory by the framework [33] includes information on cryptography types, algorithms, and key lengths per the application that they belong to. In [16], it is suggested that all of the crucial cryptographic components associated with the identified asset be recorded, including hardware, software, communication channels, and third-party services. Ultimately, the scope of the inventory is determined by its purpose.

The identification of key relevant material is already a challenge, particularly in the context of asymmetric cryptography [27]. Therefore, it is recommended for large IT systems to implement automation [16,33], whereas the identification process could be performed manually for smaller IT systems. However [2] recommends to use automation independently of the organization size. In [3,25,33] active (e.g., real-time network scanning) and passive methods for discovery with open-source and commercial tools are discussed. Furthermore, we see that it is also advised to use a combination of automated tooling with manual work [3,14,16]. Various tools have been mentioned depending on the context, as [14] provides, as also supposed by [26]. Another example is the method of database generation from the extracted data from a code base. Then using the queries on this database to detect vulnerable algorithms [25]. CI/CD pipelines could be used to some extent as well [3,25]. For the software development scenario, static and dynamic scans could be used [3]. The authors in [32] developed their own tool, called *Inventory Generator Tool (IGT)*, that processes a Java-based application binary to generate cryptographic inventory. Another approach, by [34], is to use adaptable questionnaires. The authors in [33] suggest using information on captured over cryptography, e.g., from previous audit reports, as well as PKIs.

The significance of a standardized data format for the inventory is underscored in [16,25,26] to create a comparable inventory. In large organizations, a structured and hierarchical model is particularly necessary; cf. [16]. The CBOM specification in [19] is a candidate toward the establishment of standardized asset documentation following the cryptography identification stage [3,13,14,20,33,34]. The common challenges are building and maintaining inventories for complex IT infrastructure as well as general access control or possible human errors during manual approaches [16,27]. Especially inventory maintenance is a frequently indicated task [3,14,33,34]. Per [34], access control and security around the inventory are also considerations.

In conclusion, we observe that the approach to this key stage of the migration is defined by the organization. Hence, the approach to identifying cryptography is not uniform. The level of detail on the captured data or the specifics of the utilized tooling varies. Furthermore, the format of the recorded data is a frequently discussed topic, with particular emphasis on the importance of categorizing crypto assets in a CBOM. Moreover, the maintenance and security of the inventory pose a challenge.

3.3 Dependency Analysis Approach

Another critical step in a migration strategy is a thorough analysis of the relationships between the different components of the system to be migrated. We call these relationships dependencies. These links play a central role in the feasibility, order, and complexity of cryptographic migrations. Among the publications we investigated, [13,14,16,20,32] presented an analysis method for dependencies. We analyzed the dependency analysis approaches proposed in the literature to identify what types of dependencies are considered, what models are used to represent them, and their role in the migration process.

According to our literature review, all contributions implicitly or explicitly acknowledge the significance of dependencies; however, they differ significantly in terms of objective, granularity, and formalization. Certain methods are restricted to the simple identification of dependencies within an organization only, while others suggest the use of formal graph-based models to facilitate the analysis of migration constraints. The work of [16] offers a structured analysis of security dependencies between data, systems, and cryptographic primitives. The authors model these relationships as directed graphs, based on existing organizational inventories. This method facilitates the identification of relevant dependencies between crypto assets within a cryptosystem and the selection of the appropriate level of protection based on the data's value.

Conversely, some contributions take a more organizational approach. In [14], the dependency analysis is based on identifying relationships between systems, data, algorithms, and suppliers to better understand the overall exposure of critical infrastructures. However, this approach offers neither a formal model of cryptographic dependencies nor an explicit distinction between different types of dependencies. Similarly, the CARAF framework [22] does not introduce an explicit analysis of technical dependencies but considers them as factors of organizational coupling that can slow down or complicate the transition, particularly due to a lack of crypto-agility. Other publications report on a detailed technical analysis of dependencies at the code level. The dependency analysis presented in [32] is derived from an analysis application's call graph. A static call graph is constructed from the application's Java bytecode, including internal modules and third-party libraries. It uses the *Soot* framework to generate an intermediate representation of the code and extract call relationships at the method layer. The resulting diagram is a directed diagram, with nodes representing methods and edges representing potential calls between calling and called methods.

The most formal and in-depth approach is proposed by [20]. It provides directions on estimation of the migration's complexity and how to deal with cyclic dependencies using a clustering method. The authors use a directed graph with migration constraints represented by the edges to model functional and cryptographic dependencies. It is possible to establish migration clusters that must be migrated simultaneously by identifying components that are highly connected. In medium to large systems, migration complexity is primarily determined by the mathematical structure of the dependency graph, rather than the selection of post-quantum algorithms, as this modeling demonstrates. The framework proposed by [13] presents an intermediate approach, combining an explicit approach based on dependency graphs with an organizational approach. The analysis distinguishes between intra-dependencies and inter-dependencies, revealing relationships that are invisible locally at certain department levels.

Table 2 summarizes the analysis, demonstrating that specific methodologies, such as those proposed in [14,16], provide favorable initial visibility. Formal frameworks, such as those of [13,20,32], allow robust planning at the cost of higher analytical complexity. Therefore, the selection of an approach may be contingent upon the organization's size and the complexity of its information system. Formal graph-based approaches are advantageous for large organizations with intricate infrastructures, while inventory-based approaches can yield satisfactory results for small organizations.

3.4 Risk Assessment Approach

Post-quantum cryptography migration is a difficult, time-consuming, and expensive process that cannot be completed successfully without prioritizing the assets that must be migrated. One technique that can be used to assess different migration strategies, direct choices, and distribute resources consistently is risk assessment. Together, the potential consequences of a compromise, the time and organizational constraints related to migration, and the cryptographic vulnerability to quantum attacks can be used to calculate the risk. In this subsection, we conducted an analysis of the proposed risk assessment approaches of various PQC migration frameworks. Our focus was on the risk factors identified, the assessment methods employed, and the outcomes in terms of prioritization and decision-making. Some proposed risk assessment methods proposes temporal risk models inspired by the quantum threat. The most formalized approach in this

Table 2. Overview of the approaches with recept to dependency analysis proposed in the various frameworks

Frame-Work	Proposed stages of dependency analysis		
	Dependencies analyzed factors	Dependency modelling method	Results
[13]	– Commercial assets – Cryptographic assets – Intra-departmental dependencies and inter-departmental interdependencies	– Modelling of directed dependency graphs – Two levels of analysis: interdependencies within a department and interdependencies between departments – Identification of cycles and strongly coupled subsets	– Determination of migration strategies (pure, parallel, backward compatible) – Support for gradual and controlled planning
[14]	– Critical systems – Sensitive data – Cryptographic algorithms – Suppliers and partners	– Organizational and inventory-based approach – Identification of coupling points between entities	– Overview of organizational interconnections – Assistance in assessing the exposure of critical infrastructures
[16]	– Data and its classification level – Systems and applications – Protocols, keys, algorithms, certificates, libraries, ...	– Analysis based on existing inventories – Modeling of security dependencies in the form of graphs – Nodes representing assets and cryptosystems, edges representing protection dependencies	– Identification of cryptosystems having a direct or indirect impact on the security of an asset – Relationship between dependencies and the required protection duration
[20]	– Cryptographic components and primitives – Functional and cryptographic dependencies	– Formal modelling using directed graphs – Identification of highly connected components (clusters) – Condensation of the graph into an acyclic graph to apply the properties of graph theory.	– Definition of valid migration orders – Identification of mandatory migration clusters – Highlighting the intrinsic complexity of large-scale migrations
[32]	– Application methods – Cryptographic calls	– Static analysis of source code – Construction of a call graph from Java bytecode – Use of the Soot framework	– Identification of direct and indirect cryptographic dependencies – Precise location of cryptographic usage points

category is published in [32], which introduces a quantitative risk model based on the Cox Proportional Hazards Model. Based on numerous explanatory variables, this model enables the estimation of an instantaneous risk rate. These include the type of cryptographic algorithm, the required confidentiality period for data (X), the estimated migration time (Y), and the horizon for the emergence of a quantum computer (Z). With the application Mosca's inequality ($X + Y < Z$), it is feasible to differentiate between assets that can be gradually transferred and those that necessitate immediate action. Similar temporal approaches, but less formally mathematical, are proposed in [14] and [13]. Indeed, the triplet (X, Y, Z) is employed in these publications to evaluate the compatibility between the required data protection duration, migration time, and quantum threat horizon. [14] primarily employs this modeling approach to categorize algorithms and systems based on their level of exposure, with a particular focus on critical infrastructures. The [13] framework integrates dependency constraints, probability of compromise, and impact by incorporating this temporal dimension into a more comprehensive risk analysis.

A second category of publications presents risk through the analysis of cryptographic and functional dependencies. In [16], risk arises when a dependency is identified between high-value data and cryptographic primitives whose level of security is no longer adequate in the face of the quantum threat. The risk assessment is qualitative and comparative, based on a graph analysis linking data, systems, and cryptographic mechanisms. The main result of this approach is the prioritization of asymmetric algorithms that protect sensitive and long-lived data. Complementarily, [20] shows that the structure of dependencies induces a migration risk: the existence of highly connected components makes certain partial migrations impossible and imposes strict constraints on the order and pace of the transition.

Other publications present a more organizational and strategic driven risk assessment. The CARAF framework [22] considers the risk of missing crypto-agility. The analysis is based on a qualitative assessment of the organization's maturity across several dimensions (governance, infrastructure, applications, processes, and skills). The risk increases when a organization is unable to quickly and effectively replace obsolete primitives. An intermediate approach is proposed by [25], where risk is defined as a combination of cryptographic exposure, business impact, and migration difficulty. It allows critical systems to be identified not only because they are vulnerable, but also because their migration is complex, time-consuming, or risky from an operational standpoint. Finally, [8] proposes a particularly detailed and systematic risk analysis applied to blockchains. The approach combines a functional breakdown of the architecture, a cryptographic analysis of the primitives, a threat model based on STRIDE, and explicit consideration of the different phases of migration (before, during, and after).

This analysis reveals that some strategies, such as those presented in [8,13,14,32] prioritize temporal and quantitative modeling of the quantum threat, while others (those presented in [16,20,22,25]) focus on technical dependencies and organizational impacts. We present these explicitly in Table 3.

3.5 Crypto-Agility Posture

Crypto-agility is considered a critical component of certain frameworks, such as the guidelines in [3,34], where it is considered a fundamental element of transformation and an enabler [8].

It is important to examine how frameworks define crypto-agility before looking into how they approach it. The authors of [5] present a strategic plan and the capabilities of crypto-agility. In this work, NIST evaluates the potential to replace algorithms, adapting them while maintaining the security and functionality of the systems. According to the authors [27], security is also an objective of crypto-agility. Crypto-agility features are occasionally employed and referenced without explicitly referencing the term, as evidenced by the work of [4], which discusses the flexibility of cryptographic frameworks and adjustable hardware. This could be the result of a lack of agreement on the definition of crypto-agility [26].

The authors of [1] review the various works on this subject and emphasize that there are different definitions of it depending on the context. In [5,27], the authors also underscore that the definition of crypto-agility may be actively defined by the context. Following this concept, different fixed definitions of crypto-agility are provided in [3,34] for certain settings. The work of [34] defines crypto-agility in the context of the cryptography life cycle, including the retirement algorithms stage, which is associated with retirement agility.

In [22] suggest that for the in-scope assets, the underlying cryptographic solutions must be determined, including the details of the type of cryptographic objects to some extend. Inventory is frequently mentioned in the literature as one of the steps to achieving crypto-agility; as stated in [5], inventory is a *key activity*. By conducting a vulnerability assessment and evaluating the cryptographic inventory, the authors of [16] establish crypto-agility. Similarly, [22] further emphasizes and elaborates on asset identification in their risk assessment. They recommend that the underlying cryptographic solutions for the major assets be ascertained, which includes the specifics of the type of cryptographic objects to a certain extent. Creating an inventory is the first step towards crypto-agility, though maintaining it is noted as a challenge [3].

The use of policies and architectures are common approaches for establishing crypto-agility. [5] therefore suggests that incorporating crypto-agility into policies would be a step towards a proactive approach to future changes. These would be particularly applicable to guidelines for the design and construction of systems, as well as for the collection of technology. Policies are highlighted by [3] as important for achieving crypto-agility, alongside procedural and technical approaches. [21] focuses on the PQC transition in the automotive industry and also assesses the status of specific automotive standards in relation to crypto agility. Furthermore, they emphasize that future protocol design could be influenced by standardized crypto-agility.

The topic of architectural changes to promote crypto agility is also addressed in [34]. [27] is interested in migrating to architectures offering agility, and they point out that frameworks and architectures enable crypto-agility. Although

Table 3. Overview of the proposed risk analysis approach for prioritization within the migration process.

Frame-Work	proposed risk analysis steps		
	risk analysis factors	risk analysis methods	Results
[13]	– Exposure of assets to quantum compromises – Cryptographic vulnerabilities – Migration-related constraints and dependencies – Time factors (X, Y, Z)	– Combination of traditional risk analysis (impact, probability) – Time domain modelling inspired by Mosca – Asset-level risk assessment	– Prioritisation of assets to be migrated – Iterative and reproducible migration planning
[8]	– Critical components of blockchain systems – Identified cryptographic primitives – Transitional risks associated with migration phases	– Functional and architectural decomposition – Threat modeling using the STRIDE framework – Qualitative risk assessment before, during, and after migration	– Identification of quantum threats by component and primitive – presentation of risks for hybrid architectures – mitigation measures
[14]	– Intrinsic vulnerability of cryptographic algorithms – Criticality and value of data – Regulatory constraints – Exposure duration (X, Y, Z)	– Risk modeling in the time domain – Classification of algorithms based on their quantum exposure – Explicit application of the $X + Y < Z$ rule	– Risk prioritization – Prioritization of critical infrastructure to be migrated
[16]	– Data classification – Security dependencies between data and cryptographic primitives – Vulnerability of algorithms to quantum attacks	– Qualitative risk assessment – Dependency analysis using graphs – Comparison between classical algorithms and PQCs	– Identification of high-risk situations – Prioritization of asymmetric algorithms to protect long-lived data
[20]	– Cryptographic dependencies between components – Constraints related to migration order	– Formal analysis based on graphs – Identification of highly connected components (clusters) – Reasoning about the validity of migration orders	– Determination of component groups to migrate together – Highlighting impossible partial migrations
[22]	– Internal governance, processes, and skills – Organizational crypto-agility	– Multidimensional qualitative analysis – Organizational and strategic risk-based approach – Integration of technical and commercial considerations	– Development of a migration roadmap – Prioritization of tasks based on commercial decisions
[25]	– Cryptographic vulnerability to quantum attacks – Commercial, regulatory, and operational impact – Complexity of migration due to dependencies	– Semi-quantitative risk – Combination of exposure, impact, and migration difficulty – Use of dependency analysis results	– Operational prioritization of critical systems – Identification of high value-added systems and complex migrations
[32]	– Type of cryptographic algorithm used – Required data confidentiality period (X) – Estimated migration time (Y) – Time horizon for the emergence of a relevant quantum computer (Z)	– Quantitative modeling of risk over time – Use of the Cox model (instantaneous risk rate) – Explicit application of Mosca's inequality $(X + Y \leq Z)$	– Dynamic risk estimation per asset – Decision between immediate or gradual migration – Prioritization of the most exposed assets

design and policy considerations are significant, [22] also asserts that the degree of crypto-agility of an asset is influenced by numerous design considerations and that the implementation of crypto-agility policies necessitates their enforcement. As this is closely related to design, they also mention that all subcomponents of a system must be crypto-agile for a system to be considered crypto-agile. As a result, a recurring design principle is to consider the future and consider the agility of cryptography [9,27,34,35]. Furthermore, [20] emphasizes that the implementation of mature and effective software designs can assist in surmounting technical obstacles and historically conditioned technical challenges, thereby achieving crypto agility. The authors of [33] also point out the maturity of processes and hence, directly link their PMMP framework to the Crypto-Agility Maturity Model (CAMM) [17], showing how PMMP enables the establishment of crypto-agility in CAMM level 3.

Supplier consideration is an additional aspect that is frequently discussed in relation to crypto-agility from a governance perspective. The supplier support and crypto-agility of cryptographic algorithms must be considered during the design phase, as stipulated by [21]. In [29] the authors also mention considering crypto-agility for providers, for third-party supply [22,27], and in the context of compliance of the new software [33].

In addition, we encounter a recurring connection between hybrids and crypto-agility, which means that these schemes could make crypto-agility easier [7,8,27]. In the context of hybrid schemes, interoperability also known as a property of crypto-agility is a crucial feature; cf. [5]. Similarly, [27] posits that crypto-agility is a capability, while [20] suggests that cryptographic interoperability be implemented as an additional principle. [21] considers in this context crypto-agile gateways to be an applicable solution for integrating PQC into older vehicles. The authors in [22] emphasize that a software layer or a 'gateway' application can be used between the hardware and the applications to ensure crypto-agility.

Closely linked to the design topic, hard-coded solutions are a recurring concern for crypto-agility throughout the literature; cf., [35]. According to [21], hardware with hard-coded cryptography presents in general a risk for transitions. [22] indicate that inventory shall also document how the cryptographic solutions are implemented, e.g., "hard-coded solution,". These concerns are also addressed by the authors in [9], who propose a crypto-agile architecture that supports multiple algorithms with placeholders for future algorithms. [29] approaches crypto-agility by separating application logic and cryptography algorithms, which could help in this context. Additionally, [2] emphasizes the necessity of abstraction for transitions, and [3] details the benefits of this approach in software for crypto-agility. Abstractions are identified as a subject that necessitates further investigation [27,34]. Multiple algorithm support could facilitate network protocol migrations, as noted by [20], whereas [3] regards it as crypto-agility. In the same vein, the negotiation of algorithms in blockchain smart contracts is regarded as a method of achieving crypto-agility [8], as is the negotiation of cipher suites in TLS [27]. In the case of supporting multiple algorithms, [34] suggests a centralization approach of the crypto services as a Crypto-as-a-Service.

Run-time algorithm selection, such as that deployed by the authors in [29], should be examined to ensure that insecure algorithms are not selected [34]. Automated tooling is one of the capabilities mentioned by [5]. Automating key and certificate management is recommended by [3,22]. Such tools can be implemented to use for crypto-agility principles [27].

Additionally, there are some challenges and concerns regarding crypto-agility, with [27] mentioning that crypto-agility and PQC share a common set of challenges. For instance, [6] explains that the key and ciphertext sizes of PQC algorithms may result in buffer overflow, which could potentially compromise crypto-agileness. [22] points out that due to characteristics of PQC algorithms, such as their key sizes, they bring limitations to crypto-agility. [22] considers the storage and performance impact of crypto-agility as a concern; therefore, it advises approaching crypto-agility holistically by considering all the components impacting assets. [9] claims that crypto-agility introduces governance complexity. New attack surfaces are another frequent concern encountered in this context [3,9,27,34], as well as concerns regarding legacy systems [10,27,35].

To conclude, the anticipated capabilities or definitions of crypto-agility are inconsistent. A widely agreed-upon common understanding is required to resolve this issue. On the other hand, there is consensus that crypto-agility is a critical principle for PQC migration, particularly in terms of design or architecture principles. Conversely, there are widespread apprehensions regarding the potential for an increase in attack vectors due to the implementation of crypto-agility.

3.6 Key Management

Key management is consistently acknowledged as a pertinent aspect of the transition to post-quantum cryptography (PQC) in the literature reviewed; however, its treatment is inconsistent in terms of methodological significance and depth. While the majority of frameworks concentrate on key management in the context of asset identification and inventory creation, fewer approaches incorporate it as a central, lifecycle-oriented component of the migration process. Key management is only considered at an abstract or peripheral level in numerous works. Subsequently, it is imperative to securely orchestrate the keys for the various purposes. The highly structured migration framework in [13] implicitly and continuously integrates key management. Supported by specific questionnaires, key generation is integrated into asset analysis, vulnerability assessment, dependency assessment, and risk mitigation. The framework of ETSI [13] does not distinguish key management as a distinct phase; however, its consistent inclusion in all migration phases is indicative of a comprehensive and systematic approach that aligns with corporate governance and traceability standards.

The authors in [3] discuss the importance of key management as a component of cryptographic policy definition and asset management, and it defines keys as cryptographic assets within a CBOM. Nevertheless, it does not offer any supplementary procedural information. Similar to this, key management is primarily mentioned in relation to inventory building or risk and cost assessment by [25] and [22]; they do not address handling or lifecycle considerations unique to migration. [27] references key management exclusively within the broader context of crypto-agility. Other publications explicitly recognize the significance of key management; however, they do not propose dedicated migration methodologies. Geremew et al. in [14] emphasize the importance of key management during asset identification, PQC key provisioning, and post-migration testing. This includes the implications of increased key sizes for hardware updates. As a critical migration activity, [16] underscores the importance of key updates and incorporates key management systems into dependency analysis. However, neither work establishes specific procedures for the management of lifecycles, rotation, or key deployments during migration.

On the other hand, [29] designates key management with a central operational role in the migration process. Key rotation plans are explicitly recognized as a fundamental mechanism for the exchange of cryptographic material, with a particular emphasis on the protection of archival data and the facilitation of the deprecation of vulnerable primitives. The framework of Roberts is distinguished from more abstract approaches by its practical, migration-focused perspective. Likewise, the IBM Z guidance in [34] places a significant emphasis on critical lifecycle management during the preparation and planning phases. It poses specific investigative inquiries regarding the utilization of key management systems, key origin, storage, transport, and protection relationships. The document also provides practical recommendations, including the importance of key backups before and after major operations, and it discusses the tooling support for PQC migration to inform key management decisions for deployment scenarios.

In conclusion, the literature suggests that key management is primarily addressed in a manner that is generally quite abstract; only a few publications [3,13,14,16,34] recognize it as an important part of an operational and lifecycle-aware step within the migration process with an investigative rigor.

4 Discussion

Our analysis in Sect. 3 shows that post-quantum cryptography migration frameworks offer several methods, primarily concerning asset inventory, dependency analysis, prioritization of elements to be migrated, key management, and crypto-agility posture. However, these methods are often partial and rarely integrated into a comprehensive approach covering all stages of the migration process. Additionally, there are varying interpretations of specific terms, such as crypto agility. This imprecision, with the fact that frameworks with comparable technical granularity and maturity display variations in their methodologies, renders it challenging to compare the outcomes of various frameworks.

4.1 Maturity of Methodology in Frameworks (RQ1)

It is difficult to compare existing migration frameworks in a structured way: the majority of the work is associated with the four primary stages of migration (Identify, Plan, Execute, and Maintain) [26]; however, they differ in terms of granularity and priorities. [16] and [25] are two frameworks that concentrate almost exclusively on asset identification. Conversely, [13] and [3] propose more comprehensive and iterative processes.

Concerning inventories, which we consider as the first step in the migration, most frameworks recognize the importance of identifying assets but diverge on the very definition of these assets and the level of detail required. For example, [16] relies on existing organizational records, while [13] presents structured inventories. Conversely, more organizational approaches, such as [14], remain at a more conceptual level and do not propose a precise structuring of inventories.

For dependency analysis, all implicitly or explicitly acknowledge the existence of dependencies, but few agree on how to model them. [14] or the framework CARAF [22] remain descriptive and organizational, but works like [32] and [20] propose formal models based on directed graphs, and the ETSI framework [13] adopts an intermediate position. Moreover, in all these frameworks, implicit dependencies (those that exist between keys) are missing, yet they can create system breaks because some security relations between keys from a security architectural perspective are not captured.

Finally, some frameworks like [14,32], and [13] use time-based models based on quantum threat for prioritization, using Mosca's inequality. Other methods focus on organizational maturity and crypto-agility [22] or data value and dependencies [16,20]. Unfortunately, there isn't a framework that provides a full method that includes an inventory, a risk assessment, and an analysis of dependencies to make a prioritized list that can be used by anyone. Similar findings are reported by the authors in [10], who note that although frameworks with a thorough, structured risk assessment exist, like in [3,13,16], most risk assessment methods are too theoretical and impractical in terms of operational complexity. This is especially true for highly legacy-related systems that need to be migrated.

4.2 Usage of Crypto Agility in Frameworks (RQ2)

Crypto-agility is a topic we see many times in the literature. The need for crypto-agility, along with proposed methods are presented frequently. There is even a risk assessment framework that evaluates risks from missing out on crypto-agility [22], while some work sees it as a *no-regret* move [3] or as a *milestone* [34]. After reviewing the frameworks, it is observed that there is no uniform definition for crypto-agility. Part of the literature defines crypto-agility concepts in various contexts, while some only works on the methods to achieve it. Hence, the approaches and the extent of the approaches to crypto-agility vary. This issue could be resolved by establishing a common understanding of the properties and capabilities of crypto-agility and aligning current definitions. The challenges and concerns are indicated many times, especially on the chance of new attack surfaces as possible directions for future work.

4.3 Key Management Consideration Within Frameworks (RQ3)

Only a few migration frameworks consider key management at certain stages of their migration process; cf. [3,13,14,16]. The majority of those frameworks consider it more as a source for the asset identification in the analysis activity to identify elements that need to be migrated. Only in [34] the significance of key management during the actual migration phase is addressed, with an emphasis on key provisioning only. As a result, we presume that there is a lack of comprehension regarding the importance and systematic implementation of key management in all the frameworks that have been the subject of this survey. Consequently, this could serve as a distinct direction for future research.

5 Conclusion

This publication comprises a systematic examination of current PQC migration frameworks, with an emphasis on the methodologies employed to facilitate the entire migration process. We compare various frameworks based on their structure and methodology and discuss the identified methodologies as well as missing elements, such as missing alignment in methodology and maturity to emphasize potential future directions for a structured PQC migration framework. To the best of our knowledge, no suitable framework has yet been developed, as the various phases of migration are described in very different ways, and only a few frameworks take both crypto-agility and key management into account as system characteristics. Therefore, further research is needed to develop a common framework that takes at least these characteristics into account.

Acknowledgments. This work has been funded by the German Federal Ministry of Research, Technology and Space (BMFTR) within the project PARFAIT (grant number 16KIS2144).

References

1. Alnahawi, N., Schmitt, N., Wiesmaier, A., Heinemann, A., Graßmeyer, T.: On the state of crypto-agility. In: 18. Deutscher IT-Sicherheitskongress, pp. 103 – 126. SecuMedia Verlags-GmbH (2022). ISBN: 978-3-922746-84-3. https://ia.cr/2023/487
2. Alnahawi, N., et al.: On the state of post-quantum cryptography migration. In: INFORMATIK 2021, pp. 907–941. Gesellschaft für Informatik, Bonn (2021). https://dl.gi.de/bitstreams/dba4839d-5652-4740-8fec-7b3893ee614a/download
3. Amadori, A., et al.: The PQC migration handbook: guidelines for migrating to post-quantum cryptography – revised and extended second edition. Technical report, TNO, Applied Cryptography and Quantum Algorithms and CWI, Cryptology Group and AIVD, Netherlands National Communications Security Agency (2024). https://publications.tno.nl/publication/34643386/fXcPVHsX/TNO-2024-pqc-en.pdf

4. Aydeger, A., Zeydan, E., Yadav, A.K., Hemachandra, K.T., Liyanage, M.: Towards a quantum-resilient future: strategies for transitioning to post-quantum cryptography. In: 2024 15th International Conference on Network of the Future (NoF), pp. 195–203 (2024). https://doi.org/10.1109/NoF62948.2024.10741441. ISSN: 2833-0072
5. Barker, E., et al.: Considerations for achieving crypto agility. NIST CSWP **39** (2025)
6. Baseri, Y., Chouhan, V., Ghorbani, A.: Cybersecurity in the quantum era: assessing the impact of quantum computing on infrastructure. arXiv preprint arXiv:2404.10659 (2024)
7. Baseri, Y., Chouhan, V., Ghorbani, A., Chow, A.: Evaluation framework for quantum security risk assessment: a comprehensive strategy for quantum-safe transition. Comput. Secur. **150**, 104272 (2025)
8. Baseri, Y., Hafid, A., Shahsavari, Y., Makrakis, D., Khodaiemehr, H.: Blockchain security risk assessment in quantum era, migration strategies, and proactive defense. IEEE Commun. Surv. Tutor. **28**, 2925–2964 (2026). https://doi.org/10.1109/COMST.2025.3621113
9. Campbell, R.: Hybrid post-quantum signatures for bitcoin and ethereum: a protocol-level integration strategy. J. Br. Blockchain Assoc. (2025)
10. Chammas, P., Hariss, K., Bassil, C., Chamoun, M.: Towards a comprehensive risk framework for PQC migration in legacy systems (2025)
11. Chen, L.: NISTIR 8105, "report on post-quantum cryptography", NIST (2006). https://doi.org/10.6028/NIST.IR.8105
12. European Commission: A coordinated implementation roadmap for the transition to post-quantum cryptography (2025). https://digital-strategy.ec.europa.eu/en/library/coordinated-implementation-roadmap-transition-post-quantum-cryptography
13. A Repeatable Framework for Quantum-Safe Migrations (2024)
14. Geremew, A., Mohammad, A.: Preparing critical infrastructure for post-quantum cryptography: strategies for transitioning ahead of cryptanalytically relevant quantum computing. Int. J. Eng. Sci. Technol. **6**(4), 338–365 (2024). https://doi.org/10.46328/ijonest.240
15. Grover, L.K.: A fast quantum mechanical algorithm for database search. In: Proceedings of the Twenty-Eighth Annual ACM Symposium on Theory of Computing, pp. 212–219 (1996)
16. Hasan, K.F., et al.: A framework for migrating to post-quantum cryptography: security dependency analysis and case studies. IEEE Access **12**, 23427–23450 (2024). https://doi.org/10.1109/ACCESS.2024.3360412
17. Hohm, J., Heinemann, A., Wiesmaier, A.: Towards a maturity model for crypto-agility assessment. In: 15th International Symposium on Foundations & Practice of Security. LNCS, vol. 13877, pp. 104–119 (2023). https://doi.org/10.1007/978-3-031-30122-3_7
18. ISO/IEC 27001:2022 Information security, cybersecurity and privacy protection – Information security management systems – requirements (2022). https://www.iso.org/standard/27001. International Standard
19. Kowalleck, J., Springett, S.: ECMA-424 CyclonDX Bill of material specification. Technical report, ECMA International (2025)
20. Loebenberger, D., Gazdag, S.L., Herzinger, D., Hirsch, E., Näther, C., Steghöfer, J.P.: On the Formalization of Cryptographic Migration (2024). https://doi.org/10.48550/ARXIV.2408.05997, version Number: 4

21. Lohmiller, N., Kaniewski, S., Menth, M., Heer, T.: A survey of post-quantum cryptography migration in vehicles. IEEE Access **13**, 10160–10176 (2025). https://doi.org/10.1109/ACCESS.2025.3528562
22. Ma, C., Colon, L., Dera, J., Rashidi, B., Garg, V.: Caraf: crypto agility risk assessment framework. J. Cybersecurity **7**(1), tyab013 (2021)
23. Moody, D., Perlner, R., Regenscheid, A., Robinson, A., Cooper, D.: NIST IR 8547 (initial public draft) transition to post-quantum cryptography standards (2024). https://doi.org/10.6028/NIST.IR.8547
24. National Institute of Standards and Technology: The NIST Cybersecurity Framework (CSF) 2.0. Technical report NIST CSWP 29, National Institute of Standards and Technology, Gaithersburg, MD (2024). https://doi.org/10.6028/NIST.CSWP.29
25. Newhouse, W., et al.: Migration to Post-Quantum Cryptography Quantum Readiness: Cryptographic Discovery (2023)
26. Näther, C., Herzinger, D., Gazdag, S.L., Steghöfer, J.P., Daum, S., Loebenberger, D.: Migrating software systems toward post-quantum cryptography-a systematic literature review. IEEE Access **12**, 132107–132126 (2024). https://doi.org/10.1109/ACCESS.2024.3450306
27. Ott, D., Peikert, C.: Identifying Research Challenges in Post Quantum Cryptography Migration and Cryptographic Agility (2019). https://doi.org/10.48550/arXiv.1909.07353. arXiv:1909.07353
28. Page, M.J., et al.: The PRISMA 2020 statement: an updated guideline for reporting systematic reviews. BMJ **372** (2021). https://doi.org/10.1136/bmj.n71
29. Roberts, A.: Quantum-resistant cryptography migration strategies for long-term data security in healthcare. Glob. J. Intell. Technol. **5**(3), 13–22 (2025). https://doi.org/10.64206/q6kdfq61
30. Schmitt, N., Henrich, J., Heinz, D., Alnahawi, N., Wiesmaier, A.: On criteria and tooling for cryptographic inventories. In: LNI Tagungsband GI Sicherheit 2024, pp. 49–63. Gesellschaft für Informatik e.V. (2024). https://dl.gi.de/bitstreams/f35b7164-a5bf-4c01-81e9-2accb6d01b4a/download
31. Shor, P.: Algorithms for quantum computation: discrete logarithms and factoring. In: Proceedings 35th Annual Symposium on Foundations of Computer Science, pp. 124–134 (1994). https://doi.org/10.1109/SFCS.1994.365700
32. Thakur, M.S.D., Vidhani, K., Syed, H.B., M.A., R.: Enterprise post quantum cryptography migration tools. In: 2024 16th International Conference on COMmunication Systems & NETworkS (COMSNETS), pp. 327–329 (2024). https://doi.org/10.1109/COMSNETS59351.2024.10427442
33. Von Nethen, N., Wiesmaier, A., Alnahawi, N., Henrich, J.: PMMP – PQC migration management process. In: Proceedings of the 2024 European Interdisciplinary Cybersecurity Conference, pp. 144–154. ACM (2024). https://doi.org/10.1145/3655693.3655719
34. White, B., et al.: Transitioning to Quantum-Safe Cryptography on IBM Z
35. Zhang, L., Miranskyy, A., Rjaibi, W., Stager, G., Gray, M., Peck, J.: Making existing software quantum safe: a case study on IBM Db2. Inf. Softw. Technol. **161**, 107249 (2023). https://doi.org/10.1016/j.infsof.2023.107249. http://arxiv.org/abs/2110.08661. arXiv:2110.08661

A Formal Model and Lower-Bound Intuition for Cryptographic Migration

Daniel Loebenberger[1,3(✉)], Eduard Hirsch[3], Stefan-Lukas Gazdag[2], Daniel Herzinger[2], Christian Näther[4], and Jan-Philipp Steghöfer[4]

[1] Fraunhofer Institute for Applied and Integrated Security, Hermann-Brenner-Platz 1, 92637 Weiden i.d.OPf., Germany
[2] genua GmbH, Domagkstr. 7, 85551 Kirchheim b. München, Germany
[3] OTH Amberg-Weiden, Kaiser-Wilhelm-Ring 23, 92224 Amberg, Germany
d.loebenberger@oth-aw.de
[4] XITASO GmbH, Austraße 35, 86153 Augsburg, Germany

Abstract. We present a novel approach to gaining insight into the structure of cryptographic migration problems which are classic problems in applied cryptography. We use a formal model to capture the inherent dependencies and complexities of such transitions. Using classical mathematical results from combinatorics, probability theory, and combinatorial analysis, we evaluate the challenges of migrating large cryptographic IT infrastructures. We show mathematical rigorously that for certain idealized random partitions and under some standard Erdős-Rényi-type assumptions our model exhibits a certain expected structural complexity and provide numerical data for selected parameter sets. This work paves the way for future advancements in both the theoretical understanding and practical implementation of cryptographic migration strategies.

Keywords: cryptographic migration · formal model · lower-bound intuition · structural complexity · post-quantum transition

1 Introduction

Cryptography is fundamental to ensuring information security in today's digital world and is thus an essential cornerstone of many modern dependable systems. Despite advances in cryptographic technologies, the process of migrating existing systems and IT infrastructures to new standards presents significant challenges [2]. One example is the transition from IPv4 to IPv6, which took more than 20 years and promoted technologies such as gateways and network address translation (NAT) to circumvent the actual migration. In the cryptographic realm, notable examples include updating key sizes (where RSA key sizes increased, as did integration problems) and transitioning between different hash functions (from SHA-1 to the SHA-2 family, and eventually to the SHA-3 family), with the SHA-3 family being adopted slowly as SHA-2 is still considered sufficient for most tasks. Rapid transition appears to require a strong incentive to adopt

D. Loebenberger and M. Stöttinger (Eds.): MAgiCS 2026, CCIS 3002, pp. 82–101, 2026.
https://doi.org/10.1007/978-3-032-28946-9_5

new technology. A famous example is the transition from the symmetric cipher DES to its replacements AES, driven by the need for stronger security measures due to DES's vulnerability to brute-force attacks [20]. The issue of migration is particularly prominent in the current transition towards post-quantum cryptography (PQC), which aims to protect data against future quantum computing threats. The German Federal Office for Information Security (BSI) uses the working hypothesis for the high-security sector that there likely exists a cryptographically relevant quantum computer in the early 2030s [31]. Mosca estimated more specifically that there is a 1 in 2 chance that such a computer will exist in 2031 [13]. Thus, there are numerous practical post-quantum migrations going on world-wide. The reason is that we are already running out of time: Sensitive (e.g., classified) data often has long confidentiality requirements (e.g., 25 years) and it might be possible to decrypt cryptographically protected data which is recorded today in the future. In addition, migrating the IT-infrastructure correspondingly takes a considerable amount of time [28].

Our approach to support PQC migration is to model the migration problem suitably and identify this way optimal migration strategies in general. We propose a systematic analysis to better understand the structural problems and explore which potential models are necessary for building tools to assist actual PQC migrations. Although algorithmic aspects and the details of the concrete tooling are beyond the scope of this work, we believe that a structured assessment of the migration problem provides valuable insights into the structural complexities involved. Our findings show that the dependencies of a system to be migrated usually necessitate a compatible migration order to avoid losing functionality. Within this order, there are always sets of systems which need to be migrated together – so called *migration clusters* (cf. Definition 1) – and their successive migration defines the corresponding migration strategy. As soon as the systems under evaluation exhibit non-trivial complexity, we have many or large migration clusters, and these migration clusters are expected to be interdependent, making parallelization of the different steps impossible and migration thus difficult. To facilitate the process while still allowing for rapid migration, we need tools that can identify and visualize optimal migration strategies. In order to cope with the complexity of developing such tools, we believe that a proper understanding of the underlying problem is necessary. Our work presented here provides the formal basis for this.

Contributions

Our contributions are as follows:

1. We introduce a novel graph-based formalization of cryptographic migration, along with a discussion of the structure of the resulting model (Sect. 3).
2. We then prove that any (reasonably large) migration project has an expected complex dependency structure and thus show that this structure prohibits parallelizing the migration (Sect. 4).

In an extended version of this article, we additionally explore typical graphs and patterns that occur in practice and how these patterns can support system administrators in planning a migration project. We also demonstrate there how our model can be applied to an actual migration problem as an exemplar to showcase its ability to draw conclusions about real-world migrations. We also discuss how multiple graphs on different levels of abstraction can be combined when planning the migration of a complex critical infrastructure system. Overall, the formalization proposed in this paper is an important step toward a better, more systematic understanding of migration problems. It also lays the groundwork for developing tools that will support engineers in the complex cryptographic migrations that lie ahead in the coming years.

2 Background and Related Work

2.1 Background

After the announcements of the first post-quantum public key algorithms for consideration as an international standard by the National Institute of Standards and Technology (NIST) [23–25], the transition to PQC has started in practice: in the US, there is a project run by NIST with a large consortium of industry-leading companies that explores the transition to PQC [2]. In Europe, the German Federal Office for Information Security (BSI) published a guideline concerning post-quantum migration [6] and also included certain post-quantum algorithms in their recommended suite of cryptographic algorithms [7]. The Dutch government also published a "PQC Migration Handbook" containing guidelines for migrating to PQC [1].

Despite these world-wide activities, we found little research on the general structure of migration projects and how to suitably model cryptographic migration. In fact, many people consider migrating soft- and hardware components as a best-practice task. So, people legitimately ask "Where Is the Research on Cryptographic Transition and Agility?" as David Ott did at RWC2022 (see also [18]). We show in Sect. 4 that there are combinatorial reasons why cryptographic migration is – at least in certain simplified mathematical models – inherently structurally complex. Ott et al. define the term *cryptographic agility* as "the ability to make a transition from one cryptographic algorithm or implementation to another" [18]. Our own, canonical definition [15] states that "Cryptographic Agility is a theoretical or practical approach, objective, or property which provides capabilities for setting up, identifying, and modifying encryption methods and keying material in a flexible and efficient way while preserving business continuity." Adopting cryptographic agility in this sense ensures the flexibility to transition between algorithms or implementations in response to evolving threats. Thus, in order to implement cryptographic agility we need to prepare cryptographic migration. In turn, for preparing migration, we need a step-by-step migration plan which must allow careful re-evaluation of dependencies and system integrity at each stage. This kind of approach is in line with making security solutions sustainable by allowing to adapt to changing threats and technologies.

2.2 Related Work

Our recent efforts have focused on consolidating the state-of-the-art in cryptographic migration [14] and systematically organizing knowledge on cryptographic agility [15]. Furthermore, frameworks arose that aim to support the migration process as in [30]. Also, there are few informal models of the migration problem (e.g., [5,19,27,29]). All these models have in common that they address operational aspects of cryptographic migration in various institutional contexts. This can be aligned with the above observation of structuring best-practice tasks. While these kind of analyses are clearly important and can serve as a basis for practical migration, they do not attempt to formally assess the underlying structural problem. Instead they give guidelines on how to assess the needed transition efforts, explain how to perform a suitable risk-analysis, and describe process landscapes to perform cryptographic transition.

One way of collecting the information that is necessary to build a migration model is to construct a software bill of materials (SBOM) [17] or a cryptographic bill of materials (CBOM) [10,11]. While the SBOM contains information about which software in which version is used and can also include information about dependencies that are relevant for cryptography, the CBOM contains information about the concrete cryptographic mechanisms in use. This information can be used in conjunction to plan a migration, e.g., by identifying vulnerable protocols in the communication between two assets in the CBOM and then using the SBOMs of these assets to locate the software that should be migrated. While modern tooling for SBOM and CBOM generation can identify local software dependencies and cryptographic inventories, these tools typically focus on asset management rather than strategic transition planning. The limitation of current approaches is their lack of systemic abstraction, which is addressed here.

Building an SBOM or a CBOM requires extensive tooling for (semi-)automated collection. There is a plethora of relevant tools available[1] that help either on the system level or on the network level to collect the desired information of the infrastructure. The results are typically vast: even for small setups, such an automated assembly can easily yield tens of thousands of components.

However, complex migration projects require many successive steps and in-depth strategic planning. Based on an SBOM/CBOM alone, only a simple risk-assessment and migration of components – without formal structure – based only on the highest risk exposure or when updates are available is feasible. We believe this is insufficient since it ignores the complexity of migration projects that should be based on more information than the SBOM and CBOM provide, including information about exposure, and should be based on a structured plan with a comprehensive overview rather than on ad-hoc interventions.

Initial standardization attempts with the same aim include frameworks like CARAF, a risk management approach for post-quantum migration [12]. In this framework, risks are identified, an asset inventory is set up and the risk is estimated for each asset, yielding an organizational road-map. Relating that to our

[1] See for example https://perma.cc/N8WE-QBTZ.

migration model, after the asset inventorization we also get a list of relevant components (i.e., the nodes within the graph), but the CARAF approach does not provide any information about the dependencies between the components. The draft "Repeatable Framework for Quantum-safe Migrations" of the framework ETSI published [5] approaches the migration problem from an organizational perspective. It assumes that the responsibility for migration projects is assigned internally while some form of governance regulates the interdependence of the parties involved. Local dependency structures are described in part, but an analysis of longer chains of dependencies is not conducted. Therefore, only local dependencies can be captured by this framework.

As far as we know, a formal treatment for the migration problem is still pending: While Hasan et al. [9] introduce a solid starting point for a PQC migration model by analyzing certain local dependencies in real-world migration projects, these authors do not work out the resulting composed dependency structures found in real-world interconnected systems. Instead they provide a practical framework focused on cryptographic and data inventories and a local dependency analysis within enterprise systems. Also, their analysis primarily addresses operational aspects. Building on this groundwork, our efforts enhance the theoretical rigor by formalizing migration challenges through mathematical models. Our generalization even addresses broader migration scenarios beyond PQC-specific contexts. We believe that our migration model together with its analysis and study of real-world applicability can substantially contribute to the understanding of the formal foundations of cryptographic migration.

In any case, combining different kinds of information, carving out relations and creating a model of the migration graph is still a lot of manual work and is currently not fully supported by tooling. In future work we envision tooling to support the creation and maintenance of migration graphs as well as their analysis.

3 A Model for the Cryptographic Migration Problem

Having motivated the need for a rigorous treatment of cryptographic migrations, we formulate a migration project as a directed graph whose vertices represent concrete software, hardware or organizational components which need to be migrated. Its edges capture dependencies that constrain the order of those migrations. We introduce an intuitive model, moving to a precise definition that introduces the key notions of strongly-connected migration clusters, migratable components, and the scheduling strategies that remove such clusters step-by-step. This formal framework sets the stage for the complexity analysis in Sect. 4 and underlies the practical patterns developed later in the paper.

3.1 Informal Description of the Model

Any IT infrastructure we migrate consists of a number of *migration components* or simply *components* which need to be migrated. The *migration prob-*

lem is now to migrate all migration components. However, not every component can be migrated at every point in time, because there might be dependencies between the components. For instance, an application can migrate to post-quantum algorithms only after the cryptographic libraries it relies on have been upgraded. Another example is the migration of a communicating software component, which can only be migrated if the corresponding counterparts of the communication are migrated at the same time or if we introduce some kind of interoperability. In this case the migration can be done (if there are no other dependencies) if all communicating parties of this single migration component are migrated at the same time. We call this a *migration cluster*. Components without dependencies outside its migration cluster are called *migratable components*. The *migration process* looks as follows:

1. In every migration step we select a migratable component, following a suitable *migration strategy*.
2. We then compute its migration cluster, i.e., possible interdependent components that need to be migrated at the same point in time.
3. Then, the actual migration of the migration cluster is performed and the successfully migrated migration cluster is removed from our model (together with all in-going dependencies).
4. This process is repeated until there is no migration component left and we have then solved the migration problem for this specific IT infrastructure.

The whole model is now captured in a directed graph whose vertices are the migration components and the edges are the dependencies between components, the *migration graph* of the migration problem, which we will detail in this section. Note that a migration graph's structure will vary significantly depending on the concrete IT infrastructure and the kind of model we have in mind. But also the abstraction layer and the type of migration lead to many design choices of the model. The resulting graphs will show parallels to those that already exist in several disciplines of computer science such as flowcharts, call graphs, and finite-state machines in programming, network diagrams, or software dependency graphs.

We expect that post-quantum migration is the most significant type of cryptographic migration of IT infrastructures in the near future [14]. Its specific properties introduce aspects that were less prevalent in the classical cryptography world, where examples are hybrid cryptographic schemes and more complex instantiations of cryptographically agile solutions. Also, regulatory requirements of post-quantum solutions and different views on current and future algorithm recommendations may become significantly more complicated, especially in a multinational context. All in all, post-quantum migration is the scenario that motivated our formal migration model. At the same time, it implicates several special properties which make modeling even more complex. We now specify the formal model. The concepts concerning directed graphs are partially quite standard, nevertheless we specify for the sake of completeness the full notation. Novel and unprecedented in the literature is the application to migration problems.

3.2 Formal Definition of Migration Graphs

Consider a finite set V of components in a large IT infrastructure. If the migration of a component $v \in V$ depends on the migration of a component $w \in V$, we write $v \to w$. In other words: We cannot migrate v before migrating w (but possibly at the same time). Collecting all such dependencies in a set E (without loops $v \to v$) gives us the *migration graph* $G = (V, E)$ modeling the *migration project* we have in mind. Canonically, we extend the relation $v \to w$ to sets $M_1, M_2 \subseteq V$ and write $M_1 \to_G M_2 := \{v \to w; (v,w) \in E, v \in M_1, w \in M_2\}$. If G is clear from the context, we omit the subscript and only write $M_1 \to M_2$. For a dependency $e = v \to w \in E$ we write $\mathit{source}(e) := v$ and $\mathit{target}(e) := w$, again with canonical extension to sets. For later use, we write for a set $M \subseteq V$ for the *restricted graph* $G|_M = (M, M \to M)$. The *direct dependencies* of $v \in V$ are precisely given by the set $\mathit{target}(v \to V)$. We define the *dependencies of* v as $\mathit{dep}(v) := \mathit{target}(v \to^* V)$, where $\to^*$ is the reflexive and transitive closure of the relation $\to$. A simple example of a migration graph can be found in Fig. 1.

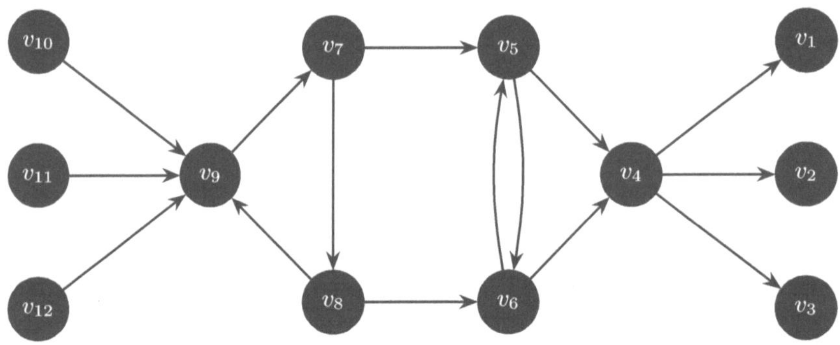

Fig. 1. An example of a simple migration graph on twelve components $v_1, \ldots, v_{12}$.

3.3 Migration Clusters and Migratable Components

Definition 1 (Migration Cluster). *Let* $G = (V, E)$ *be a migration graph and* $v \in V$*. The* migration cluster $c(v)$ of v *is set of all components* $w \in V$ *such that* $w \in \mathit{dep}(v)$ *and* $v \in \mathit{dep}(w)$*.*

In the literature, the migration clusters are classically called the *strongly connected components* of G. For sake of exposition we stick to the term *migration cluster* in the context of cryptographic migration. Intuitively, the elements of $c(v)$ are precisely those components that have to be migrated at the same time as v due to mutual dependencies. The migration clusters specify how complex single *migration steps* of a *migration project* are. Additionally, the properties of the migration clusters inside a migration graph G shed light on the complexity of the resulting *migration problem* which we will describe below. In fact, we have the following important characteristics:

1. The *size* s of the cluster $s(v) := \#c(v)$.
2. The *degree* $cdeg(v) := max_{w \in c(v)} deg(w)$, where $deg(w)$ is the out-degree of the component w.

Clearly, if $cdeg(v) = 0$, then $deg(w) = 0$ for all $w \in c(v)$. Hence no vertex in $c(v)$ has an outgoing edge. If $s(v) = \#c(v) > 1$, then for $w_1 \neq w_2 \in c(v)$ there exists a path $w_1 \to^* w_2$, which must start with an outgoing edge of w_1, a contradiction. Thus $s(v) = 1$. Conversely, if $s(v) = 1$ then $cdeg(v) = 0$ since $c(v)$ consists of a single component only and has no edges. In practice this case occurs in the situation where we have a single component that simply can be migrated without any dependencies on other components. This is the easiest case in a migration process.

In the case $cdeg(v) = 1$ the migration cluster $c(v)$ is a cycle. In practice this case often occurs for $s(v) = 2$ when there are two components that communicate using the same protocol. A migration of the protocol can only be done successfully if both components are migrated at the same time. The set $m(v)$ of *migratable components around* v is given by

$$m(v) = \begin{cases} c(v) & , \text{if } c(v) \to \bar{c}(v) = \emptyset \\ \emptyset & , \text{otherwise} \end{cases}$$

where we write $\bar{c}(v) = V \setminus c(v)$. The set $m(v)$ specifies exactly which components can be migrated in G when we attempt to migrate $v \in V$. If v has dependencies outside its migration cluster, i.e., v cannot be migrated, then $m(v) = \emptyset$. If there are no direct dependencies of v, then $m(v) = \{v\}$. Also, in all other cases $m(v) = c(v)$, i.e., the whole migration cluster. If $m(v) \neq \emptyset$, we call v *migratable* (in G).

Now, in a migration project, there might be several subsequent steps to fully migrate all involved components, i.e., solve the migration problem the migration graph poses. We write $G^{(v)} = (V \setminus m(v), E \setminus (V \to m(v)))$ for the graph after a migration attempt of v. If v is not migratable, then $G^{(v)} = G$. Generally, $G^{(v)}$ is exactly the graph restricted to the components outside the migratable components around v. Using similar to above the notation $\bar{m}(v) = V \setminus m(v)$, we can thus alternatively write $G^{(v)} = G|_{\bar{m}(v)} = (\bar{m}(v), \bar{m}(v) \to \bar{m}(v))$. We now show

Lemma 1. *In any (finite and non-empty) migration graph $G = (V, E)$ there is at least one component $v \in V$ that is migratable.*

Proof. Suppose there is no migratable component, i.e., $m(v) = \emptyset$ for all $v \in V$. By definition, $c(v) \to \bar{c}(v)$ is always non-empty, i.e., there is always a dependency to a component outside the migration cluster of v. Call such a dependency $w \in \bar{c}(v)$. Since w is outside the migration cluster of v, w cannot depend on elements of $c(v)$ and all dependencies of w reside in the (strict) subgraph $G|_{\bar{c}(v)}$, which also has by the assumption on G no migratable component. Repeating this process, after a finite number of steps, we end-up in a graph which only contains a single migration cluster $c(u)$ and $u \in V$ is migratable in G contradicting our assumption. $\square$

3.4 Migration Strategies

We will now define *migration strategies of* G. Formally, a strategy $S = (v_1, \ldots, v_\ell) \in V^\ell$ for $\ell \in \mathbb{N}$ is a sequence of components that are migrated one by one (of course together with their respective migration clusters). ℓ is the *length* of the strategy. For $1 \leq i \leq \ell$ denote by G_i the graph after successively migrating $v_1, \ldots, v_i$, i.e., $G_i := G_{i-1}^{(v_i)}$, where $G_0 = G$. The strategy S is *reasonable* if for all $1 \leq i \leq \ell$, we have $m(v_i) \neq \emptyset$ in the graph G_{i-1}. That means that the component v_i is in fact migratable in the graph G_{i-1} and, therefore $G_i \subsetneq G_{i-1}$, i.e., the migration of v_i yields a smaller graph. S is *successful*, if G_ℓ is the empty graph. By Lemma 1 there is a reasonable, successful strategy for any migration graph G.

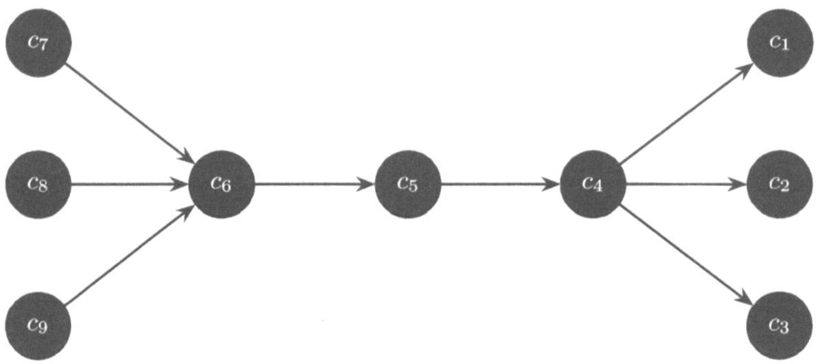

Fig. 2. The acyclic condensation graph G/c on nine clusters $c_1, \ldots, c_9$ of the migration graph from Fig. 1.

Theorem 1. *All reasonable, successful strategies* $S = (v_1, \ldots, v_\ell)$ *for a migration graph* $G = (V, E)$ *have the same length* ℓ.

Proof. Consider two reasonable, successful strategies $S_1 = (v_1^1, \ldots, v_{\ell_1}^1)$ and $S_2 = (v_1^2, \ldots, v_{\ell_2}^2)$ with $\ell_2 \geq \ell_1$. Since S_1 is successful, $V = \biguplus_{1 \leq i \leq \ell_1} m(v_i)$ partitions into the migration clusters given by S_1. Note that all $m(v_i) = c(v_i)$ are non-empty since S_1 is reasonable. Now, consider the (sub-)strategy $S_3 = (v_1^2, \ldots, v_{\ell_1}^2)$ of the strategy S_2. By the partition property, there is for each $1 \leq j \leq \ell_1$ an $1 \leq i \leq \ell_1$ such that $v_j^2 \in c(v_i^1)$. Furthermore, for each $1 \leq j_1 < j_2 \leq \ell_1$ and corresponding $1 \leq i_1, i_2 \leq \ell_1$, we have $i_1 \neq i_2$ since otherwise $v_{j_2}^2 \in m(v_{j_1}^2) \neq \emptyset$. The non-emptiness of $m(v_{j_1}^2)$ follows from the assumption that S_2 is reasonable. But then $\sum_{1 \leq j \leq \ell_1} s(v_j^2) = \#V$ and the strategy S_3 is already successful. $\square$

Due to Theorem 1 the *migration length* $\ell(G)$ as a property of the migration graph G is well-defined. It basically expresses how many independent migration steps one has to perform in order to fully migrate a system. Equivalently, we see that the set of components V partitions into the migration clusters of its components, i.e., $V = \bigcup_{v \in V} c(v)$ and for all $v_1, v_2 \in V$, we either have $c(v_1) = c(v_2)$ or $c(v_1) \cap c(v_2) = \emptyset$. In other words the relation $v_1 \sim_c v_2 :\Leftrightarrow c(v_1) = c(v_2)$ is an equivalence relation. Another important measure of the complexity of a migration project is the *migration depth* of the migration graph G. Clearly, migratable independent components, i.e., migratable $v_1, v_2 \in V$ with $c(v_1) \neq c(v_2)$ can in practice either be migrated in parallel or sequentially. As it turns out there is a *canonical strategy* $S(G)$ (up to isomorphism) that specifies how in practice a migration project should be performed optimally. The idea is to specify a directed acyclic graph $G/c = (V/c, E/c)$, classically called the *condensation of* G, containing as nodes the migration clusters $c(v)$ that is $V/c = \{c(v); v \in V\}$ with an edge $c(v_1) \to c(v_2)$ iff there is an edge between a member of $c(v_1)$ and a member of $c(v_2)$, i.e., $E/c = \{c(v_1) \to c(v_2); v_1 \to v_2 \in E\}$, see Fig. 2. We now have $\#(V/c) = \ell(G)$. We state the simple and well-known lemma:

Lemma 2. *For a migration graph $G = (V, E)$ the graph G/c is acyclic.*

Proof. Assume G/c is not acyclic, that is, there are $v_1, v_2 \in V$ such that $c(v_1) \to^+ c(v_2) \in (E/c)^+$ and $c(v_2) \to^+ c(v_1) \in (E/c)^+$ as usual denoting by the superscript $+$ the irreflexive transitive closure of the dependency relation. But then, by definition of c, we have $c(v_1) = c(v_2)$. □

Notions like migratability can now also be considered for the graph G/c. We define the *canonical migration time* of $c(v) \in V/c$ as

$$t(c(v)) := \ max\{1 \leq k \leq \ell(G) \mid c(v) \to^k V/c \neq \emptyset\}$$

where $\to^k$ denotes paths of length k via the relation $\to$. The canonical migration time is the position in the topological order of the directed acyclic graph G/c. Migratable migration clusters have $t(c(v)) = 1$, all other clusters have $t(c(v)) > 1$. Write $T(k) := \{c(v) \in V/c; t(c(v)) = k\}$ for the set of all migration clusters with canonical migration time k. The *canonical strategy* is now to first migrate all migration clusters in $T(1)$ then in $T(2)$ and so on. A canonical strategy is thus given by $S(G) = (T(1), \dots, T(d(G)))$. We call $d(G) := \ max_{c(v) \in V/c} t(c(v))$ the *migration depth* of G. In other words, the migration depth specifies how many migration steps successively depend on each other in the worst case. Note that for all $1 \leq i \leq d(G)$ we can arbitrarily order the elements of the set $T(i)$. Thus, there are exactly $\prod_{1 \leq i \leq d(G)} \#T(i)!$ many canonical strategies. Since all of them are isomorphic (w.r.t. the dependency relation on G/c), our notation for $S(G)$ is sound.

The overall structure of the migration graph G is thus as follows (cf. Fig. 3):

1. G partitions acyclically into its migration clusters.
2. The migration clusters have only acyclic dependencies between each other.

3. The migration clusters have thus a canonical position in the migration process depending on how deep in the graph they are located.

Note that there are also non-canonical migration strategies, where a migration of a component $v \in V$ removed a dependency of another component $w \in V$ and even though there were other migratable components in the first place the migration of w is done next.

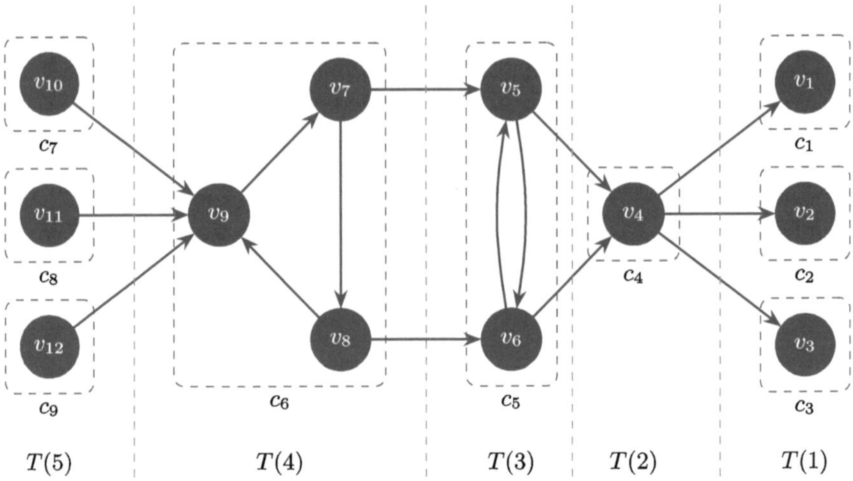

Fig. 3. The migration graph from Fig. 1 with its migration clusters (denoted by dashed boxes) and canonical migration times. In this example with 12 components, we have $\ell(G) = 9$ and $d(G) = 5$.

4 Assessing the Structural Complexity of the Migration Problem

We now prove some expected properties of certain "random" migration graphs. The results shed light on a general lower-bound intuition of the migration problem, but do not impose claims on the nature of real-word system structure. In that model, we show that, expectedly, any sufficiently large migration project splits into many dependent migration steps that cannot be parallelized and provide a formal proof of this statement.

From classical results in combinatorial analysis we know the following about random decompositions of the migration graph into its clusters.

4.1 Random Migration Clusters

Since every migration graph decomposes disjointly into its migration clusters, we now study the expected properties of these migration clusters. Let n be the number of components. There are B_n different possible partitions of n components in disjoint subsets, where

$$B_{n+1} = \sum_{k=0}^{n} \binom{n}{k} B_k = \frac{1}{e} \sum_{k=0}^{\infty} \frac{k^n}{k!}$$

is the nth Bell number and $B_0 = 1$. More precisely, there are $\left\{ {n \atop k} \right\}$ partitions of our components in k distinct non-empty subsets, where $\left\{ {n \atop k} \right\}$ are called the *Stirling numbers of the second kind.* Obviously, we have $B_n = \sum_{1 \le k \le n} \left\{ {n \atop k} \right\}$.

Consider now a migration project with m different sub-projects and suppose each of our n components is assigned to one of the m sub-projects uniformly at random. Let Π_{nm} be the random variable defining the resulting partition π of our components. We have:

$$prob(\Pi_{nm} = \pi) = \frac{m^{\underline{k}}}{m^n}$$

if $\#\pi = k$, where $m^{\underline{k}} = m \cdot (m-1) \cdots (m-k+1)$ is the falling factorial function. In other words: if there are k different sub-projects with at least one component, then the probability of creating one such partition is given by the formula above. For the distribution of the number of non-empty different sub-projects we have

$$prob(\#\pi = k) = \left\{ {n \atop k} \right\} \frac{m^{\underline{k}}}{m^n}.$$

Note that for arbitrary migration graphs, we do not know the distribution of the different partitions. We have the following

Theorem 2 (Proposition 2 in [21]). *Let M be the random variable with values in $\mathbb{N}_{\ge 1}$ and suppose given $M = m$ that n balls labeled by $\mathbb{N}_{\le n}$ are thrown independently and uniformly at random into m boxes. Then the following two statements are equivalent:*

1. *M is distributed via $prob(M = m) = m^n p_m / B_n$ for $m \in \mathbb{N}_{\ge 1}$, where p_m is a probability distribution on $\mathbb{N}_{\ge 0}$ whose first n factorial moments are identically equal to 1. One may for example take $p_m = 1/(em!)$.*
2. *Π_{nM} has uniform distribution over the set of all partitions of n components.*

The Theorem gives a constructive way of uniformly generating a migration cluster: First sample $m \in \mathbb{N}_{\ge 1}$ following the above distribution, then distribute the n components uniformly in m bins. The resulting partition π will be a uniformly selected partition of our n components. We will now study the expected properties of the outcome. In the following $logn$ is always the natural logarithm. Studying the distribution of random partitions of sets with n elements is a classical problem. Set into the context of migration problems, we state.

Theorem 3 (Summary of [16] and Chapter 4, Theorem 1.1 in [26]). *The number of migration clusters M is expectedly $\mathsf{E}(M) \sim n/\ \log n$ and the expected size of each migration cluster is $\log n$. Also, almost all partitions have approximately $e \log n$ distinct cluster sizes. More specifically the distribution of the number of migration clusters M converges asymptotically to a normal distribution with mean $\mu = n/\ \log n$ and standard deviation $\sigma = \sqrt{n}/\ \log n$ for $n \to \infty$.*

Furthermore, the expected maximum size of a migration cluster is, for growing n, asymptotic to $er - \ \log\sqrt{r}$, where $r \cdot \ exp(r) = n$ and $r = \ \log n - (1 + o(1))\ \log\ \log n \sim \ \log n$ [22]. This means that we typically expect lots of small clusters and we do not expect exceptionally large ones. Results on the speed of convergence are beyond the scope of this article. We now compute an upper bound on the expected number of migration clusters when looking independently at s randomly selected migration projects.

Theorem 4. *The expected maximal number of migration clusters when looking independently at s randomly selected migration projects is bounded above by*

$$\frac{n}{\log n} + \frac{\sqrt{2n\ \log s}}{\log n}.$$

Proof. Let $M_1, \ldots, M_s$ be the resulting numbers of migration clusters and define $X = \max_{1 \le i \le s} M_i - \mu$. Note that generally $\mathsf{E}(X) > 0$.

Since for a fixed real constant $t > 0$ the function $x \mapsto \exp(tx)$ is convex and increasing, by Jensen's inequality we have:

$$\begin{aligned}
\exp(t\mathsf{E}(X)) &\le \mathsf{E}(\exp(tX)) \\
&= \mathsf{E}\left(\max_{1\le i\le s} \exp(t(M_i - \mu))\right) \\
&\le \sum_{i=1}^{s} \mathsf{E}(\exp(t(M_i - \mu))) \\
&= s\exp(t^2\sigma^2/2)
\end{aligned}$$

Here, the last equality follows from the fact that the moment generating function $\mathsf{E}(\ exp(t(M_i - \mu)))$ for a normal distribution with mean zero is equal to $exp(t^2\sigma^2/2)$ and in particular independent of the index-variable i. Rewriting this, $\mathsf{E}(X) \le \frac{\log s}{t} + \frac{t\sigma^2}{2}$. This bound is minimal at $t = \frac{\sqrt{2\ \log s}}{\sigma}$ since its derivative in direction t is $\frac{\sigma^2}{2} - \frac{\log s}{t^2}$. Thus, $\mathsf{E}(X) \le \sigma\sqrt{2\ \log s}$. □

In practice, the Lemma implies that we would have to sample exponentially many migration graphs (in the number of components n) in order to expectedly observe graphs with asymptotically more than $n/\ \log n$ migration clusters. Thus, the statement from Theorem 3 applies in practice all the time, at least for sufficiently large n. It remains to study the dependencies between the migration clusters, i.e., the structure of the condensation modulo the migration clusters.

Table 1. Numerical evaluation of the expected behavior of migration clusters for migration projects with n components rounded to the nearest integer. We observe that we do not expect large clusters, but the expected number of independent clusters is vast and the chain-dependencies are also large when we bound the number of migration clusters with fixed canonical migration time by $w(n') = logn'$ in the fifth and $w(n') = \sqrt{n'}/\ logn'$ in the sixth column, respectively. Here, as in Theorem 6, $n' = \mathsf{E}(\#(G/c)) = \frac{n}{logn}$. For readability, we only specify the asymptotic description of $d(G)$ (in the number of components n) for the specified choices of w in the last two columns of the table.

$\#V$	$\mathsf{E}(\#c(v))$	$\mathsf{E}(\#(G/c))$	$\mathsf{SD}(\#(G/c))$	$\sim d(G)$	
n	$logn$	$\frac{n}{logn}$	$\frac{\sqrt{n}}{logn}$	$\frac{n}{log^2 n}$	$\sqrt{n\ logn}$
10	2	4	1	2	5
100	5	22	2	5	21
1 000	7	145	5	21	83
10 000	9	1 086	11	118	303
100 000	12	8 686	27	754	1 073
1 000 000	14	72 382	72	5 239	3 717
10 000 000	16	620 421	196	38 492	12 696
100 000 000	18	5 428 681	543	294 706	42 919
1 000 000 000	21	48 254 942	1 526	2 328 539	143 956

4.2 Properties of the Condensation Graph

According to Theorem 3, we consider a condensation graph, i.e., the directed acyclic graph resulting from the migration graph on n components modulo its strongly connected components, with expectedly $n' = n/\ logn$ vertices. Since we are considering a single migration project, we can assume that this graph is connected. How can we model this graph?

A first idea would be to use the standard Erdős-Rényi model [4], where the graph is constructed by connecting the components independently at random with a fixed probability p. One can ensure that the result is acyclic by defining any linear order on the vertices and include a directed edge only if it obeys the selected ordering. Each such edge is included in the graph with probability p, independently from every other edge. For such graphs, we have

Theorem 5 (Theorem 4.1 in [8], a variant of Theorem 1 in [3]). *Let G_{n,p_n} be a random n-vertex graph, where each arc is present with probability $p_n = \frac{logn+c_n}{n}$. Then, for growing n, the probability that G is connected is given by*

$$\lim_{n\to\infty} prob(G_{n,p_n}\ connected) = \begin{cases} 0 & ,\ if\ c_n \to -\infty \\ e^{-e^{-c}} & ,\ if\ c_n \to c\ const. \\ 1 & ,\ if\ c_n \to \infty \end{cases}$$

Note that we can directly apply this Theorem to our directed acyclic graph situation, since such a graph is connected if and only if the undirected variant of it is connected.

As our goal is to prove a lower bound on the number of edges in the condensation graph (with n' vertices!) in our model, we assume now the sparsest case $c_{n'} \to c$ constant for which the graph is connected with high probability. Note that the doubly-exponential term in Theorem 5 approaches 1 already for comparatively small c very quickly. For example, already for $c = 10$, the value of $e^{-e^{-c}} \geq 0.99995$. But also for any $c > 0$, we obtain for the number of edges in the condensation graph expectedly asymptotically

$$\begin{aligned} \frac{logn' + c_{n'}}{n'} \cdot \frac{n' \cdot (n'-1)}{2} &= \frac{1}{2}((n'-1)(\ logn' + c_{n'})) \\ &\sim \frac{1}{2} n'\ logn'. \end{aligned}$$

That means that even in the sparsest case, we expect a considerable number of dependencies between the migration clusters.

We now analyze what happens if we bound for any k the number $\#(c(v) \to^k V/c)$ of clusters with a common ancestor of distance k, the *width* w of the migration graph G, by a small function $w(n') = o(n')$ in the size n' of the condensation graph G/c.

Theorem 6. *Let $w : \mathbb{R} \to \mathbb{R}$ be a smooth function in a real variable with $w \in o(n')$, e.g., $w(n') =\ logn'$. Assume for any cluster $c(v)$ in a condensation graph G/c with $n' \sim \frac{n}{logn}$ components, we have for each $k \geq 0$ the bound $\#(c(v) \to^k V/c) \leq w(n')$. Then $d(G) \geq n'/w(n')$. In other words, the width of the migration graph has a trade-off with the depth of the migration graph.*

Proof. Without loss of generality we can assume that G/c has a single source $c(v)$. Otherwise take the set of sources and consider the one with the longest path in $c(v) \to^* V/c$. This path has length $d(G)$. For $0 \leq k < d(G)$ define $W_k := c(v) \to^k V/c$. Since G/c has only a single source, the disjoint union $\biguplus_{0 \leq k < d(G)} W_k = V/c$, i.e., $n' = \#(V/c) = \# \biguplus_{0 \leq k < d(G)} W_k = \sum_{0 \leq k < d(G)} \#W_k$. By assumption $\#W_k \leq w(n')$ for all $0 \leq k < d(G)$. Thus $n' \leq d(G) \cdot w(n')$ and the claim follows. □

If, e.g., in the Theorem $w(n') =\ logn'$, we obtain expectedly $d(G) \geq \frac{n'}{logn'} = \frac{n}{(\ logn-\ log\ logn)\ logn} \sim \frac{n}{log^2 n}$, that is, large chains of dependencies of the migration clusters. Of course one can trade depth $d(G)$ vs. the bound $w(n')$, but then the complexity of at least one migration step will increase.

4.3 Discussion

In this section we discuss alternative earlier versions of the model, explain which limitations we see when applying our model to real-world migration projects, summarize our findings in a less formal wording, and discuss the different implicit assumptions. During the genesis of this work, our primary goal was to model dependencies of migrations suitably and to understand why migration projects seem to be structurally complex in almost all practical use-cases. In this endeavor, graphs emerged quite naturally. To understand the structural complexity better, we wanted to give a quantitative mathematical explanation and give a first general lower-bound intuition. Thus, we tried to find a model that reflects reality at least approximately. We started in a very early version of the manuscript with classical Erdős-Rényi graphs and the study of properties there. This clearly did not reflect reality, because Erdős-Rényi graphs either fall apart in many disconnected subgraph or quickly produce a giant component. The idea that the clusters might emerge randomly and the following analysis of this assumption yielded the proposed model.

We explicitly do not claim that real-world scenarios follow the randomness assumptions made in the model, but we tried to understand whether our mathematical model fits real-world examples at least in principle, starting from the `GitLab` architecture described in an extended version of this article. It turned out that the model works, but there needs to be much more refinement to fit everything to specific real-word examples. A more complicated example, the analysis of emerging graphs in critical infrastructural systems is our second real-world candidate. As it will turn out, modeling real-world systems is a very challenging task and the details are beyond the scope of this foundational article. We believe that there is much more work to be done to actually understand the complexities of real-world interdependent IT architectures. Nonetheless, also a theoretical study of other distributions as the one based on random set-partitions would clearly be very interesting, but is beyond the scope of the current manuscript.

We now summarize the proposed model. In the previous sections we analyzed how the graph structure stemming from certain random choices for such a graph affects the expected properties of the migration problem. To do so, we looked at random partitions of components, i.e., random migration clusters, arguing that a random migration project stemming from such a process should exhibit a certain clustering behavior and the remaining directed acyclic condensation should also have a random structure. Thereby, we found several mathematical arguments that underline the fact that migration is structurally complex in general. Specifically, for a random (large) migration graph with n components, we showed a number of theorems which are combined into the following.

Corollary 1. *In expectation (of the random variables involved), we have:*

1. *Partitions can be efficiently sampled (Theorem 2), i.e., we can easily observe different random migration graphs.*
2. *The migration graph decomposes in $n/\log n$ migration clusters of size $\log n$ with standard deviation $\sqrt{n}/\log n$ (Theorem 3).*
3. *Even after observing many migration projects, we do not expect to observe any with considerably more than $n/\log n$ migration clusters (Theorem 4).*
4. *The condensation graph is connected and thus not sparse (Theorem 5).*
5. *If for each node the number of dependencies is suitably bounded, the condensation graph has large depth, i.e., many migration clusters that successively*

depend on each other and cannot be parallelized. Stated the other way around, we have at least one migration step with many dependencies if we assume small depth (Theorem 6).

We thus showed that in our model informally we have

Fact 1. *Any sufficiently large migration project splits into many dependent migration steps that cannot be parallelized. The migration of these clusters either takes many successive steps or includes at least one particularly difficult one.*

The statement tells us that a "random" migration project exhibits a certain structural complexity. If we bound the number of clusters at each canonical migration time then we expect larger chains of successive dependencies. Conversely, one might argue that having many independent clusters in a single step is not as difficult as large dependency chains, since one might potentially freely migrate all single clusters at the same time and the difficulty of the migration then purely comes from the number of clusters to migrate, not from the structure of the graph. In other words, one might potentially be able to parallelize the migration steps. Indeed, with parallelization large width might be much more preferable than large depth. This issue deserves future analyses, especially in the context of real-world systems.

We now revise the assumptions made of the above Fact: The first assumption is that in any practical migration project, partitions (i.e., clustering) of components appear uniformly from the set of all partitions. Another assumption is that the structure of the condensation graph follows the Erdős-Rényi model, i.e., that dependencies appear with a fixed probability independently of each other. Finally, our third assumption is that the two modeling steps are structurally independent. All assumptions seem valid for the generic complexity assessment of the model. In practice, of course, we do not have asymptotic objects or expected behaviors of concrete migration graph examples. Nevertheless, the mathematical model provides a sound basis for understanding the structure of migration projects in general.

Actually, there is also a less explicitly stated fourth assumption in our model: We assume that migration graphs are connected. The reason for this assumption is that we needed the property for the estimation on the (large) number of edges in the condensation graph. However, there is no valid reason why this should hold in general – migration projects might actually decompose into several sub-projects. Nonetheless, the statements here are valid for indecomposable migration problems and there are quite standard techniques for deriving asymptotic estimates for decomposable instances. We reserve this for future analyses.

We summarize these results with a numerical evaluation of the relevant estimates in Table 1. In the table, we compute the numerical outcomes for different migration projects with $n = 10^i$ components for $i \in \{1, \ldots, 9\}$, give the expected size of the migration clusters, the expected number of migration clusters with its standard deviation and numerical values of the expected depth of the graph for different bounds of the width $\#(c(v) \to^k V/c) \leq w(n)$.

5 Conclusion

In this work, we used classical mathematical results from graph theory, probability theory, and combinatorial analysis to assess the structural complexity of a very practical problem: cryptographic migration of large IT infrastructures. We formulated a formal model of cryptographic migrateability in terms of directed graphs and showed several expected properties of these graphs. This approach not only elevates the discussion to a scientific level but also establishes a foundation for further research on more efficient migration strategies. We showed that sufficiently large migration projects expectedly have an intrinsic complexity due to many dependent, comparatively small migration clusters which successively depend on each other.

Our work sets the stage for future research aimed at refining these models, integrating them with real-world data, and ultimately creating more adaptive, user-friendly tools that support real-world migration. We therefore aim here to scientifically substantiate migration approaches. By emphasizing the relevance of this formal approach, we hope to support the development of more robust migration strategies and (open-source) tooling that can keep pace with the evolving landscape of cryptographic standards. Still, there is a lot of work to be done when it comes to practical migration projects, especially how to obtain useful migration graphs in practice and how to deduce concrete cost estimates for migration project in general. A further important line of applied research is to actually implement tooling for semi-automated analysis. Practical migrations are too large to handle with a purely manual approach. Our formal model serves as a starting point for tool-supported analysis of systems and tool-supported planning of migrations.

Acknowledgments. This work is supported in part by funds from the German Federal Ministry of Education and Research (# 16KIS1818). We thank the anonymous referees for their valuable suggestions on earlier drafts of this work.

References

1. Amadori, A., et al.: The PQC Migration Handbook: Guidelines for Migrating to Post-Quantum Cryptography – Revised and Extended Second Edition. Technical report, TNO, Applied Cryptography and Quantum Algorithms and CWI, Cryptology Group and AIVD, Netherlands National Communications Security Agency (2024)
2. Barker, W., Polk, W., Souppaya, M.: Getting Ready for Post-Quantum Cryptography: Exploring Challenges Associated with Adopting and Using Post-Quantum Cryptographic Algorithms. Technical report, National Institute of Standards and Technology (2021)
3. Erdős, P., Rényi, A.: On random graphs I. Publ. Math. Debrecen **6**(12), 290–297 (1959)
4. Erdős, P., Rényi, A.: On the evolution of random graphs. Publ. Math. Inst. Hung. Acad. Sci **5**(1), 17–60 (1960)

5. ETSI Technical Committee. ETSI TR QSC 0024 v0.0.6: CYBER – A Repeatable Framework for Quantum-Safe Migrations (2024)
6. Federal Office for Information Security: Migration to Post Quantum Cryptography: Recommendations for action by the BSI. Technical report, Federal Office for Information Security (2021)
7. Federal Office for Information Security. Cryptographic Mechanisms: Recommendations and Key Lengths. Technical Guideline BSI TR-02102-1, BSI (2025)
8. Frieze, A., Karoński, M.: Introduction to Random Graphs. First edition: Cambridge University Press (2024). https://www.math.cmu.edu/~af1p/BOOK.pdf
9. Hasan, K., et al.: A framework for migrating to post-quantum cryptography: security dependency analysis and case studies. IEEE Access **12**, 23427–23450 (2024)
10. Hess, B., Körtge, N.: Standardization of cryptography bill of materials in OWASP CycloneDX. In: ETSI/IQC Quantum Safe Cryptography Conference (2024)
11. Leirimaa, K.: Supporting PQC migration and cryptographic agility with automated CBOM generation. Master thesis, University of Jyväskylä (2024)
12. Ma, C., Colon, L., Dera, J., Rashidi, B., Garg, V.: CARAF: crypto agility risk assessment framework. J. Cybersecurity **7**(1), tyab013 (2021)
13. Mosca, M.: Cybersecurity in an era with quantum computers: will we be ready? IEEE Secur. Priv. **16**(5), 38–41 (2018)
14. Näther, C., Herzinger, D., Gazdag, S.L., Steghöfer, J.P., Daum, S., Loebenberger, D.: Migrating software systems towards post-quantum cryptography – a systematic literature review. IEEE Access 132107–132127 (2024)
15. Näther, C., Herzinger, D., Steghöfer, J.-P., Gazdag, S.-L., Hirsch, E., Loebenberger, D.: SoK: Towards a Common Understanding of Cryptographic Agility (2024)
16. Odlyzko, A.M., Richmond, L.B.: On the number of distinct block sizes in partitions of a set. J. Comb. Theory Ser. A **38**(2), 170–181 (1985)
17. O'Donoghue, E., Hastings, Y., Ortiz, E., Redempta Manzi Muneza, A.: Software Bill of Materials in Software Supply Chain Security A Systematic Literature Review (2025)
18. Ott, D., Paterson, K., Moreau, D.: Where is the research on cryptographic transition and agility? Commun. ACM **66**(4), 29–32 (2023)
19. Ott, D., Peikert, C., et al.: Identifying Research Challenges in Post Quantum Cryptography Migration and Cryptographic Agility (2019)
20. Patil, P., Narayankar, P., Narayan, D.G., Meena, S.M.: A comprehensive evaluation of cryptographic algorithms: DES, 3DES, AES, RSA and blowfish. Procedia Comput. Sci. **78**, 617–624 (2016)
21. Pitman, J.: Some probabilistic aspects of set partitions. Am. Math. Mon. **104**(3), 201–209 (1997)
22. Pittel, B.: Random set partitions: asymptotics of subset counts. J. Comb. Theory Ser. A **79**(2), 326–359 (1997)
23. Raimondo, G.M., Locascio, L.E.: FIPS-203: module-lattice-based key-encapsulation mechanism standard. Fed. Inf. Process. Stan. Publ. **203**, 1–56 (2025)
24. Raimondo, G.M., Locascio, L.E.: FIPS-204: module-lattice-based digital signature standard. Fed. Inf. Process. Stan. Publ. **204**, 1–65 (2025)
25. Raimondo, G.M., Locascio, L.E.: FIPS-205: stateless hash-based digital signature standard. Fed. Inf. Process. Stan. Publ. **205**, 1–61 (2025)
26. Sachkov, V.N.: Probabilistic Methods in Combinatorial Analysis. Encyclopedia of Mathematics and its Applications. Cambridge University Press (1997)

27. Schmitt, N., Henrich, J., Heinz, D., Alnahawi, N., Wiesmaier, A.: On criteria and tooling for cryptographic inventories. In: GI Sicherheit 2024, pp. 49–63. Gesellschaft für Informatik e.V. (2024)
28. Sowa, J., et al.: Post-Quantum Cryptography (PQC) Network Instrument: Measuring PQC Adoption Rates and Identifying Migration Pathways (2024)
29. Von Nethen, N., Wiesmaier, A., Alnahawi, N., Henrich, J.: PMMP-PQC migration management process. In: Proceedings of the 2024 European Interdisciplinary Cybersecurity Conference, EICC 2024, pp. 144–154. Association for Computing Machinery, New York, NY, USA (2024)
30. Wiesmaier, A., et al.: On PQC Migration and Crypto-Agility (2021)
31. Wilhelm, F., Steinwandt, R., Zeuch, D., Lageyre, P., Kirchhoff, S.: Status of quantum computer development. Technical report, Federal Office for Information Security (2024)

Scaling of Memory and Bandwidth Requirements of Post-quantum Signatures with Message Size

Falko Strenzke(✉)

MTG AG, Darmstadt, Germany
falko.strenzke@mtg.de

Abstract. In this work we analyse the qualitative memory and bandwidth efficiency properties of the currently standardised post-quantum signatures as such and of their protocol integrations mainly in the X.509 context. The term "qualitative" in this respect refers to how memory and bandwidth requirements scale with the size of the signed message. Specifically, we address the question in how far the algorithms support online-computations, a.k.a streaming, with respect to the signed message in the signing and verification operations. Further, we review the possibilities for the pre-computation of a short message representative outside the cryptographic module responsible for the signing or verification operation of the different signature schemes. We also give a preview on the corresponding cryptographic API of the PKCS#11 standard which introduces numerous PQC signature algorithms in the upcoming version 3.2. We demonstrate that for specific realistic use cases, the qualitative memory and bandwidth efficiency of the PQC signature schemes in protocol use is widely varied and by tendency substantially degraded compared to the traditional signature schemes based on RSA and elliptic curves, which always allow for the pre-computation of a short message representative in the form of a hash value. Our results are relevant to PQC migrations of existing applications using traditional RSA or elliptic curve schemes.

1 Introduction

The standardisation of PQC signatures schemes has reached a state where not only finalized cryptographic algorithm specifications from NIST for ML-DSA and SLH-DSA [1,2] and previously existing RFCs specifying the stateful hash-based signature schemes XMSS and LMS [3,4] are available, but where also the standards specifying their use in the X.509 [5] context are completed or close to finalisation. In the LAMPS working group of the IETF, RFCs specifying the use of XMSS, LMS, ML-DSA and SLH-DSA in X.509 [6–8] and the Cryptographic Message Syntax (CMS) [9–11] have been finalized. Drafts for X.509 and CMS, specifying ML-DSA composite signatures, combining the lattice-based PQC signature scheme with RSA and ECC-based signature algorithms have been finalized by the working group and entered the IETF publication process [12,13].

D. Loebenberger and M. Stöttinger (Eds.): MAgiCS 2026, CCIS 3002, pp. 102–120, 2026.
https://doi.org/10.1007/978-3-032-28946-9_6

In this work we analyse how the memory and bandwidth requirements scale with the size of the signed message for the PQC signature schemes. This pertains to their "raw" form, i.e., based on the respective algorithm standard from NIST or the IETF, but also to their protocol integrations in the X.509 protocol. We further address the integration of PQC signatures in the cryptographic message formats CMS [14] and OpenPGP [15]. The analyses of these protocol integrations turns out to be relevant, as the protocol specifications can on the one hand restrict the usage of the PQC signature schemes compared to the respective genuine cryptographic algorithm specification and on the other hand modify their security and performance characteristics. A further aspect we take into account is the integration of the PQC signature schemes into the current and upcoming PKCS#11 standard [16,17], which is the most widely used programming API to communicate with a middleware for cryptographic hardware and potentially also software modules. We will learn that the upcoming version addresses an important efficiency aspect by the introduction of a new function interface for signature verification but also imposes artificial restrictions that negatively affect memory and bandwidth efficiency.

It should be noted that our analysis, as explained above, is qualitative in nature and thus does not present any quantitative results. This is because for the scaling of memory and bandwidth requirements with the message size, there are only two cases: either the respective requirement scales fully with the message, i.e., the required memory size on a processing device or the transmitted message has the size of the message or it is constant, i.e., independent of the message size. The case where the full message has to be stored or transmitted can have significant impacts in at least these three different scenarios: First, a memory-constrained device may be unable to store even small messages such X.509 certificates or revocation lists. Second, even powerful infrastructure components can suffer from memory exhaustion when extraneously large message have to be signed. Third, increased bandwidth, even though not accompanied by the problem of memory exhaustion on the involved machines, can be a cost factor as it can lead to the need of scaling up the network infrastructure.

The basic reason for the arising of such memory efficiency issues for the PQC signature schemes is the deviation from the traditional hash-then-sign paradigm in the new schemes in favor of what we refer to as *direct signing*. A signature algorithm that is based on hash-then-sign first hashes ("digests") the message with a cryptographic hash algorithm and then signs the hash value ("message digest") with the underlying core signature algorithm. This approach applies to RSA and elliptic curve based signature schemes. The modern design approach, on the other hand, is to input the message to the signature algorithm directly. In this work, we refer to such schemes as *direct signature* schemes or *direct signing*.

Direct signature schemes also always perform an internal hashing step before applying the signature function of the underlying primitive. However, this internal hashing step prefixes a set of parameters to the message, the structure of which varies from signature scheme to signature scheme. The purpose of direct signing is to have weaker security assumptions regarding the collision resistance of the employed hash function. While ML-DSA restricts the exploitability of a single hash collision to a single key, SLH-DSA, XMSS, and LMS remain secure even if the collision resistance of the employed hash function is broken. This property makes these algorithms especially interesting for applications with long-term security requirements. These properties are obviously lost when the pre-hash variants of the NIST algorithms, which turn the schemes into hash-then-sign schemes, are used or the direct signature scheme is used in a protocol to sign a message hash.

The main motivation for this work is to help designers to tackle the challenge that lies in the PQC migration of systems currently relying on traditional public-key signatures that arises due to the message-size-scaling effects in the PQC schemes. Besides message hashes in the hash-then-sign, potentially, depending on the particular signature scheme or even implementation, other mechanisms to achieve a *short message representative* may be available. The latter is a term for the token that can be transmitted to a cryptographic module to perform the signature. Thus its availability is a key factor in achieving bandwidth efficiency. While the increase in artifact sizes, namely public key and signature sizes, for PQC signature schemes is well-known and is already considered a burden, the associated cost increase is constant, that is, not scaling with message size. To make a concrete example for the effects of increased cryptographic artifact size and message-size-scaling, let us assume the transition from RSA-3072 to SLH-DSA-128 "fast" parameters – the most size intensive of the currently standardised PQC signature schemes at the equivalent security level of roughly 128 bit. The increased artifact size gives a ratio for the sums of signature and public key sizes of $(17088 + 32)/(2 * 384) = 22.29$.

For a message of 1 MB, the ratio of the transmission size for transmitting the full to-be-signed data to the signing module and transmitting a short message representative given through a SHA-256 hash value, is $1,000,000/32 = 31,250$. This comparison, where the cost increase is more than 10,000 fold higher for the message-size-scaling effect compared to that of the increased artifact sizes, clearly shows the relevance of considering the former even for moderately sized messages.

In the following subsections, we explain further the aspects of our analysis.

1.1 Short Message Representative

As outlined above, a short message representative is a token that can be computed outside the signature module, i.e., without the knowledge of the private key, and provided to the signature module to compute the signature. Equivalently, it can be sent to a cryptographic module for the purpose of signature verification. A short message representative is thus in this respect equivalent to the message digest in signature schemes that adhere to the hash-then-sign paradigm.

Pre-hash variants, as they have been specified for ML-DSA and SLH-DSA [1,2] give the simplest and most straightforward form of short message representatives. Their use reverts the respective signature scheme back to the security assumptions of the hash-then-sign paradigm. External-μ, addressed in Sect. 2.1, is another such mechanism defined specifically for ML-DSA, which preserves the security assumptions, as it is merely an implementation variant of the direct signing or pure variant of ML-DSA.

The ability to use a short message representative in the signing function reduces the bandwidth requirements in the communication with the signing module compared to sending the full message. The concrete technical realization in the PKCS#11 interface is given through the use of a mechanism like `CKM_RSA_PKCS` [18], which sends an externally computed hash value to the cryptographic module in a signature generation or verification operation.

1.2 Online Property of the Signing and Verification Function with Respect to the Message

It is important to note that the traditional hash-then-sign paradigm, besides providing a means to transfer a short message representative to a cryptographic module in the form of the message hash, has another performance-relevant aspect. This is the ability to start the hash computation with the receipt of the message to be signed or verified without the need for any further information than the hash algorithm to use. The hash computation can be continued incrementally with only the need for a relatively small constant amount of memory until the whole message has been received. This is what is referred to as an *online* or *streaming* algorithm, computation, or implementation.

As the message to be signed is potentially unlimited in size, the ability of the cryptographic module performing the signing operation to consume the message in chunks is another performance-critical aspect that becomes relevant when short message representatives are not available in the application context.

For the signature verification, the relevance of the online computation is potentially wider. The verification operation typically does not require the use of a specific cryptographic module. Nevertheless, even for infrastructure systems, the means of accessing the message data for verification may be limited by the software architecture. This can be seen from the example of a command line application which receives the message data on the standard input file descriptor. In this case, the signature verification has to be conducted in a single pass over the message. In case the algorithm does not allow for online computation, the whole message will have to be buffered in memory before the verification can be carried out.

For memory-constrained devices, on the other hand, the lack of the ability to perform the signature verification in an online manner, can be significant. We demonstrate this in particular for the certificate path validation in Sect. 3.1.

As we show in our analysis, the ability to perform the PQC signature verification in an online manner is generally dependent on whether the public key or the signature is available prior to receiving the message. Furthermore, as we learn, ML-DSA using the external-μ mechanism for computing a short message representative does not solve the problem of performing the signature verification in an online manner in all cases, as demonstrated in Sect. 3.1.

1.3 A Note on PKCS#11

Due to its broad relevance in cryptographic applications, we address the interface functions that the PKCS#11 standard prescribes for PQC signature schemes. The current PKCS#11 v3.2 Committee Specification Draft [17] introduces the PQC signature algorithms XMSS, ML-DSA, SLH-DSA. LMS and its multi-tree variant HSS are already included in the current version 3.1 of PKCS#11. The v3.2 draft accounts for the memory-efficiency challenges of the PQC signature algorithms by introducing new interface functions for the signature verification, namely the C_VerifySignature interface with its functions C_VerifySignatureInit, C_VerifySignature, C_VerifySignatureUpdate, and C_VerifySignatureFinal. These functions enable the caller to set the signature prior to feeding the message, possibly in a multi-part operation using C_VerifySignatureUpdate as shown in Fig. 1. The previously existing C_Verify interface allows to set the signature only after the message in the C_VerifyFinal interface function.

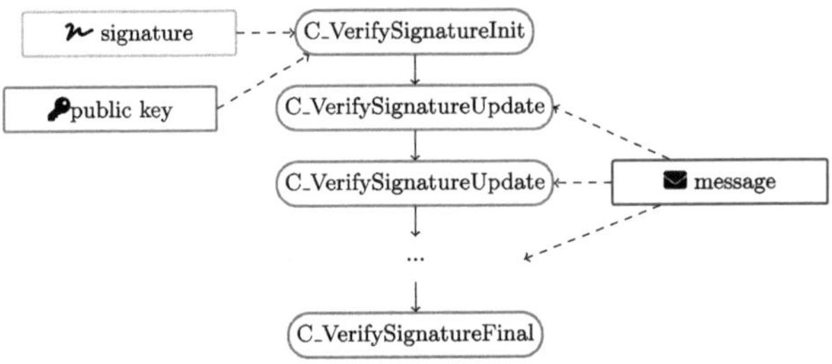

Fig. 1. Depiction of the incremental, i.e., online, processing of a message for signature verification in the current draft for PKCS#11 v3.2 [17] using the newly introduced C_VerifySignature interface.

2 Cryptographic Algorithm Specifications

In this section we provide a concise description of the operations of the individual signature algorithms that are relevant to our analysis. These are limited to the initial transformation of the message until the computation of what can be called the inner message digest, which forms the data input to the actual signature primitive. Please note that our description is agnostic towards concrete encodings or actual lengths of various parameters such as random byte strings, or concrete instances of hash functions, since these aspects are of no relevance to our analysis. The omission of elements of data structures not relevant to our analysis will be indicated by ellipsis ("...").

2.1 ML-DSA

ML-DSA is specified in FIPS-204 [1]. The pure variant of ML-DSA, performing direct signing, is defined as

$$M' \leftarrow \text{0x00} \parallel \text{byte\_length}(\text{ctx}) \parallel \text{ctx} \parallel M \tag{1}$$

$$\text{tr} \leftarrow \text{SHAKE256}(\text{pk}, 512)$$

$$\mu \leftarrow \text{SHAKE256}(\text{encode}(\text{tr}) \parallel M', 512) \tag{2}$$

$$\text{sig} \leftarrow \text{ML-DSA-primitive-sign}(\mu, \text{rnd}, \text{sk})$$

where M is the signed message, ctx is a user-specified context parameter that is by default empty[1], pk is the public key, rnd is a 32 byte array which in case of the so-called hedged variant is chosen uniformly at random and all zero in case of the deterministic variant, SHAKE256(x, y) denotes the application of the SHAKE256 function to the data x with an output of length of y bits and ML-DSA-primitive-sign() takes as arguments the message to be signed, a random seed, and the private key in that order.

Pre-hash Variant. NIST specifies a pre-hash variant of ML-DSA alongside with the pure variant [1]. While the pure variant given above signs the message directly, the pre-hash variant takes an externally computed message digest in place of the message as the data to be signed. The pre-hash signature operation is defined analogously to the direct-signing or pure variant with only the following alternate first step replacing Eq. (1):

$$M' \leftarrow \text{0x01} \parallel \text{byte\_length}(\text{ctx}) \parallel \text{ctx} \parallel \text{OID} \parallel \text{PH}(M), \tag{3}$$

where OID is the OID of the hash algorithm used to compute the pre-hash PM(M) of the message.

μ-ML-DSA. FIPS-204 further specifies that the value μ, computed in Eq. (2), may be computed in a different cryptographic module than the signature.[2] This allows to compute a short message representative in the form of μ which can be sent to a signing module instead of the message.

PKCS#11. The upcoming PKCS#11 version 3.2 will introduce ML-DSA in the pure and pre-hash variant. Providing external-μ as the input to the signature or verification function will be specified in version 3.3[3].

---

[1] This is the case for the use of ML-DSA in the X.509 and CMS context, but ML-DSA-composite schemes [12] employ the context parameter to achieve domain separation from standalone use of ML-DSA in the same protocol.

[2] https://csrc.nist.gov/csrc/media/Projects/post-quantum-cryptography/documents/faq/fips204-sec6-03192025.pdf.

[3] https://github.com/oasis-tcs/pkcs11/issues/58.

Message-Related Memory Efficiency. The signature operation can straightforwardly be performed in an online manner. For the signature verification, the computation of μ in ML-DSA requires the public key as an input prior to being able to start consuming the message.[4] It is thus only an online operation if the public-key is available before the receipt of the message.

Since certificate chains are typically provided in the sequence from the end-entity to the root certificate, verification with ML-DSA requires to store each certificate in memory until the signer certificate is received and the signature can be verified. This is for instance the case in the TLS protocol. The memory-efficiency of the X.509 certificate path validation is analysed in Sect. 3.1.

Also in the case of cryptographic message formats, the availability of the public key is not necessarily given at the point where the message is received. In a protocol supporting PKI, the public key of the sender is typically provided as part of the signed message and authenticated against a trust anchor. In the case of the Cryptographic Message Syntax [14], and thus also for S/MIME [19], it is indeed the case that the signer's public key is provided after the signed message. Thus also here message streaming is generally not possible. See our discussion of CMS in Sect. 3.3.

2.2 Composite ML-DSA Signatures in draft-ietf-lamps-pq-composite-sigs

Version 14 of draft-ietf-lamps-pq-composite-sigs [12], which has been finalized by the LAMPS working group of the IETF and is in the IETF publication process, defines various composite schemes combining ML-DSA with RSA and elliptic curve based signature schemes. The signature process transforms the message as follows before applying the signature function of the component schemes:

$$\begin{aligned} M' &= \text{Prefix}||\text{Label}||\text{byte\_length}(\text{ctx})||\text{ctx}||\text{PH}(M), \\ \text{mldsaSig} &= \text{ML-DSA.Sign}(\text{key} = \text{sk}_{\text{mldsa}}, \text{message} = M', \text{ctx}_{\text{mldsa}} = \text{Label}) \\ \text{tradSig} &= \text{Trad.Sign}(\text{key} = \text{sk}_{\text{trad}}, \text{message} = M') \end{aligned}$$

where M is the message supplied by the user, M' is the message that is fed into the component algorithms, and PH(M) is a pre-hash of the message. "Prefix" is a fixed string, "Label" is an algorithm and security parameter specific byte string, and ctx is a user-supplied context string. The important observation here is that the construction allows to compute PH(M) as a short message representative without any dependency on other values than M and the employed hash function for computing PH(M), which defined by the algorithm identifier.

Message-Related Memory Efficiency. There are no dependencies on values other than the message and the algorithm identifier for the online-processing of the message during signature generation or verification.

[4] This has been pointed out by Samuel Lee on the PQC-Forum mailing list: https://groups.google.com/a/list.nist.gov/g/pqc-forum/c/GPtJRsk67TY/m/8vbWxGbrAAAJ.

2.3 SLH-DSA

SLH-DSA, defined in [2], is the stateless hash-based digital signature standard. Besides the pure variant also a pre-hash variant is specified.

The pure, i.e. direct signing, variant of SLH-DSA transforms the signed message according to the following steps:

$$R = \mathrm{PRF}_{\mathrm{msg}}(\mathrm{SK.prf}, \mathrm{opt\_rand}, M) \tag{4}$$

$$M' \leftarrow 0x0 \,\|\, \mathrm{byte\_length}(\mathrm{ctx}) \,\|\, \mathrm{ctx} \,\|\, M \tag{5}$$

$$\mathrm{digest} = H_{\mathrm{msg}}(R, \mathrm{PK.seed}, \mathrm{PK.root}, M')$$

$$\mathrm{signature\_SLH\text{-}DSA} = \{R, \ldots\}$$

Here, opt_rand is a byte array which in the case of the hedged variant is chosen uniformly at random and all zeroes in the case of the deterministic variant of SLH-DSA. SK.prf is part of the secret key, while PK.seed and PK.root are parts of the public key. $\mathrm{PRF}_{\mathrm{msg}}$ and H_{msg} represent either applications of SHAKE256 or SHA-2 based constructions depending on the concrete parameter set.

Pre-hash Variant. The pre-hash variant of SLH-DSA defined in FIPS-205 is equivalently defined to the pre-hash variant of ML-DSA. It is realized by replacing Eq. (5) with the following step:

$$M' \leftarrow 0x1 \,\|\, \mathrm{byte\_length}(\mathrm{ctx}) \,\|\, \mathrm{ctx} \,\|\, \mathrm{OID} \,\|\, PH(M),$$

The pre-hash variant is also available for X.509 objects [7], but not for CMS [9].

Message-Related Memory Efficiency. By hashing the message in the computation of the randomizer R in Eq. (4), the scheme achieves resilience against flawed random bit generation. At the same time, this feature leads to the requirement of processing the message twice. A device performing the signature generation thus is required to either hold the whole message in memory during the operation or to receive it twice. Refer to Sect. 3.1 for the concept of two-pass algorithms to circumvent memory limitations in the context of X.509 certificate path validation and the security measure specified there to ensure consistency of the input data in both passes.

The signature verification of SLH-DSA requires the availability of the public key and the randomizer R from the signature prior to online-processing of the message. With the pre-hash variant of SLH-DSA, these memory-performance issues can be circumvented at the expense of independence of the security assumptions from collision resistance of the underlying hash function.

2.4 XMSS and LMS

XMSS and LMS are stateful hash-based signature schemes. When we are referring to XMSS and LMS, this is meant to equally address their respective multi-tree variant, namely $\text{XMSS}^{\text{MT}}$and HSS for LMS. The statefulness property means that the private key carries an internal state which has to be updated in each signature generation. If ever the same private key state is used to sign two messages, either of these scheme becomes insecure and signatures verifiable by that private key can be forged [20].

Message Preprocessing in XMSS. For the signature generation first the value M' is computed as

$$\text{randomizer} = \text{PRF}(\text{secret-key-part}, \text{idx\_msg})$$
$$M' = H_{\text{msg}}(\text{randomizer}||\text{pk}||\text{idx\_msg}, M)$$
$$\text{signature}_{\text{XMSS}} = \{\text{idx\_msg}, \text{randomizer}, \ldots\}$$

where pk denotes the public key and idx_sig, the index of the signature, which is incremented for each generated signature for a particular key. The signature contains the values of the randomizer and the idx_msg.

Then the internal signature is generated on M'.

Message Preprocessing in LMS. In LMS, the message is transformed as follows during the signature generation:

$$C = \text{random\_bytes}()$$
$$Q = H(I||\text{idx\_msg}||\text{D\_MESG}||C||M),$$
$$\text{signature}_{\text{LMS}} = \{C, \text{idx\_msg}, \ldots\}$$

where I is a part of the public (and private) key and D_MESG is a constant. The function random_bytes() designates a function that returns a random byte array with the help an RNG. The randomizer C is hashed before the message.

PKCS#11. As of the current draft for PKCS#11 v3.2, multipart signature generation and verification is not supported for XMSS and LMS. The introduction of multi-part signature support for these algorithms is considered for PKCS#1 v3.3[5].

Message-Related Memory Efficiency. XMSS and LMS exhibit the same efficiency properties. These algorithms have no mechanism for a short message representative, i.e., the whole message has to be provided to the signature module. Their signature generation operation can be performed in an online manner. The signature verification can only be performed in an online manner after the signature and the public key are available.

[5] https://github.com/oasis-tcs/pkcs11/issues/44 and https://github.com/oasis-tcs/pkcs11/issues/32.

3 Protocol Integrations of the PQC Signature Schemes

We review the protocol integrations of the PQC signature schemes in X.509, CMS, and OpenPGP as the most basic and widespread asynchronous cryptographic message protocols and that already have an advanced state of the integration of PQC signatures. Table 1 gives an overview.

3.1 X.509 Certificates

The X.509 standard, RFC 5280 [5], defines the data structures and processing rules for X.509 public key certificates and certificate revocation lists (CRL). The X.509 certificate path validation is one of the crucial applications of X.509 certificates and typically has to be carried before any usage of a public key certificate. RFC 5280 defines the path validation in the order from the trust anchor to the end-entity certificate, however, in practice, the order in which certificate chains are provided is often inverted. This was the case for TLS prior to TLS 1.3 [21]. TLS 1.3 allows different orderings here, but requires the end-entity certificate to be provided as the first in any case. Thus at least at the beginning of the TLS certificate chain, the ordering is from end-entity certificate to the issuer. Algorithm 1 describes a memory-optimized path validation routine for this chain ordering in the case of direct signing schemes. Since the currently specified direct signing schemes ML-DSA, SLH-DSA, XMSS, and LMS all require the public key prior to the message processing during signature verification, the TBS data (the certificate body, refer to Fig. 2 for structure of an X.509 certificate) of a certificate has to be stored until the reception of the public key in the issuer certificate. This means that the peak memory requirement for path validation resulting from the involved cryptographic artifacts is

$$\text{size}(c_{i-1}) + \text{size}(p_i),$$

which amounts to 5 kB for ML-DSA-44. In comparison, for a hash-then-sign algorithm, it is not necessary to store the certificate c_i at all. Instead, it can be processed in an online manner with a parallel computation of the hash of the TBS data. The hash function is specified early in the TBS data in the *signature* field which defines the signature algorithm. The computed hash is then input to the signature verification in the next iteration.

The memory cost of the path validation is especially relevant in the case of ML-DSA, since this algorithm is, under consideration of the absolute signature and public key sizes and the running time performance, the most cost-effective and thus presumably by tendency the preferred choice for resource-constrained devices.

In case resource-constrained devices are operating in a heterogeneous PKI environment, where the key sizes of the certificates in the peer certificate chain may vary, the implementation of a straightforward fallback mechanism for the case of a memory exhaustion suggests itself. This is achieved by resorting to a two-pass processing where in the first pass the following values are computed and stored: firstly, keyed-hashes, i.e., hashes with secret random prefix generated on the device, of all certificates received for the path validation; secondly, internal states of the signature-algorithm-internal hash operations for the signature verification of each certificate that has to be verified. The saved hash state is the state after having received the required public key and signature elements and thus is ready to receive the TBS data of the certificate to verify.

Algorithm 1. Certificate path validation from the end-entity certificate c_0 to the trust anchor c_n with any number of intermediate certificates for ML-DSA certificates. Here p_i and s_i denote the public key and signature of c_i, respectively. For simplicity, the description ignores the modelling of trust anchor trust.

Algorithm VALIDATE-CERT-PATH(certificate-chain $c_0, \dots c_n$)
  receive c_0 and store it in memory
  apply c_0 or its public key p_0 in protocol or store it in memory for later use
  for i = 1 to n **do**
    start to receive c_i
    process leading part of c_i until subject public key p_i
    ensure verify(message = TBS_data(c_{i-1}), public_key = p_i, signature = s_{i-1})
    release c_{i-1} from memory
    process the final part of c_i
    after complete receipt of c_i, store the whole certificate in memory
  end for
end Algorithm

The process for the two-pass verification in given Algorithm 2. The two-pass property here means that receipt of the certificate chain has to occur twice. In reality, this is simply achieved by a retry from the client after a failed TLS handshake during the first pass. The memory-constrained device causing the failure in the first pass may either be the server or the client. In case it has the role of the client, the initiation of the second handshake attempt happens at its own discretion. In case it is the server, a successful handshake requires a second handshake attempt by the client.

For simplicity, Algorithm 2 is written such that two-pass verification is always realized. In reality, an implementation of the path validation would implement the two-pass verification only as fallback option when the regular verification according to Algorithm 1 fails due to memory exhaustion. For this purpose, the algorithm specifications of Algorithm 1 would have to be merged with the specification of the first pass in Algorithm 2 appropriately.

Algorithm 2 removes the requirement to store any certificate in full at any time during the algorithm execution. The keyed hashes y_i computed during the first pass are used to ensure that the same certificate chain is received in the second pass. The precomputed hash states t_i allow for an online computation of the TBS data hash in the second pass. This algorithm achieves basically the same memory requirements as those for the path validation with signature schemes adhering to the hash-then-sign paradigm, since it ensures that in the second pass the hash computations required for the verification of the certificate signature can be performed in an online manner. There is only a small overhead in storing a hash values and an internal hash state for each level of the certification path.

Algorithm 2. Two-pass certificate path validation from the end-entity certificate c_0 to the trust anchor c_n with any number of intermediate certificates for ML-DSA certificates. The function verify$_\mu$ refers to the ML-DSA verification based on externally computed μ.

Algorithm TWO-PASS-VALIDATE-CERT-PATH(certificate-chain $c_0, \ldots c_n$)
  x_0 = random_bytes()
  receive c_0
  incrementally compute $y_0 = \text{hash}(x_0||c_0)$ and store (x_0, y_0)
  for i = 1 to n **do**
    x_i = random_bytes()
    start to receive c_i
    incrementally compute $y_i = \text{hash}(x_i||c_i)$ and store (x_i, y_i)
    compute and store t_{i-1} =hash-state(SHAKE256(encode(tr$_i$))) using tr$_i$ from p_i
  end for
  start to receive c_0
  incrementally compute $y'_0 = \text{hash}(x_0||c_0)$ and ensure equality to y_0 after complete receipt
  apply c_0 or its public key p_0 in protocol or store it in memory for later use
  store s_0, the signature in c_0
  for i = 1 to n **do**
    start to receive c_i
    incrementally compute $y'_i = \text{hash}(x_i||c_i)$ and ensure equality to y_i after complete receipt
    if $(i < n)$ **then** restore t_i and incrementally continue hash computation μ_i = SHAKE256(encode(tr$_{i+1}$) || ...) with the TBS data of c_i
    incrementally process c_i until receipt of p_i starts
    ensure verify$_\mu$($\mu = \mu_{i-1}$, public_key = p_i, signature = s_{i-1})
    release s_{i-1} from memory
    incrementally process the final part of c_i
    if $(i < n)$ **then** store s_i
  end for
end Algorithm

Algorithm 2 can be adapted to the case of the hash-based schemes SLH-DSA, XMSS, and LMS in a straightforward manner. Only the precomputation of the hash states t_i differs in that it also requires elements from the signature. These can be collected during the first pass of the certificate receipt as well.

3.2 X.509 CRLs

The considerations about the memory efficiency in processing X.509 certificates given in Sect. 3.1 equally apply to the processing of CRLs. However, since CRLs can grow to considerable size, the ability for online processing on memory-constrained devices is even more critical than in the case of X.509 certificates. The concept of two-pass processing can be equally applied for CRLs, where especially for the hash-based schemes the elements from the signature have to collected and processed into a stored hash state during the first pass.

```
Certificate ::= SEQUENCE {
      tbsCertificate       TBSCertificate,
      signatureAlgorithm AlgorithmIdentifier,
      signatureValue       BIT STRING }

   TBSCertificate ::= SEQUENCE {
      version          [0]  EXPLICIT Version DEFAULT v1,
      serialNumber          CertificateSerialNumber,
      signature             AlgorithmIdentifier,
      issuer                Name,
      validity              Validity,
      subject               Name,
      subjectPublicKeyInfo SubjectPublicKeyInfo,
      issuerUniqueID  [1]  IMPLICIT UniqueIdentifier OPTIONAL,
                            -- If present, version MUST be v2 or v3
      subjectUniqueID [2]  IMPLICIT UniqueIdentifier OPTIONAL,
                            -- If present, version MUST be v2 or v3
      extensions       [3]  EXPLICIT Extensions OPTIONAL
                            -- If present, version MUST be v3
      }
```

Fig. 2. ASN.1 definition of an X.509 certificate.

3.3 CMS

CMS effectively supports pre-hashing on the protocol layer by the use of the so-called Signed Attributes [14]. Signed Attributes are a collection of attribute-value pairs in an encoded structure, one of which represents the hash of the signed message. Signing with Signed Attributes is the approach recommended by the LAMPS working group of the IETF [22]. Allowing only a single variant of signing with or without Signed Attributes per protocol is necessary to avoid subtle security vulnerabilities existing in this protocol [23]. Signing with Signed Attributes effectively amounts to applying a protocol specific pre-hash to the message. Accordingly, a short message representative is available at least for modern protocols using CMS or those being modernized in this respect. Accordingly, in applications using the modern recommended signature mechanism of CMS, memory and bandwidth efficiency issues are entirely avoided. However, as noted in the introduction, this effectively reverts the signature scheme to the hash-then-sign paradigm and makes its security dependent on the collision resistance of the underlying hash function.

3.4 OpenPGP

The draft for the PQC integration of OpenPGP [24], which has entered the IETF publication process, defines only ML-DSA-composite combinations with elliptic curve signature schemes and SLH-DSA as standalone. The OpenPGP protocol [15] design inherently depends on the hash-then-sign paradigm, and thus adheres to this also in the use of the PQC signature algorithms. However, v6 signatures, based on which PQC signatures are defined, prefix a randomizer to the signed data and thus achieve independence of the signature scheme's security from the collision resistance of the hash function.

Table 1. Overview of the features of the protocol integrations of PQC signatures schemes. By "direct signing" and "pre-hash" we do not necessarily refer to the use of the pure and pre-hash variant of the algorithm, but rather how the signature algorithm is effectively embedded in the respective protocol. ✓ and ✗ indicate availability and unavailability of the feature in question, respectively. The symbols 🎲 indicate that the message digestion has a randomizer prefixed – either in the signature algorithm internally or on the protocol level – and ~~🎲~~ indicates deterministic hashing of the message. The latter implies that the signature scheme's security depends on hash-collision resistance of the underlying hash function. The third and forth columns describe CMS signatures with and without the use of Signed Attributes, respectively.

Algorithm	**X.509**	**CMS (w/SA)**	**CMS (w/o SA)**	**OpenPGP**
ML-DSA / direct signing	✓ ~~🎲~~	✗	✓ ~~🎲~~	✗
ML-DSA-comp. / pre-hash	✓ ~~🎲~~	✓ ~~🎲~~	✓	✓ 🎲
ML-DSA / pre-hash	✗	✓ ~~🎲~~	✗	✗
SLH-DSA / direct signing	✓ 🎲	✗	✓ 🎲	✗
SLH-DSA / pre-hash	✓ ~~🎲~~	✓ ~~🎲~~	✗	✓ 🎲
XMSS / direct signing	✓ 🎲	✗	✓ 🎲	✗
XMSS / pre-hash	✗	✓ ~~🎲~~	✗	✗
LMS / direct signing	✓ 🎲	✗	✓ 🎲	✗
LMS / pre-hash	✗	✓ ~~🎲~~	✗	✗

4 Summary and Mitigating Measures

Table 2 gives an overview of the message-related memory and bandwidth efficiency aspects of the PQC signature algorithms as such and in the context of the X.509 formats that we determined in Sects. 2 and 3.

As our results show, the PQC signature schemes, besides their well known increased signature size, and, in the case of ML-DSA, also public key size, exhibit considerable challenges in terms of scaling of bandwidth and memory requirements with message size. The two main relevant critical scenarios we have identified are the execution of the signing operation on a possibly remote cryptographic module and the signature verification for messages that are large in relation to the memory capacity of a device receiving the message through an external interface.

The use of the existing mechanisms to obtain a short message representative, namely resorting to pre-hash variants or using ML-DSA with external-μ can be used to address both of these scenarios. However, with the exception of external-μ, this reverts the security assumptions of the signature scheme to that of a hash-then-sign scheme. Further, external-μ fails to improve the challenge of performing the signature verification in an online manner, since the dependence of the operation on the early availability of the public key remains.

Table 2. Overview of the Message-related memory efficiency aspects of PQC signature schemes. N/A denotes that a feature is not relevant for efficient processing. The symbol 🔑‖✉/✉‖🔑 means that the feature is given if the public key is available before the message is processed, while ✍🔑‖✉/✉‖✍🔑 indicates that both the public key and the signature have to be available beforehand. The feature description in the last three columns refer to the current draft for PKCS#11 v.3.2 except where noted otherwise.

	Algorithm specification (NIST, IETF)			X.509 (cert, CRL) spec. (IETF/LAMPS WG)			PKCS#11 v3.2 draft / v3.3		
	short msg. repr.	**sign-online**	**verify-online**	**short msg. repr.**	**sign-online**	**verify-online**	**supported**	**sign multi-part**	**verify multi-part**
ML-DSA	✗	✓	🔑‖✉/✉‖🔑	✗	✓	🔑‖✉/✉‖🔑	✓	✓	✓
μ-ML-DSA	✓ (μ)	✓	🔑‖✉/✉‖🔑	✓ (μ)	✓	🔑‖✉/✉‖🔑	(✓) (v3.3)	N/A	N/A
Hash-ML-DSA	✓ (hash)	✓	✓	N/A	N/A	N/A	✓	N/A	N/A
ML-DSA-comp.	✓ (hash)	✓	✓	✓ (hash)	✓	✓	N/A	N/A	N/A
SLH-DSA	✗	✗	✍🔑‖✉/✉‖✍🔑	✗	✗	✗	✓	✓	✍🔑‖✉/✉‖✍🔑
Hash-SLH-DSA	✓ (hash)	✓	✓	✓ (hash)	✓	✓	✓	N/A	N/A
XMSS/LMS	✗	✓	✍🔑‖✉/✉‖✍🔑	✗	✓	✍🔑‖✉/✉‖✍🔑	✓	✗	✗

[1] To be corrected (see https://github.com/oasis-tcs/pkcs11/pull/63) in a future PKCS#11 version, this aspect is still under discussion. Note that executing the signature verification in a cryptographic module is typically not required.
[2] The feature for using external-μ computation with ML-DSA will be added in PKCS#11 v3.3 (see Sect. 2.1).

For the stateful schemes XMSS and LMS, in the general setting, neither of the two scenarios can be effectively addressed using the available algorithm variants. Due to the lack of any mechanism for a short message representative in these cases, the whole message has to be transmitted to the signing module. As an unnecessary artifact, when bound to a PKCS#11 v3.2 interface as specified in the current Committee Specification Draft, not even incremental message transmission is possible. The verification operation of these algorithms requires both the availability of the signature and the public key before the message can be processed.

In the following subsections, we address possible mitigating measures to resolve the memory and bandwidth restrictions of the PQC signature schemes.

4.1 Two-Pass Processing

Two-pass processing incurring repeated message transfers was addressed as an option for signing modules in Sect. 2.3 and for the certificate path validation in memory-constrained devices in Sect. 3.1. This measure suggests itself only as a last resort in scenarios where better mitigations are unavailable or as a reaction to rarely expected large messages or protocol data structures. It generally causes doubled bandwidth and in the case of repeated handshake attempts, incurs observable protocol errors which may trigger warnings in network monitoring systems and subsequently manual investigations and bear the risk of other unintended side effects.

4.2 Resorting to Pre-hashing in the Algorithm Choice or Protocol Design

As previously pointed out, resorting to one of the specified pre-hash variants of the PQC signature algorithms effectively addresses the memory efficiency. Note that in the case of ML-DSA, which does not support the pre-hash variant in the X.509 protocol, resorting to ML-DSA-composite is a possible option, as it is a hash-then-sign algorithm type. In cases where no viable option exists to use a specified pre-hash variant, but where the protocol or application design can be modified, it is possible to simply apply a pre-hashing step on the protocol layer and supply the message digest as the message to the direct signing algorithm. Such a design choice requires care, since in the case that the same protocol allows direct signing of the message and at the same time direct signing of a hash of the message and, further, the specification of the variant is not part of the signed data, the protocol will at least formally be susceptible to signature forgeries. An example for such a problem is the presence or absence of the Signed Attributes in CMS [23].

Prefixing a randomizer on the protocol level, like realized in OpenPGP's v6 signatures, achieves independence of the signature's scheme security from the collision resistance of the message digest algorithm.

4.3 Early Supply of Missing Information in Protocols

The observed memory-efficiency problems of the signature verification are solely caused by the delayed availability of information that has to be extracted from the signature or the signer's public key. A straightforward measure to solve these restrictions for all PQC signature algorithms is the inclusion of the required information in the transmitted protocol data before the message. For X.509 certificates and CRLs, this could be achieved by using the *signature* field in the *TBSCertificate* which announces the signature algorithm. For RSA and ECC-based signature schemes, this identifier also announces the hash algorithm and thus allows to start incremental hashing of the TBS data after the receipt of a few bytes. To achieve the same feature for the direct signing PQC signature schemes, a new algorithm identifier could be defined, which internally contains as parameters the existing defined identifier for the respective scheme and further contains all elements from the signature and the public key, that are needed to start the internal hash computation. In case of ML-DSA, this is for instance only the hash value tr.

4.4 Custom Interfaces for Short Message Representatives

A further mitigating measure is to enable the concept of a short message representative with preservation of direct signing as it has been done by NIST for ML-DSA with the external-μ mechanism. For instance Thales provides a proprietary extension of the PKCS#11 interface which enables the host to retrieve the data required for starting the XMSS and LMS internal message hash computation from the cryptographic module.[6].

5 Conclusion

In this work we investigate the problem of the qualitative memory-efficiency of the currently standardised PQC signature schemes in terms of how well bandwidth and memory usage scales with message size. As the two main critical scenarios, we considered the signing operation on an external cryptographic module and the signature verification for messages that are large in relation to the device's memory capacity. We have shown that the PQC signature schemes all have different characteristics in this respect with the only exception of XMSS and LMS, which qualitatively behave identically. Further, we analysed the integration of PQC signature schemes in the X.509 protocol based on finalized and almost finalized IETF standards as well as in the upcoming version of the PKCS#11 interface specification and demonstrated that both induce further restrictions on their memory and bandwidth efficiency. We provided a number of mitigating measures that can be applied by application and protocol designers to achieve memory-efficiency.

Most importantly, in our view, the presentation of these characteristics of the PQC signature algorithms can help system architects in the planning of the PQC migration. There is a considerable risk that the new algorithms are only gauged in terms of their obvious performance characteristics, namely artifact sizes and running times of the operations, but not with respect to the less obvious memory and bandwidth related features. The latter clearly do not surface in all applications contexts of signature schemes, but in the critical cases we have identified, can lead to problems that either increase operational costs at a far greater scale than the increased artifact sizes – as shown by the example in the introduction – or require fundamental re-engineering of existing applications or protocols.

For a sound and cost-aware planning of the PQC migration, the cryptographic architecture needs to be modelled through all the relevant layers of the cryptographic algorithm, the cryptographic protocol, and programming as well as hardware module interfaces. This requires a comprehensive understanding of the relevant security and efficiency notions and a detailed knowledge of the existing implementation landscape and the concrete options offered by employed third party components – in many cases still not fully implemented or even specified. Thus a merely conceptional approach seems as a fragile option. As a consequence, our work reinforces the urgency of early practical experience and evaluation of concepts in the PQC migration in order to rule out conceptional oversights.

[6] https://thalesdocs.com/gphsm/luna/7/docs/network/Content/sdk/extensions/pqc/PQC_external_hash.htm.

References

1. NIST – National Institute of Standards and Technology: FIPS 204 – Module-Lattice-Based Digital Signature Standard (2024)
2. NIST – National Institute of Standards and Technology: FIPS 205 – Stateless Hash-Based Digital Signature Standard (2024)
3. Huelsing, A., Butin, D., Gazdag, S.L., Rijneveld, J., Mohaisen, A.: XMSS: eXtended Merkle Signature Scheme. RFC 8391 (2018)
4. McGrew, D., Curcio, M., Fluhrer, S.: Leighton-Micali Hash-Based Signatures. RFC 8554 (2019)
5. Boeyen, S., Santesson, S., Polk, T., Housley, R., Farrell, S., Cooper, D.: Internet X.509 Public Key Infrastructure Certificate and Certificate Revocation List (CRL) Profile. RFC 5280 (2008)
6. Massimo, J., Kampanakis, P., Turner, S., Westerbaan, B.: Internet X.509 Public Key Infrastructure – Algorithm Identifiers for the Module-Lattice-Based Digital Signature Algorithm (ML-DSA). RFC 9881 (2025)
7. Bashiri, K., Fluhrer, S., Gazdag, S.L., Geest, D.V., Kousidis, S.: Internet X.509 Public Key Infrastructure – Algorithm Identifiers for the Stateless Hash-Based Digital Signature Algorithm (SLH-DSA). RFC 9909 (2025)
8. Geest, D.V., Bashiri, K., Fluhrer, S., Gazdag, S.L., Kousidis, S.: Use of the HSS and XMSS Hash-Based Signature Algorithms in Internet X.509 Public Key Infrastructure. RFC 9802 (2025)
9. Housley, R., Fluhrer, S., Kampanakis, P., Westerbaan, B.: Use of the SLH-DSA Signature Algorithm in the Cryptographic Message Syntax (CMS). RFC 9814 (2025)
10. S, B., R, A., Geest, D.V.: Use of the ML-DSA Signature Algorithm in the Cryptographic Message Syntax (CMS). RFC 9882 (2025)
11. Housley, R.: Use of the HSS/LMS Hash-Based Signature Algorithm in the Cryptographic Message Syntax (CMS). RFC 9708 (2025)
12. Ounsworth, M., Gray, J., Pala, M., Klaußner, J., Fluhrer, S.: Composite ML-DSA for use in X.509 Public Key Infrastructure. Internet-Draft draft-ietf-lamps-pq-composite-sigs-14, Internet Engineering Task Force (2026) Work in Progress
13. Ounsworth, M., Gray, J., Klaußner, J., Geest, D.V.: Composite ML-DSA for use in Cryptographic Message Syntax (CMS). Internet-Draft draft-ietf-lamps-cms-composite-sigs-04, Internet Engineering Task Force (2026) Work in Progress
14. Housley, R.: RFC 5652 – Cryptographic Message Syntax (CMS) (2009). https://tools.ietf.org/html/rfc5652
15. Wouters, P., Huigens, D., Winter, J., Yutaka, N.: OpenPGP. RFC 9580 (2024)
16. OASIS: PKCS#11 cryptographic token interface specification version 3.1 (2023) Edited by Dieter Bong and Tony Cox
17. OASIS Open: PKCS #11 Specification Version 3.2 – Committee Specification Draft 01 (2025)
18. Gleeson, S., Zimman, C.: PKCS #11 Cryptographic Token Interface Current Mechanisms Specification Version 2.40 (2015)
19. Schaad, J., Ramsdell, B., Turner, S.: RFC 8551: Secure/Multipurpose Internet Mail Extensions (S/MIME) Version 4.0 Message Specification (2019). https://www.rfc-editor.org/rfc/rfc8551.html
20. Groot Bruinderink, L., Hülsing, A.: "Oops, i did it again" – security of one-time signatures under two-message attacks. In: Adams, C., Camenisch, J. (eds.) SAC 2017. LNCS, vol. 10719, pp. 299–322. Springer, Cham (2018). https://doi.org/10.1007/978-3-319-72565-9_15

21. Rescorla, E.: The Transport Layer Security (TLS) Protocol Version 1.3. RFC 8446 (2018)
22. Geest, D.V., Strenzke, F.: Best Practices for Signed Attributes in CMS Signed-Data. Internet-Draft draft-ietf-lamps-cms-euf-cma-signeddata-01, Internet Engineering Task Force (2026) Work in Progress
23. Strenzke, F.: ForgedAttributes: An existential forgery vulnerability of CMS signatures. Cryptology ePrint Archive, Paper 2023/1801 (2023)
24. Kousidis, S., Roth, J., Strenzke, F., Wussler, A.: Post-Quantum Cryptography in OpenPGP. Internet-Draft draft-ietf-openpgp-pqc-17, Internet Engineering Task Force (2026) Work in Progress

Apples, Oranges, and Signatures
Pitfalls and Methodology in ML-DSA Benchmarking

Sebastien Riou[1(✉)], Jong-Yeon Park[2], Liga Anwar[2], Axel Poschmann[1], and Michael Hutter[1,2]

[1] PQShield Inc., Prama House, 267 Banbury Rd, Oxford, UK
{sebastien.riou,axel.poschmann}@pqshield.com
[2] University of the Bundeswehr Munich, Werner-Heisenberg-Weg 39, 85579 Neubiberg, Germany
{jongyoun.park,liga.anwar,michael.hutter}@unibw.de

Abstract. Cryptographic migration, particularly in the post-quantum setting, poses significant practical challenges and requires reliable performance data to support sound engineering decisions. For ML-DSA, however, existing benchmarking practices often produce misleading or non-comparable results, complicating migration and cryptographic agility efforts. This paper analyzes common pitfalls in benchmarking ML-DSA signature operations, including subtle inconsistencies when comparing security levels. We show that execution-time variability of the ML-DSA signing algorithm—an inherent property due to rejection sampling and other data-dependent components—makes commonly used straightforward metrics, e.g., *min*/*average*/*max*, unsuitable for migration planning. To address this gap, we propose a robust benchmarking methodology based on standardized input data sets and clearly qualified reporting metrics. The proposed approach enables fair comparison across hardware and software implementations and supports designers of real-time systems to assess the worst-case execution time.

Keywords: Post-Quantum Cryptography (PQC) · ML-DSA · Worst-case execution time (WCET) · Cryptographic Migration · ASIL · Benchmarking Methodology · Cryptographic Agility

1 Introduction

Benchmarking cryptographic primitives has a long history. Early efforts such as eBACS and SUPERCOP established unified benchmarking harnesses for classical cryptography [4], enabling cross-platform comparisons under controlled conditions. Similar goals motivated post-quantum benchmarking frameworks and reference platforms, notably the Open Quantum Safe project [19] and the PQM4 framework [9], which support systematic evaluation of post-quantum algorithms on embedded platforms. In practice, the resulting performance figures often guide product selection, architectural design, and cryptographic migration decisions, and these initiatives have strongly shaped current benchmarking practice.

D. Loebenberger and M. Stöttinger (Eds.): MAgiCS 2026, CCIS 3002, pp. 121–142, 2026.
https://doi.org/10.1007/978-3-032-28946-9_7

Building on this foundation, several recent works have highlighted methodological limitations in existing benchmarking practices for post-quantum cryptography, particularly on constrained platforms. Howe et al. [7] evaluate lattice-based post-quantum signatures on ARM Cortex-M7 and show the strong impact of implementation choices, platform characteristics, and input sizes on measured performance, while also illustrating the difficulty of comparing results without a standardized methodology. Kris Gaj [5] explicitly frames post-quantum benchmarking as a methodological challenge, identifying sources of misleading comparisons such as variable-time behavior, differences in side-channel protection, ambiguous metrics, and limited reproducibility. A complementary perspective is provided by Kaps et al. [10], who propose a framework for fair and efficient benchmarking of lightweight cryptographic hardware. Although not focused on post-quantum schemes, their emphasis on clear measurement boundaries, standardized inputs, and avoiding cherry-picked operating points is directly applicable.

In this paper, we address a gap that remains largely unfilled in post-quantum signature benchmarking: the lack of a scheme-specific and rigorously defined methodology for benchmarking NIST FIPS 204 ML-DSA signature generation [14], arguably the most important quantum-safe signature algorithm. While prior frameworks and studies provide valuable performance data and general guidance, even after a decade of scrutiny they do not resolve the concrete ambiguities that arise when benchmarking ML-DSA, which combines multiple standardized interfaces, operation modes, variable-size inputs, and rejection-based execution. As a result, published benchmarks are often difficult to interpret or compare in a fair and migration-relevant manner. To the best of our knowledge, this is the first work to systematically analyze these ML-DSA-specific issues and to propose a concrete methodology enabling fair, reproducible, and meaningful performance comparison of ML-DSA signature implementations in post-quantum cryptographic migration contexts.

Contributions. This work makes the following contributions:

1. An analysis of algorithm-intrinsic sources of execution-time variability in ML-DSA, explaining why commonly reported average and worst-case performance figures can be ambiguous or misleading.
2. A systematic identification and formalization of benchmarking pitfalls specific to ML-DSA.
3. A novel benchmarking methodology specifically crafted for ML-DSA sign operation.
4. Reproducible artifacts including the first publicly verifiable WCET [21] benchmarking results for ML-DSA signing.

The remainder of this paper is organized as follows. Section 2 introduces ML-DSA, benchmarking concepts, WCET and ASIL context, and defines the scope of this work. Section 3 examines algorithmic sources of execution-time variability, while Sect. 4 discusses benchmarking pitfalls specific to ML-DSA signature generation. Section 5 presents a robust benchmarking methodology and reporting

Table 1. ASIL level target FIT rates

ASIL Level	PMHF
ASIL A	None
ASIL B	$\leq$ 100 FIT
ASIL C	$\leq$ 100 FIT
ASIL D	$\leq$ 10 FIT

Table 2. Maximum signing rate vs. ASIL level and timeout probability (signatures/s)

ASIL Level	Failure Probability		
	2^{-32}	2^{-48}	2^{-64}
ASIL B and C	0.0012	78.2	5.12 M
ASIL D	0.0001	7.8	512.40 K

guidelines. Section 6 reports benchmarking results obtained using this methodology, and Sect. 7 concludes the paper, outlining what is left as future work.

2 Background and Scope

We begin by outlining the industrial and real-time system context relevant to benchmarking, before introducing ML-DSA-specific considerations.

Benchmarking, WCET, and ASIL. The automotive industry adopts the ISO 26262 standard [1] and its Automotive Safety Integrity Levels (ASIL) to quantify system reliability, ranging from ASIL A (least stringent) to ASIL D (most stringent). Reliability is expressed using the Probabilistic Metric for Random Hardware Failure (PMHF), measured in Failures in Time (FIT), which estimates the number of failures per billion operating hours. The PMHF budget applies to the entire electronic control unit, and individual components are therefore allocated only a fraction of the FIT numbers given in Table 1; for example, Microchip reports that an MCU typically consumes about 10 % of the total FIT budget [12].

In real-time systems with a Worst-Case Execution Time (WCET) [21] constraint, an ML-DSA signing operation that exceeds its time budget constitutes a failure. Although such timeouts arise from the algorithm's statistical behavior and are therefore systematic rather than random hardware faults, they still contribute to the PMHF. This contribution depends on both the signing rate over the product lifetime and the probability of a timeout. Table 2 summarizes the maximum admissible signing rates for different ASIL levels, assuming that 1 % of the total FIT budget is allocated to ML-DSA signing. What is an acceptable timeout probability depends very much on the targeted application. Nevertheless it is clear that a failure probability of 2^{-32} is already too high for most applications at ASIL B or above, while probabilities around 2^{-48} should be adequate for most use cases at ASIL B and C. High-intensity use cases such as V2X at ASIL D may require failure probability below 2^{-48}. This highlights the importance of benchmarking rare execution-time cases and explicitly reporting both their execution times and associated probabilities of occurrence.

ML-DSA. ML-DSA, standardized by NIST [14], is a post-quantum digital signature scheme that balances security, performance, and implementation complex-

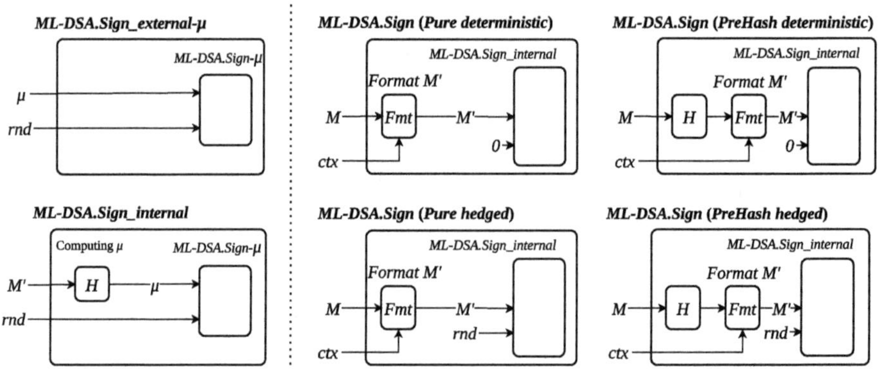

Fig. 1. Diagrams distinguishing ML-DSA.Sign variants.

ity. The specification includes three parameter sets corresponding to distinct NIST security levels:

- ML-DSA-44: NIST security level 2 (comparable to SHA-256)
- ML-DSA-65: NIST security level 3 (comparable to AES-192)
- ML-DSA-87: NIST security level 5 (comparable to AES-256)

Figure 1 illustrates the variants of ML-DSA.Sign specified in [14] and ML-DSA.Sign_external-μ. The left part describes building blocks while the right part describes the current *External interfaces*, i.e., standardized operations suitable for usage at application level. We introduced the ML-DSA.Sign-μ building block to show the relation between ML-DSA.Sign_external-μ and ML-DSA.Sign_internal. This highlights that ML-DSA.Sign-μ is the core operation for all variants.

The four variants of external interfaces affect only how the formatted message M' and how *rnd* are constructed. In *Pure* interface, the message M is formatted directly, whereas in *Pre-hash* interface (HashML-DSA) it is first hashed; apart from this step, both interfaces follow the same control flow and invoke the same internal signing algorithm. Both *Pure* and *Pre-hash* exist in *deterministic* and in *hedged* variants. In *deterministic* variant, the value of *rnd* is fixed to all zeros whereas in *hedged* variant it is randomized. Together, Fig. 1 and Algorithm 1 show that the external interface is responsible only for constructing μ—including optional pre-hashing, hash-function selection, and incorporation of *ctx* (an application-defined context string) —while all security-critical operations are performed by a single common internal algorithm [14].

3 Sources of Execution-Time Variability in ML-DSA

We first analyze the dominant source of execution-time variability in ML-DSA signature generation, followed by a discussion of other variable-time components.

Algorithm 1. ML-DSA.Sign_internal(sk, M', rnd)

Input: private key sk, formatted message $M' \in \{0,1\}^*$, $rnd \in \mathbb{B}^{32}$
Output: signature σ

$(\rho, K, tr, \mathbf{s}_1, \mathbf{s}_2, \mathbf{t}_0) \leftarrow \mathsf{skDecode}(sk)$
$\hat{\mathbf{s}}_1 \leftarrow \mathsf{NTT}(\mathbf{s}_1),\quad \hat{\mathbf{s}}_2 \leftarrow \mathsf{NTT}(\mathbf{s}_2),\quad \hat{\mathbf{t}}_0 \leftarrow \mathsf{NTT}(\mathbf{t}_0)$
$\hat{\mathbf{A}} \leftarrow \mathsf{ExpandA}(\rho)$ ▷ $\mathbf{A}$ generated/stored in NTT form
$\mu \leftarrow H(\mathsf{BytesToBits}(tr) \parallel M', 64)$
$\rho'' \leftarrow H(K \parallel rnd \parallel \mu, 64),\quad \kappa \leftarrow 0,\quad (\mathbf{z}, \mathbf{h}) \leftarrow \perp$ ▷ random seed and counter
while $(\mathbf{z}, \mathbf{h}) = \perp$ **do** ▷ rejection sampling loop
  $\mathbf{y} \in R_q^\ell \leftarrow \mathsf{ExpandMask}(\rho'', \kappa)$
  $\mathbf{w} \leftarrow \mathsf{NTT}^{-1}(\hat{\mathbf{A}} \circ \mathsf{NTT}(\mathbf{y}))$
  $\mathbf{w}_1 \leftarrow \mathsf{HighBits}(\mathbf{w})$ ▷ signer's commitment
  $\tilde{c} \leftarrow H(\mu \parallel \mathsf{w1Encode}(\mathbf{w}_1), \lambda/4)$
  $\hat{c} \leftarrow \mathsf{NTT}(\mathsf{SampleInBall}(\tilde{c}))$
  $\langle\langle c\mathbf{s}_1 \rangle\rangle \leftarrow \mathsf{NTT}^{-1}(\hat{c} \circ \hat{\mathbf{s}}_1),\quad \langle\langle c\mathbf{s}_2 \rangle\rangle \leftarrow \mathsf{NTT}^{-1}(\hat{c} \circ \hat{\mathbf{s}}_2)$
  $\mathbf{z} \leftarrow \mathbf{y} + \langle\langle c\mathbf{s}_1 \rangle\rangle,\quad \mathbf{r}_0 \leftarrow \mathsf{LowBits}(\mathbf{w} - \langle\langle c\mathbf{s}_2 \rangle\rangle)$ ▷ signer's response
  if $\|\mathbf{z}\|_\infty \geq \gamma_1 - \beta$ **or** $\|\mathbf{r}_0\|_\infty \geq \gamma_2 - \beta$ **then**
    $(\mathbf{z}, \mathbf{h}) \leftarrow \perp$ ▷ validity checks failed
  else
    $\langle\langle c\mathbf{t}_0 \rangle\rangle \leftarrow \mathsf{NTT}^{-1}(\hat{c} \circ \hat{\mathbf{t}}_0)$
    $\mathbf{h} \leftarrow \mathsf{MakeHint}(-\langle\langle c\mathbf{t}_0 \rangle\rangle,\ \mathbf{w} - \langle\langle c\mathbf{s}_2 \rangle\rangle + \langle\langle c\mathbf{t}_0 \rangle\rangle)$
    if $\|\langle\langle c\mathbf{t}_0 \rangle\rangle\|_\infty \geq \gamma_2$ **or** $\#1(\mathbf{h}) > \omega$ **then**
      $(\mathbf{z}, \mathbf{h}) \leftarrow \perp$
    end if
  end if
  $\kappa \leftarrow \kappa + \ell$ ▷ increment counter
end while
return $\sigma \leftarrow \mathsf{sigEncode}(\tilde{c},\ \mathbf{z} \bmod {}^{\pm}q,\ \mathbf{h})$

Rejection Sampling and Signature Repetitions. Independently of the selected variant and signing interface, ML-DSA signature generation exhibits inherently variable execution time, even when all input sizes are fixed. This variability stems from the algorithm's structure, which repeatedly generates candidate signatures until validity conditions are met, causing the number of signing-loop repetitions to vary across signatures. This rejection-driven variability poses a fundamental challenge for benchmarking. While few rejections are common, much higher counts are not exceptional, and even a few hundred measurements may show large execution-time fluctuations. Widely used benchmarking infrastructures such as SUPERCOP [4], the Open Quantum Safe tools in `liboqs` [19], and PQM4 [9] assume that such variability can be averaged out as measurement noise. Although reasonable on high-performance systems, this assumption becomes impractical on low-end and edge devices, where executions are slow.

For ML-DSA, this assumption does not hold even in principle. Execution-time variability is algorithm-intrinsic, heavy-tailed, and sensitive to input selection and repetition statistics. Applying standard benchmarking workflows without additional qualification can therefore produce misleading or non-comparable results. This does not reflect a limitation of existing frameworks, but rather underscores the need for scheme-specific benchmarking methodologies for post-quantum algorithms with intrinsic variable-time behavior.

Other Variable-Time Components. Beyond the rejection-driven variability of the signing loop, several additional components contribute to execution-time variation even when input sizes are fixed:

- *Public-key–dependent variability.* Some variable-time components depend only on the public key. In particular, `ExpandA` relies on rejection sampling in `RejNTTPoly`, introducing execution-time variability independent of the message or signature and present before message-dependent processing.
- *Message- and secret-key–dependent variability.* Other components exhibit data-dependent behavior influenced by the message, context, and secret key, including `HighBits`, `LowBits`, `SampleInBall`, and `MakeHint`. In addition, failed validity checks may cause early termination or additional processing, further increasing execution-time variability.
- *Signature-dependent variability.* Execution time may also depend on the signature itself. The `SigEncode` stage, particularly `HintBitPack`, may process a variable number of coefficients, causing variability even after the signing loop completes.
- *Implications for benchmarking.* These effects show that execution-time differences are not solely determined by signing-loop rejections. Benchmarking ML-DSA implementations must therefore account for both repetition-driven and data-dependent timing behavior.

4 Pitfalls in ML-DSA Signature Benchmarking

In this section, we discuss benchmarking pitfalls relevant to ML-DSA signature generation. We first examine general pitfalls applicable to cryptographic benchmarking (Pitfalls 1 to 3), and then focus on pitfalls that arise from ML-DSA-specific design choices (Pitfalls 4 to 14).

Pitfall 1: Comparison of Different Key Sizes. Like many standardized cryptographic schemes, ML-DSA is specified for multiple security levels, corresponding to the parameter sets ML-DSA-44, ML-DSA-65, and ML-DSA-87, which differ substantially in computational cost, memory footprint, and security strength. Consequently, their performance characteristics are not directly comparable.

A common benchmarking pitfall is to compare signature generation performance across different ML-DSA parameter sets without clearly stating the security level. Such comparisons are misleading, as apparent performance gains often stem from lower security parameters rather than superior implementations. Performance results must be reported separately for each ML-DSA parameter set, and comparisons are only valid when the same security level is used. This best practice is exemplified by [2], where results are consistently presented per NIST security level.

Pitfall 2: Protected vs. Unprotected Implementations. In cryptographic benchmarking, the distinction between protected and unprotected implementations is often overlooked. Although not mandated by the specification, such protections are essential under many real-world threat models [8,11,17].

A common pitfall is to compare implementations with different levels of protection against side-channel attacks (SCA) and fault-injection attacks (FIA) without explicitly accounting for these differences. Countermeasures such as masking or hiding can introduce substantial overhead and may interact non-trivially with rejection sampling and randomness generation.

For meaningful evaluation, benchmarks should jointly report performance, footprint, and security claims against SCA and FIA. When multiple configurations exist, all metrics should be given for each considered configuration, rather than, for example, reporting performance of the *maximum-performance* configuration, footprint of the *minimum-footprint* configuration, and security claims of the *maximum-security* configuration.

Pitfall 3: Measurement Boundaries. Benchmarking results depend critically on how measurement boundaries are defined. For ML-DSA signature generation, these boundaries are not uniquely specified and vary across implementations, particularly with respect to input parsing, hashing or pre-hashing, randomness generation, signature encoding, and memory transfers.

Comparing performance figures obtained with different, often undocumented, boundaries is a common pitfall. Benchmarks may exclude preprocessing or randomness generation, or measure only the cryptographic core while omitting data transfers, substantially affecting reported performance even for the same ML-DSA parameter set. For fair and reproducible benchmarking, measurement boundaries must be clearly defined and applied consistently. Otherwise, reported results may reflect benchmarking scope rather than true implementation efficiency.

Pitfall 4: Comparison Across ML-DSA Interfaces. A common benchmarking pitfall is to compare performance across these interfaces as if they were equivalent. Such comparisons are misleading: the *Internal* and *External-*μ interfaces omit computations mandatory for a standard-compliant signature, such as message formatting and hashing, and therefore cannot be meaningfully compared to the *Pure* or *Pre-hash* interfaces. Apparent speedups reflect reduced computational scope rather than superior implementation efficiency.

For fair benchmarking, it is essential to distinguish between application-level signature interfaces (*Pure* and *Pre-hash*) and internal building blocks (*Internal* and *External-*μ). Performance comparisons are only meaningful when the same ML-DSA interface is used and all required computations are included.

Table 3. Inputs of the different ML-DSA signing interface as defined in FIPS 204.

Input	Size (Bytes)	Pure	Pre-hash	Internal	External μ
sk (secret key)	Fixed	✓	✓	✓	✓
ctx (context)	0–255	✓	✓	–	–
M (message)	Variable	✓	✓	–	–
M′ (formatted msg)	Variable	–	–	✓	–
rnd (randomness)	32	–	–	✓	✓
μ (msg representative)	64	–	–	–	✓

Pitfall 5: Ambiguous Input Sizes. Benchmarking of digital signature schemes often varies only the message size, implicitly assuming all other inputs have fixed length. For ML-DSA, this assumption is incorrect and can lead to misleading results. Depending on the signing interface, ML-DSA exposes multiple variable-length inputs, including the context string, formatted message, and per-message randomness.

Table 3 summarizes the inputs required by the different ML-DSA signing interfaces. As shown, the *Pure*, *Pre-hash*, and *Internal* interfaces each include at least one variable-size input beyond the message itself. In particular, the *Internal* interface operates on a formatted message whose size depends on standard-defined preprocessing, and the context input may range from zero to several hundred bytes, directly affecting signing cost.

Ignoring these variable-size inputs, or silently fixing them to convenient values, can distort benchmarking results. Performance figures that qualify only the message length are therefore insufficient. For meaningful benchmarking, all variable-size inputs relevant to the selected ML-DSA interface must be explicitly specified and consistently controlled.

Pitfall 6: Comparison of *Hedged* and *Deterministic* Variants. The ML-DSA standard supports both *hedged* and *deterministic* variants of signature generation. In the *hedged* variant, the per-message randomness input *rnd* is filled with fresh random data, whereas in the *deterministic* variant it is fixed to a constant.

A common benchmarking pitfall is to compare *hedged* and *deterministic* measurements without clearly qualifying the variant and signing interface. For the *Internal* and *External-*μ interfaces, *rnd* is provided explicitly and processed identically by the signing algorithm in both variants; any performance difference between *hedged* and *deterministic* variants in this case stems from external randomness generation rather than the ML-DSA implementation itself. In contrast, for the *Pure* and *Pre-hash* interfaces, randomness generation is performed internally and may introduce non-negligible overhead, conflating randomness costs with the intrinsic signing cost.

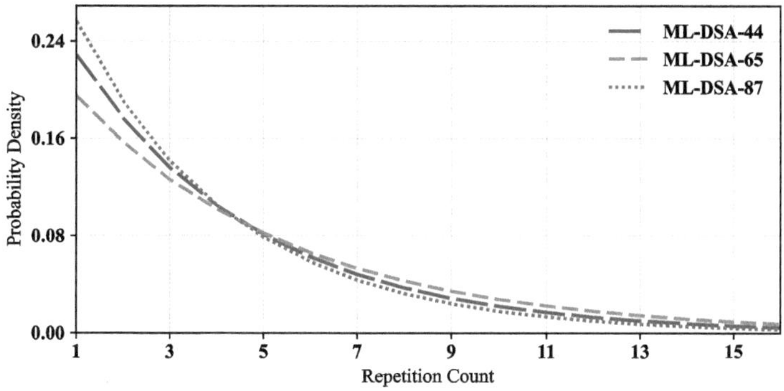

Fig. 2. Empirical distributions of ML-DSA signing-loop repetition counts over 20 million signatures for different parameter sets. See also Sect. 5.1 of https://datatracker.ietf.org/doc/draft-ietf-pquip-pqc-hsm-constrained/04/.

For fair benchmarking, the selected variant must be explicitly stated and applied consistently. Performance comparisons are only meaningful when the same ML-DSA interface and the same variant—*hedged* or *deterministic*—are used.

Pitfall 7: Assuming *Deterministic* is Always Faster. It is often assumed that *deterministic* ML-DSA signing is faster than the *hedged* variant because it avoids fresh randomness, but this assumption does not generally hold. In software implementations, randomness generation may add overhead, whereas many hardware accelerators take *rnd* as an input even for the *Pure* and *Prehash* interfaces, leaving signing time unchanged. In addition, rejection-sampling variability can dominate overall cost, eliminating any systematic advantage of *deterministic* signing.

Randomized signing can even improve performance in protected implementations by providing implicit masking against DPA [11]. As shown at the NIST Fourth PQC Standardization Conference [3], masked implementations using randomized signing achieve significant speedups (approximately 1.6×–1.7×) over *deterministic* designs. Consequently, assuming *deterministic* variants are always faster is a benchmarking pitfall.

Pitfall 8: Ambiguous use of *Average* and *Maximum* Execution Time. Section 3 highlighted the intrinsic timing variability of ML-DSA sign operation. A common benchmarking practice is to execute the algorithm repeatedly on random inputs of fixed size and report statistics such as minimum, average, or maximum execution time. While suitable for mitigating environmental measurement noise, this approach is ill-suited when execution-time variability is heavy-tailed, like Fig. 2 illustrates. In the case of ML-DSA, it has several drawbacks:

- *Observed maxima are not true worst cases.* They reflect only the worst outcome encountered during measurement and may significantly underestimate the algorithmic worst case.

- *Results depend on sample size.* Benchmarks based on different numbers of executions are not directly comparable, as larger samples are more likely to expose rare high-rejection events.
- *Results are sensitive to input selection.* For some signing interfaces and variants, inputs can be chosen to statistically favor low rejection counts, yielding overly optimistic performance figures.

Without careful qualification, averages and maxima can therefore be misleading. For ML-DSA, execution-time variability must be treated as an explicit algorithmic property and incorporated into the benchmarking methodology, rather than averaged away as measurement noise.

Pitfall 9: Misinterpreting Maximum Repetition Bound. A natural question when benchmarking a variable-time algorithm is how to interpret its worst-case execution time. For ML-DSA signature generation, a standard-conforming implementation may perform up to 814 rejection iterations before aborting, as specified in FIPS 204 Appendix C [14]. This bound is a theoretical safety limit to guarantee termination, not a realistic execution scenario.

Treating this limit as a meaningful worst case is a serious benchmarking pitfall. The probability of reaching such an extreme number of rejections is vanishingly small—on the order of 2^{-256}. In practice, we observed a maximum of only 106 signing-loop iterations over 1.6 trillion ML-DSA-44 signatures, making the specification-defined abort bound grossly pessimistic and unsuitable for system sizing or performance comparison.

More generally, system-level guidelines caution against loop constructs that are theoretically bounded yet effectively non-terminating in practice. For example, the SEI CERT C Coding Standard (MSC21-C) stresses analyzable termination guarantees [18]. A similar issue arises in RSA key generation, where standards bound Miller–Rabin rounds but not the number of candidates tested [13], underscoring that probabilistic cryptographic procedures must be evaluated with real system constraints in mind.

Pitfall 10: Computing Average over Skewed Data. We analyze subsets of consecutive ML-DSA-87 signatures and compute the sum of repetitions for different sample sizes. Table 4 summarizes the results.

Table 4. Cumulative repetition variation for consecutive ML-DSA-87 signature subsets.

Sample size	Min. sum	Max. sum	Theoretical
10	12	108	38.5
100	270	579	385.0
1,000	3,543	4,293	3,850.0
10,000	37,979	40,143	38,500.0

Even when benchmarking with 10,000 *hedged* signatures, two independent and well-intentioned benchmarks of the same implementation may report average execution times that differ by several percent. In the example above, one benchmark may observe an average corresponding to approximately 99 % of the theoretical value, while another may report 104 %. Put differently, results for a single implementation may vary by around 5 % solely due to statistical effects, despite using identical parameters and sample sizes.

Pitfall 11: Extrapolating from Repetition Counts. One frequently proposed approach to address Pitfall 10 is to extrapolate execution time from a measured *time per repetition*. In this method, the signing time is measured for cases with one and with two repetitions, a nominal $Time_{repetition}$ is derived from the difference, and overall performance is estimated using the expected repetition count. Although this approach appears attractive and difficult to game, it is fundamentally flawed. In most implementations, $Time_{repetition}$ is itself variable. The signing loop may terminate at different points in Algorithm 1, each involving multiple conditional checks, and some implementations employ early-abort mechanisms that stop processing as soon as a failure is detected. As a result, there is no single, well-defined execution time for a single repetition.

Extrapolating overall signing performance from repetition counts and a nominal $Time_{repetition}$ therefore constitutes a benchmarking pitfall. Such extrapolation obscures intrinsic algorithmic variability and produces results that are neither robust nor comparable across implementations.

Pitfall 12: Verifiable but Incorrect Signatures. In ML-DSA, a signature that was not produced by a correct signing execution may still be accepted by the verification algorithm. This does not indicate a flaw, but reflects a structural property of the scheme: verification checks only a subset of the conditions enforced during signing.

During signing, ML-DSA applies norm bounds and rejection sampling to maintain its security properties, whereas verification focuses only on algebraic consistency and selected public bounds, as dictated by the Fiat–Shamir-with-aborts construction. As a result, successful verification alone does not guarantee that a signature was generated by a compliant signer.

A concrete example is the rejection condition in line 19 of Algorithm 1,

$$\left[\left\|\langle\langle ct_0\rangle\rangle\right\|_\infty \geq \gamma_2\right] \vee [\#1(h) > \omega] \tag{1}$$

which is enforced only during signing. Signatures violating this condition may still verify, even though they would never be produced by a correct implementation. Such violations are extremely rare—none were observed in over one billion signatures—making them unlikely to be detected by random sign–verify tests. Consequently, sign–verify consistency alone is insufficient to validate an ML-DSA implementation. Correctness testing must also ensure enforcement of signing-side constraints, such as norm bounds, rejection conditions, and randomness handling, to prevent implementations that appear correct while weakening the scheme's security guarantees.

Pitfall 13: Unspecified *Pre-hash* Function Selection. In the *Pre-hash* interface of ML-DSA, the choice of the pre-hashing function is part of the signing interface and has a direct impact on performance. A common benchmarking pitfall is to report *Pre-hash* results without specifying the hash function used.

To ensure meaningful and reproducible benchmarking, results for the *Pre-hash* interface must explicitly state the hash function and relevant implementation details; otherwise, comparisons can be misleading.

Pitfall 14: Pre-computations in Key Generation. A part of the sign operation can be precomputed as part of key generation function. It is therefore important to cover also the key generation in the benchmark otherwise implementations which adopt this strategy appear better than they really are.

5 Towards Fair and Reproducible ML-DSA Benchmarking

This section outlines the guiding principles and practical recommendations required for fair and reproducible benchmarking of ML-DSA implementations.

5.1 What *fair Benchmarking* Means

In the context of ML-DSA, we define *fair benchmarking* along two complementary dimensions:

1. *Fairness towards readers:* Reported performance figures must not mislead the reader into an overly optimistic interpretation. In particular, benchmark results should reflect realistic operational behavior rather than best-case or artifact-driven measurements.
2. *Fairness towards vendors (IP providers):* Benchmarking results should be robust against metric selection and configuration choices. In particular, an implementation with inferior or equal intrinsic performance should not be able to advertise better results by exploiting alternative metrics or benchmark setups, and repeating the benchmark on the same implementation should yield comparable results within expected statistical variation.

These objectives are partially conflicting, particularly when reporting *worst observed* execution times. Including higher rejection counts improves coverage of extreme behavior but increases the risk of unfair comparisons if competing benchmarks exclude such cases. This tension must therefore be managed through explicit reporting: benchmarks should state both the maximum observed number of signing-loop repetitions and the associated occurrence probability.

Table 5 summarizes repetition counts for selected target probabilities. A good benchmarking data set should reach the same occurrence probability for each

Table 5. Repetition counts for ML-DSA and occurrence probabilities.

Algorithm	Occurrence Probability		
	2^{-32}	2^{-48}	2^{-64}
ML-DSA-44	83	125	166
ML-DSA-65	102	153	204
ML-DSA-87	74	111	148

key size, otherwise one may end up with a *worst observed* execution times higher for ML-DSA-44 than ML-DSA-65 for example. Similarly the average number of repetitions should match the theoretical average given in [14] Table 1:

- ML-DSA-44: 4.25 repetitions on average
- ML-DSA-65: 5.10 repetitions on average
- ML-DSA-87: 3.85 repetitions on average

Ideally, benchmarking data sets would include test vectors with occurrence probabilities of 2^{-48} or lower. Since generating such vectors is resource intensive, practical benchmarks may target higher probabilities, but the chosen probability must always be explicitly documented.

5.2 Handling the *hedged* Variant

Constructing a fixed input data set with a prescribed average repetition count is not feasible for the *hedged* variant, due to the fresh randomness used for each signature. Its performance can instead be inferred from the *deterministic* variant, since the only algorithmic difference is the generation of 32 bytes of random data.

We propose measuring the *hedged* variant on random inputs of the same sizes and stopping once a zero-rejection signature is observed, estimating the randomness overhead as the timing difference between the *hedged* and *deterministic* variants. Although this does not capture all signing-loop variability, it avoids the error amplification inherent in repetition-based extrapolation. For implementations that do not support the *deterministic* variant, fair benchmarking requires exposing the number of signing-loop repetitions (Algorithm 2), at the cost of a resource-intensive search for suitable executions.

Algorithm 2. Benchmark procedure for *hedged*-only signing implementation

Input: a set of test vectors tvs
Output: minimum, average, and worst observed cycles

$remaining \leftarrow \mathsf{Repetitions}(tvs)$ ▷ List of repetitions occurring in tvs
$sk \leftarrow tvs.sk, \quad m \leftarrow tvs.messages[0], \quad ctx \leftarrow tvs.contexts[0]$
$sum \leftarrow 0, \quad cycles_{\min} \leftarrow \infty, \quad cycles_{wob} \leftarrow 0, \quad \mathrm{NP} \leftarrow |remaining|$
while $remaining$ **is not empty do**
  $(cycles, repetitions) \leftarrow \mathsf{Implementation.Sign}(sk, m, ctx)$ ▷ inputs are fixed
  if $repetitions \in remaining$ **then**
    remove $repetitions$ **from** $remaining$ ▷ avoid duplicate measurements
    $sum \leftarrow sum + cycles$
    $cycles_{\min} \leftarrow \min(cycles_{\min}, cycles), \quad cycles_{wob} \leftarrow \max(cycles_{wob}, cycles)$
  end if
end while
$cycles_{\mathrm{avg}} \leftarrow sum/\mathrm{NP}$ ▷ one measurement per one test vector
return $cycles_{\min}, cycles_{\mathrm{avg}}, cycles_{wob}$

5.3 Rare Rejection Path Test Vectors

Test vectors for rare signing-side rejection paths are necessary because these paths are infrequent yet performance-critical, making them easy to omit or mis-implement. Developers may intentionally bypass such checks to improve apparent performance or inadvertently skip them due to misunderstandings or aggressive optimizations. Because these conditions are unlikely to be triggered by random inputs, standard benchmarking and validation procedures may fail to detect such deviations.

Without targeted test vectors, implementations that violate the signing specification may therefore appear faster while still passing verification-based tests, undermining fair performance evaluation. Alternatively, benchmark reports may document the results of dedicated functional test suites such as NIST's ACVP-Server [15] or Project Wycheproof [6].

5.4 Optimal Message Sizes

Optimal message size for the *internal* interface. Message size directly affects signature and verification performance. For the Internal signing interface, FIPS 204 defines the computation of the message representative as

$$\mu \leftarrow H\big(\mathrm{BytesToBits}(\mathtt{tr}) \,\|\, M'\big),$$

where $\mathtt{tr} \in \mathbb{B}^{64}$ is defined in Algorithm 1 and

$$H(\mathrm{str}, \ell) = \mathsf{SHAKE\text{-}256}(\mathrm{str}, 8\ell).$$

To minimize execution time, the goal is to ensure that μ is generated with a single invocation of the KECCAK permutation. Let the input length to H be

$$|\texttt{tr}| + |M'| = 64 + |M'|$$

Accounting for the suffix overhead of SHAKE-256 (4 bits) and the `pad10*1` rule (2 bits), this corresponds to one byte of overhead in byte-oriented implementations. The maximum formatted message length is therefore

$$|M'| = \frac{1600 - 512}{8} - 64 - 1 = 71 \text{ bytes.}$$

Thus, messages up to 71 bytes yield optimal performance for Internal ML-DSA signing.

Optimal Message Size for the *Pure* Interface. For the Pure signing interface defines the formatted message as

$$M' \leftarrow \text{BytesToBits}\big(\text{IntegerToBytes}(0, 1) \,\|\, \text{IntegerToBytes}(|\texttt{ctx}|, 1) \,\|\, \texttt{ctx}\big) \,\|\, M$$

With a zero-length context, this gives $|M'| = 2 + |M|$. Using the same reasoning as above, the maximum message size yielding optimal performance is

$$|M| = 71 - 2 = 69 \text{ bytes.}$$

Optimal Message Size for the *pre-hash* interface. For the *pre-hash* interface (Algorithm 4 in [14]) applies a *pre-hash* function PH to the message. When using PH=SHAKE-128 and a zero-length context, the only dependency on message size arises from the input to SHAKE-128. Accounting for padding, the maximum message size processed with a single KECCAK permutation is

$$|M| = \frac{1600 - 256}{8} = 168 \text{ bytes.}$$

Messages up to 168 bytes therefore achieve optimal performance for *pre-hash* ML-DSA signing.

For substantially larger messages (e.g., kilobytes or megabytes), reducing the number of KECCAK invocations yields diminishing returns and has little impact on overall benchmark results.

5.5 Benchmarking ML-DSA.Sign: Practical Recommendations

Based on the pitfalls identified in this paper, we derive practical recommendations for benchmarking and reporting ML-DSA signature performance to support fair comparison, reproducibility, and informed deployment decisions.

Complete Qualification of Benchmarked Operations. To avoid Pitfall 1, Pitfall 2, Pitfall 4, Pitfall 6 and Pitfall 13, benchmark reports should fully qualify the benchmarked operation and provide performance figures for all interfaces and variants supported by the product. At a minimum, the following parameters should be explicitly stated:

1. *Key size:* ML-DSA-44, ML-DSA-65, ML-DSA-87
2. *Signing interface: pure, pre-hash, internal, external-μ*
3. *Pre-hash algorithm:* e.g., SHAKE-256, SHA-512
4. *Variant: hedged, deterministic*

Explicitly Describe the Benchmarking Boundaries. Precise reference to algorithms in [14] helps to avoid Pitfall 3.

Cover Key Expansion. Report figures for Algorithm 6 in [14] to avoid Pitfall 14.

Explicit Reporting of Input Sizes. To avoid Pitfall 5, benchmark reports should always specify the input sizes used for benchmarking and, where applicable, select the optimal sizes for the corresponding signing interface:

- 69 bytes message, 0 byte context for *Pure*
- 168 bytes message, 0 byte context for *Pre-hash*
- 71 bytes formatted message for *Internal*
- For *External-μ*, message size is fixed by FIPS 204 via the message representative μ.

Dataset-Based Performance Reporting. To avoid Pitfall 7, Pitfall 8, and Pitfall 9, performance figures should be derived from a standardized input data set rather than ad hoc measurements. Reports should include cycle counts over this data set with clearly labeled metrics such as *best observed*, *average*, and *worst observed.* The *worst observed* should have a documented probability of occurence. To avoid ambiguity, the benchmarking data set should be publicly accessible.

Constraints on Standardized Input Data Sets. For each key size, the standardized data set should target the *deterministic* variant and satisfy the following constraints:

- Include a best-case test vector with 0 rejections, including in `SampleInBall`.
- Exhibit an average repetition count matching the theoretical expectation (avoid Pitfall 10, Pitfall 11).
- Include a case with the highest number of rejections happening with the target probability.
- Include cases with rare rejection paths or mandate to pass an extensive functional test suite.

Table 6. Maximum repetition count for ML-DSA signing over 2 trillions signatures.

Algorithm	Occurrence Prob.			
	2^{-37}	2^{-39}	2^{-41}	2^{-43}
ML-DSA-44	96	-	106	-
ML-DSA-65	119	127	-	-
ML-DSA-87	86	-	-	100

Table 7. Maximum signing rate with 2^{-37} probability of timeout vs. ASIL level, 1 % of total FIT.

ASIL Level	Max. signatures/s
ASIL B and C	0.0382
ASIL D	0.0038

Implications for Product Comparison and Cryptographic Migration. Adhering to these recommendations enables meaningful and fair comparison between competing ML-DSA implementations across platforms and vendors. Reliable and reproducible benchmarking is also a prerequisite for cryptographic migration decisions, where performance data directly influences architectural choices, resource provisioning, and risk assessment during the transition to post-quantum cryptography.

6 Implementation Results

Test vectors to benchmark ML-DSA.Sign. Using an instrumented version of `mldsa-native` [16], we searched for executions exhibiting high signing-loop repetition counts in ML-DSA *Pure deterministic* signature generation. For this search, the message length was fixed to 69 bytes and the context length to 0 bytes. Table 6 summarizes the results; the column headers indicate the corresponding probabilities of occurrence.

As we found a case with a probability of occurrence of 2^{-37} for each key size, we use those cases to build our test vectors. Our search is far from reaching the target probability of 2^{-64} or even 2^{-48} so we will keep searching. Table 7 shows the number of signatures per second tolerable in ASIL levels for an application which would fail if the signature times out. We see that a probability of 2^{-37} is probably too high for ASIL B and C as it allows only 0.0382 signature per second. We intend to find lower probability test vectors in future works. For each key size, we add to the following test vectors (still with 69 bytes messages and 0 byte context):

- A zero-rejection case with zero rejection in `SampleInBall` (best case).
- Additional cases to reach an average repetition count matching the theoretical expectation for the target key size.

Finally, for each key size, we include a single zero-rejection test vector for two message lengths: 10 KB and 1 MB. All test vectors use a zero-length context. Each test vector is generated in four formats—C, Python, SystemVerilog, and JSON (following NIST's KAT format)—to facilitate reuse across software and hardware implementations. The complete set of test vectors is then bundled into a single archive and released publicly[1], together with the software used to generate them. The archive is named `mldsa-p37-m108-r96-1-1-119-1-1-86-1-1`, which encodes high-level information about the contained test vectors, i.e.,

- *p37*: probability of occurrence of worst case is 2^{-37}.
- *m108*: it contains 108 test vectors in total.
- *r96-1-1-119-1-1-86-1-1*: highest observed repetition counts per parameter set, namely 96 for ML-DSA-44, 119 for ML-DSA-65, and 86 for ML-DSA-87 on a 69-byte message, with a single repetition for both 10 KB and 1 MB messages in all cases.

We choose to not include cases with rare rejection paths. Instead we require the implementation to pass all test vectors from NIST's ACVP-Server [15] and from Project Wycheproof [6] test suites to maintain a clean separation between test vectors for functional validation and test vectors for performance benchmark. Benchmarking of the *hedged* variant is handled separately, as discussed in Sect. 5.2.

Benchmark on NUCLEO-U5A5 of ML-DSA.Sign ***pure deterministic*****.** We use the test vectors `mldsa-p37-m108-r96-1-1-119-1-1-86-1-1` to benchmark software implementations on a NUCLEO-U5A5 development board [20]. This board integrates an STM32U5A5 microcontroller featuring an ARM Cortex-M33 CPU. All experiments are conducted at the maximum clock frequency of 160 MHz, with both instruction and data caches enabled. While operating the processor at a lower frequency would trivially yield smaller absolute cycle counts, such artificially reduced figures are less informative for practitioners seeking to determine whether a given implementation satisfies real-world timing constraints.

All software components are compiled using `arm-none-eabi-gcc` (`xPack GNU Arm Embedded GCC x86_64` version `14.2.1 20241119`), with the exception of the `stm32pqc` library, which is provided by STMicroelectronics in precompiled binary form (we evaluated the version v1.0.1). The measurement boundaries match Algorithm 6 in [14] for `key-exp`, *deterministic* variant of Algorithm 2 in [14] for `sign` and Algorithm 3 in [14] for `verify`. All software involved is publicly released[2].

Table 8 presents the performance of ML-DSA-44 and ML-DSA-87 according to our methodology. It shows that even with its relatively high probability of occurrence, our worst case test vector for `sign` is about 20 times slower than the average execution time. Table 9 presents the memory footprint of ML-DSA-44 and ML-DSA-87. `Stack` and `Heap` contains the maximum size when calling successively `key-exp`, `sign` and `verify`. The `Static RAM` contains private and public keys in the native format of each implementation. We observe large variations from one library to another as various performance-memory trade-offs are possible in ML-DSA implementation.

[1] https://github.com/sebastien-riou/BTVG-MLDSA.

[2] https://github.com/sebastien-riou/crypto-benchmark,
https://github.com/sebastien-riou/crypto-benchmark-stm32u5

Table 8. Performance for a 69-byte message and zero-length context (in million cycles).

Implementation	Level	Operation	Minimum	Average[a]	Worst observed[b]
`pqcrystals-lowram`	44	key-exp	3.55	3.65	3.70
	44	sign	6.99	22.01	446.48
	87	key-exp	11.29	11.44	11.74
	87	sign	18.56	53.92	1061.51
`stm32pqc-lowram`	44	key-exp	2.25	2.27	2.28
	44	sign	4.20	14.61	308.69
	87	key-exp	6.46	6.47	6.50
	87	sign	9.95	32.99	691.94
`wolfssl-lowram`	44	key-exp	2.93	2.96	2.97
	44	sign	4.27	16.28	355.35
	87	key-exp	8.54	8.56	8.61
	87	sign	11.87	42.60	926.04

[a] Match long term average for `sign`. [b] Probability of occurrence is 2^{-37} for `sign`.

Table 9. Memory footprint for key generation, signing and verification (in KiB).

Implementation	Level	Stack	Heap	Static RAM	Read-only
`pqcrystals-lowram`	44	5.30	0.00	3.77	12.52
	87	8.30	0.00	7.30	12.21
`stm32pqc-lowram`	44	1.20	0.00	14.88	17.20
	87	1.20	0.00	26.41	17.04
`wolfssl-lowram`	44	1.98	28.01	20.32	25.94
	87	1.98	79.01	20.32	25.94

None of the benchmarked implementations have claims about SCA or FIA. We leave the validation of those implementation with the functional validation suites as future work.

7 Conclusions

This paper examined the challenges of benchmarking ML-DSA signature generation and showed that conventional metrics can be misleading when methodological choices are left implicit. We identified 14 key pitfalls related to standardized interfaces, variable-size inputs, and rejection sampling that hinder fair performance comparison. We proposed a fair and reproducible benchmarking methodology based on publicly available input data sets, clearly qualified configurations, and reporting metrics, enabling fair comparison and more reliable performance data for post-quantum deployment and migration. We also presented the first

ML-DSA signing benchmarks reporting worst-case execution time with associated occurrence probabilities, released the supporting software, and outlined future work extending these results to lower-probability test vectors and to HashML-DSA. While this work focuses on ML-DSA, the identified issues are not unique to this scheme. Other post-quantum signature and key encapsulation mechanisms similarly combine multiple standardized variants, variable-size inputs, and data-dependent execution paths. As a result, comparable benchmarking ambiguities are likely to arise unless scheme-specific methodologies are adopted. ML-DSA therefore serves as a concrete and timely case study illustrating a broader class of challenges in post-quantum cryptographic benchmarking.

Acknowledgments. This work has received funding from the EU's Horizon Europe research and innovation programme under grant agreement No. 101225722 (FORTRESS).

References

1. ISO 26262-1:2018 Road vehicles – Functional safety – Part 1: Vocabulary (2018) edition 2, 2018-12
2. Abbasi, M., Cardoso, F., Váz, P., Silva, J., Martins, P.: A practical performance benchmark of post-quantum cryptography across heterogeneous computing environments. Cryptography **9**(2), 32 (2025)
3. Azouaoui, M., Bronchain, O., Cassiers, G.: Leveling dilithium against leakage, revisited: Sensitivity analysis and improved implementations. In: Presentation at the Fourth NIST Post-Quantum Cryptography Standardization Conference (2022) available at the NIST Computer Security Resource Center (CSRC)
4. Bernstein, D.J., Lange, T.: eBACS: ECRYPT benchmarking of cryptographic systems. http://bench.cr.yp.to
5. Gaj, K.: Challenges and rewards of implementing and benchmarking post-quantum cryptography in hardware. In: Chen, D., Homayoun, H., Taskin, B. (eds.) Proceedings of the 2018 on Great Lakes Symposium on VLSI, GLSVLSI 2018, Chicago, IL, USA, May 23–25, 2018, pp. 359–364. ACM (2018)
6. Google Security Team: Project Wycheproof: Cryptographic Test Vectors. https://github.com/C2SP/wycheproof. Accessed 28 Jan 2026
7. Howe, J., Westerbaan, B.: Benchmarking and Analysing the NIST PQC Lattice-Based Signature Schemes Standards on the ARM Cortex M7. In: Mrabet, N.E., Feo, L.D., Duquesne, S. (eds.) Progress in Cryptology - AFRICACRYPT 2023 - 14th International Conference on Cryptology in Africa, Sousse, Tunisia, July 19-21, 2023, Proceedings. Lecture Notes in Computer Science, vol. 14064, pp. 442–462. Springer (2023)
8. Hutter, M., Tunstall, M.: Constant-time higher-order Boolean-to-arithmetic masking. J. Cryptogr. Eng. **9**(2), 173–184 (2019). https://doi.org/10.1007/s13389-018-0191-z
9. Kannwischer, M.J., Rijneveld, J., Schwabe, P., Stoffelen, K.: pqm4: testing and benchmarking NIST PQC on ARM Cortex-M4. In: Workshop Record of the Second PQC Standardization Conference (2019). https://cryptojedi.org/papers/#pqm4

10. Kaps, J., Diehl, W., Tempelmeier, M., Farahmand, F., Homsirikamol, E., Gaj, K.: A Comprehensive Framework for Fair and Efficient Benchmarking of Hardware Implementations of Lightweight Cryptography. IACR Cryptol. ePrint Arch. p. 1273 (2019). https://eprint.iacr.org/2019/1273
11. Kocher, P., Jaffe, J., Jun, B.: Differential power analysis. In: Advances in Cryptology-CRYPTO'99: 19th Annual International Cryptology Conference, pp. 388–397. Springer (1999)
12. Lassen, J.L.: Importance of the failure mode effect and diagnostics analysis when designing safety critical applications. Microchip (2020). https://ww1.microchip.com/downloads/en/DeviceDoc/Failure-Mode-Effect-Diagnostics-Analysis-DS00003638A.pdf
13. National Institute of Standards and Technology: Digital Signature Standard (DSS). FIPS PUB 186-5 (2023). https://nvlpubs.nist.gov/nistpubs/FIPS/NIST.FIPS.186-5.pdf
14. National Institute of Standards and Technology: FIPS 204: Module-Lattice-Based Digital Signature Standard (Aug 2024). https://doi.org/10.6028/NIST.FIPS.204
15. National Institute of Standards and Technology (NIST): ACVP-Server: Automated Cryptographic Validation Protocol Server. https://github.com/usnistgov/ACVP-Server. Accessed 28 Jan 2026
16. PQ-Code-Package Project: MLDSA-native: Native Implementation of ML-DSA. https://github.com/pq-code-package/mldsa-native. Accessed 28 Jan 2026
17. Sasdrich, P., Bilgin, B., Hutter, M., Marson, M.E.: Low-latency hardware masking with application to AES. IACR Trans. Cryptogr. Hardw. Embed. Syst. **2020**(2), 300–326 (2020). https://doi.org/10.13154/TCHES.V2020.I2.300-326
18. SEI CERT: MSC21-C: Use Robust Loop Termination Conditions. SEI CERT C Coding Standard (2023). https://wiki.sei.cmu.edu/confluence/display/c/MSC21-C.+Use+robust+loop+termination+conditions
19. Stebila, D., Mosca, M.: Post-quantum key exchange for the internet and the open quantum safe project. In: Avanzi, R., Heys, H.M. (eds.) Selected Areas in Cryptography - SAC 2016 - 23rd International Conference, St. John's, NL, Canada, August 10-12, 2016, Revised Selected Papers. Lecture Notes in Computer Science, vol. 10532, pp. 14–37. Springer (2016). https://doi.org/10.1007/978-3-319-69453-5_2
20. STMicroelectronics: NUCLEO-U5A5ZJ-Q Evaluation Board. https://www.st.com/en/evaluation-tools/nucleo-u5a5zj-q.html. Accessed 28 Jan 2026
21. Wilhelm, R., et al.: The worst-case execution-time problem - overview of methods and survey of tools. ACM Trans. Embed. Comput. Syst. **7**(3), 36:1–36:53 (2008). https://doi.org/10.1145/1347375.1347389

Policy Externalization in 5G-PKI: Enabling Scalable and Quantum-Ready IoT

Manish Paudel(✉), Maryna Veksler, and Kemal Akkaya

Virginia Commonwealth University, Richmond, VA, USA
{paudelm,vekslerm,akkayak}@vcu.edu

Abstract. The widespread deployment of Internet of Things (IoT) devices within cellular infrastructure (i.e., 5G) has greatly expanded the attack surface and introduced new security challenges. One of such challenges arises due to the lack of a standardized Public Key Infrastructure (PKI) capable of handling the massive scale of IoT environments. For instance, the existing 5G PKIs lack the agility to manage dynamic and diverse policies required for billions of interconnected devices. These PKIs embed security policies directly into X.509 certificates, leading to critical architectural and scalability issues. Any change in policy necessitates mass certificate revocation and reissuance. Additionally, identical policy data is redundantly replicated across millions of certificates, wasting bandwidth and storage, while routine policy updates result in an overwhelming increase in revocation list size. This instability is further compounded by the emerging threat of quantum computing, where the larger signatures required for Post-Quantum Cryptography (PQC) cannot coexist with the current certificate bloat. This paper proposes a novel backward-compatible 5/6G-PKI infrastructure that fundamentally restructures certificate management by decoupling identity from policy. We introduce an External Policy Management (EPM) framework that replaces embedded policy extensions with lightweight Object Identifier references. This approach enables dynamic policy updates without the need for certificate reissuance, reduces the certificate size, minimizes redundant data exchange during authentication processes, and facilitates practical integration of PQC. Our evaluation reveals significant improvements in the speed of policy updates, substantially reduced authentication latency and bandwidth, thereby creating a scalable foundation for future 5/6G networks while ensuring PQ security.

Keywords: 5/6G · Public Key Infrastructure · Internet of Things · Certificate Management · Policy Updates · Post-Quantum Cryptography

D. Loebenberger and M. Stöttinger (Eds.): MAgiCS 2026, CCIS 3002, pp. 143–164, 2026.
https://doi.org/10.1007/978-3-032-28946-9_8

1 Introduction

Traditional cellular networks (3G/4G) managed billions of User Equipment (UE) devices through centralized Mobile Network Operators (MNOs), relying on cryptographic credentials like SIM cards for device authentication [35]. 5G networks move beyond the "human-to-human" focus of 4G to a "machine-to-machine" model to support massive machine type communications (mMTC), introducing billions of unattended devices (sensors, actuators, smart meters, etc.) that operate autonomously without human supervision [29]. While the architecture remains centralized, mMTC alters key management requirements since these devices cannot respond to certificate alerts or conduct frequent re-authentication. Unlike smartphone users who can respond to certificate expiration alerts or complete re-authentication through device interfaces, mMTC sensors deployed in inaccessible locations (e.g., underground infrastructure) may operate for several years without physical access [26]. Failed certificate updates in remote deployments may require costly physical service calls or permanent device disconnection.

This unattended IoT deployment introduces two critical challenges: first, the scale of mMTC can reach up to one million devices per square kilometer [36], significantly increasing the number of certificates mobile network operators (MNOs) manage. Second, the need for autonomous certificate management complicates updates and revocations, which previously relied on user action in 4G networks. Additionally, device diversity ranges from low-power sensors to advanced gateways, with lifecycles from just days to over a decade [26]. These resource-limited unattended devices are more vulnerable to attacks due to limited security processing capabilities, infrequent security updates, and extended deployment lifecycles in physically accessible locations. At the same time, different network slices require specific security based on dynamic policies, with devices able to shift between different service categories. To manage this scale and heterogeneity, 5G architectures rely on PKI and digital certificates rather than static SIMs.

However, a critical architectural design decision in the 5G Public Key Infrastructure (PKI) standard, which is inherited from Internet PKI (X.509) [12], limits scalability as it embeds all policies within certificates. X.509 certificates contain policy extensions (300–500 bytes) that define operational permissions on the protocols that the device can use (e.g., IoT protocols, HTTP), the network resources it can access, and the allowed cryptographic operations [3]. While this design is manageable for attended devices, it poses three critical problems for unattended IoT devices requiring frequent policy changes:

1-Policy rigidity arises because security policies are cryptographically embedded in certificates through the Certificate Authority (CA), which means that any policy modifications invalidate the certificate [6]. This necessitates certificate revocation and reissuance, a process involving certificate generation, certificate revocation list (CRL) updates, distribution, and device reconfiguration [4], which can take hours for large-scale deployments. A simple policy change, such as allowing the HTTP protocol for smart city sensors affecting thousands of devices, or migrating those devices to a different network slice requires revocation and reissuance of all certificates [4], which can take hours and risk service disruption.

2-Massive redundancy occurs when millions of identical devices each carry the same 300–500 bytes of policy data, resulting in duplicate information transmitted initially and during every authentication handshake [24]. This results in energy waste and congestion of cellular radio channels.

3-Revocation of certificates in traditional cellular networks occurs ideally for legitimate security events (lost/stolen phones, detected compromises, device decommissioning). However, because any policy update requires certificate reissuance (which first requires revocation of the old certificate), the CRL grows with policy-related revocations unrelated to actual security compromises. CRLs grow linearly at approximately 26 bytes per entry [12], which every Network Function (NF) must download and search during device authentication.

This structural inefficiency is further compounded by the emerging threat of quantum computing. Post-Quantum Cryptography (PQC) algorithms like NIST-standardized ML-DSA (Dilithium) require significantly larger signatures (2,420 bytes vs 256 bytes for RSA-2048) [5]. Hence, the massive scale and heterogeneity [34], structural inefficiency, and the threat of quantum computing cannot be handled by existing PKI systems [11,19,20,37].

To address these converging challenges, we present a novel and backward-compatible approach optimizing certificate management operations (certificate size, policy update, revocation frequency, computational overhead) for 5G/6G IoT at massive scale while providing quantum resistance. Our core contribution is fundamentally restructuring PKI by **decoupling policy from the certificate** structure. We introduce an **External Policy Management (EPM)** framework where, instead of embedding 300–500 bytes of static policy extensions in each certificate, certificates carry a lightweight Policy object ID (OID) pointers (approximately 80 bytes) that reference a mutable policy stored in an external database managed by the MNO's CA infrastructure.

Our methodology maintains full backward compatibility with existing 5G infrastructure through utilizing existing Certificate Policies extension of X.509 certificate standard, existing certificate revocation interfaces, and TLS protocols, enabling incremental deployment without requiring wholesale infrastructure replacement or simultaneous device updates across millions of endpoints. The specific contributions of this paper are as follows:

I. **EPM Framework:** We propose a framework that separates security policies from digital certificates, challenging the existing architectural design choices. This minimizes policy overhead per certificate and allows for dynamic, real-time policy updates across millions of devices, improving scalability and efficiency by removing the need for reissuance in traditional PKI.
II. **Regulated Certificate Revocation:** By storing policies externally and referencing them via immutable OIDs, we bring a new perspective to certificate revocation. When policies change, only the external database is updated

while certificate OIDs remain unchanged, eliminating policy-driven revocations regardless of the underlying revocation mechanism.

III. **Enabling Post-Quantum Cryptographic Integration:** By externalizing policies (300–500 bytes) from certificates, our framework reduces both certificate size to accommodate larger PQC signatures (e.g., ML-DSA's vs RSA's) and transmission frequency. Reclaiming the policy overhead partially offsets the PQC signature increase, and eliminating policy-induced certificate reissuance restricts the transmission of large PQC certificates to only initial enrollment and rare key compromise events. This will enable practical PQC adoption for bandwidth-constrained IoT devices.

IV. **Implementation, Threat Model and Evaluation:** We provide a complete working implementation over an open-source 5G infrastructure, including CA infrastructure, an external policy database with multi-CA security verification, certificate revocation, and IoT device simulators. Our threat model analyzes database security concerns and demonstrates automated compromise detection and recovery. Performance evaluation demonstrates the effectiveness and scalability of our design.

The remainder of this paper is organized as follows. Sections 2 and 3 provide background and related work overview on 5G digital certificates, policy extensions, and revocation mechanisms. Section 4 describes the problem statement. Section 5 provides the threat model of our approach. Section 6 details the proposed framework. Section 7 provides security analysis, and Sect. 8 evaluates performance across multiple metrics and deployment scale, and provides discussion on real-world deployment. Section 9 concludes the paper.

2 Background and Preliminaries

This section provides background on 5G IoT network architecture, current PKI implementations, certificate structures, revocation mechanisms, and PQC.

5G Architecture and IoT: 5G marks a significant shift from traditional phone systems to a versatile, software-defined infrastructure designed to facilitate hyper-connectivity through three primary use cases: massive Machine-Type Communications (mMTC), Ultra-Reliable Low-Latency Communications (URLLC), and Enhanced Mobile Broadband (eMBB), as shown in Fig. 1. The mMTC is particularly crucial for IoT, as it enables the simultaneous connection of billions of resource-constrained devices across smart cities and industrial settings. To achieve this, 5G uses a service-based architecture (SBA) and technologies such as software-defined networking, Network Function (NF) Virtualization, edge computing, and enormous Massive Multiple-Input Multiple-Output (MIMO) [2]. These technologies allow the creation of *network slices*, which are isolated logical networks tailored to specific IoT requirements, such as separating low-power sensor traffic from high-bandwidth autonomous vehicle streams.

The 5G architecture has three main components: UEs, base stations, and core network. The core network uses an SBA with key functions such as the Access and Mobility Management Function (AMF) for device certificate validation, the

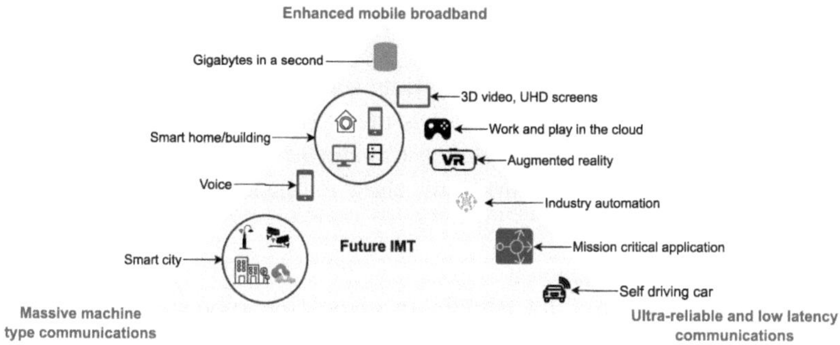

Fig. 1. 5G Use Case Services.

Security Anchor Function (SEAF) for authentication, and the Network Slice Selection Function (NSSF) for assigning devices to slices.

5G Key Management Infrastructure: To ensure security, 5G networks implement a PKI to manage the entire lifecycle of cryptographic keys and certificates, including key generation, distribution, storage, rotation, revocation, and archival. In 5G ecosystems, PKI is operationalized through hierarchical X.509 architecture, typically managed by the MNO through in-house CA infrastructure or in partnership with trusted third-party PKI service providers [4], [20]. The hierarchical structure is: **Root CA → Intermediate CA → End-Device Certificates**, where end-device certificates include both device certificates (for IoT sensors, gateways) and NF Certificates (for AMF, SMF, UPF) [4]. The certificate lifecycle in traditional PKI workflow for 5G IoT devices includes: 1) device enrollment with key pair generation and Certificate Signing Requests (CSRs), (2) CA policy assignment where device types are determined and policy extensions are embedded into certificates, (3) certificate issuance and distribution, (4) authentication involving certificate chain validation and revocation checks, and (5) revocation of compromised certificates [20].

Digital Certificate Structure: To manage the identity of billions of devices, 5G IoT relies on the X.509 version 3 certificate standard [9]. This structure binds a cryptographic key to an identity through a CA's digital signature. As shown in Fig. 2, an X.509 certificate contains core identity fields (Subject, Issuer, Serial Number), public key, validity period, policy extensions, and CA signature.

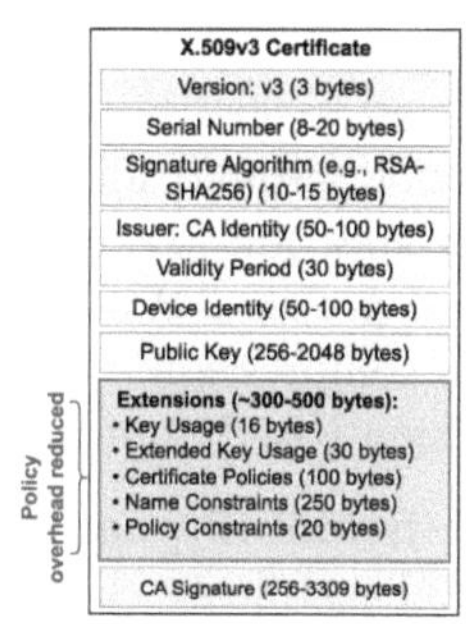

Fig. 2. X.509 certificate

The **policy extensions** rigidly embed security policies directly into the certificate's *Extensions* field. Key extensions include Key Usage, Extended Key Usage, Certificate Policies, Name Constraints, and Policy Constraints, which establish operational constraints. *Key Usage* specifies allowed cryptographic operations (e.g., digital signatures, key encipherment), *Extended Key Usage* defines the certificate's purpose (e.g., client authentication, server authentication), *Name Constraints* restrict accessible domain names or IP ranges (e.g., only *.5g.network domains or other networks), and *Policy Constraints* enforce validation requirements. In typical 5G IoT configurations, these extensions add about 300 to 500 bytes of overhead per certificate [9].

Revocation Mechanisms:
Traditional mechanisms for certificate revocation rely on CRLs, which are linear lists of revoked serial numbers, or OCSP, which provides real-time status via server queries. Both mechanisms face scalability challenges in massive IoT deployments. CRLs suffer from unbounded linear growth leading to bandwidth exhaustion [9], while OCSP introduces latency and privacy leakage by exposing device lookup patterns to the CA [8].

PQC: PQC aims to develop algorithms resistant to both quantum and classical attacks. NIST is leading efforts to standardize PQC algorithms, having selected two lattice-based signature schemes, CRYSTALS-Dilithium and Falcon, along with a stateless hash-based scheme, SPHINCS+SHA [28]. However, adoption of PQC with traditional embedded-policy certificates is structurally infeasible for bandwidth-constrained, storage-limited IoT devices.

3 Related Work

Traditional PKI scalability has been studied extensively, but existing solutions fail to address the convergent challenges of 5G IoT scale, policy agility, and quantum readiness.

Certificate Size Reduction: Previous work has extensively explored reducing certificate overhead through compact certificate formats and compression techniques. Standard X.509 compression via schemes like CBOR (RFC 7049) and Deflate typically achieves 30–40% size reduction by encoding optimizations [15]. More aggressive approaches, such as Implicit Certificates (ECQV), can reduce sizes by nearly 80% but strictly bind the public key to the identity, preventing key rotation without identity re-issuance [24]. Recent proposals for compressed X.509 profiles for IoT improve transmission efficiency but maintain statically embedded policies. While our approach achieves comparable size reduction to standard compression, we uniquely enable dynamic policy updates, which static compression-based approaches cannot support.

PKI Scalability and 5G Security: Hierarchical PKI systems leverage multi-level certificate chains to distribute trust management, but this structure inherently increases validation latency and storage requirements at the edge [20]. Lightweight PKI frameworks have been proposed to reduce computational overhead for constrained devices by minimizing certificate fields and validation paths, yet they largely retain the traditional embedded-policy model [20,32]. Alternative decentralized trust models, such as blockchain-based PKI overlays, offer decentralized trust but require fundamental protocol changes that are incompatible with existing 5G 3GPP standards [23]. Existing 5G security research predominantly focuses on authentication protocols (AKA), network slicing isolation, and edge computing security [14,18,39]. However, these works generally assume a traditional PKI infrastructure for device identity [30] and do not address certificate management scalability for billions of IoT devices requiring dynamic policy changes. 5G Network slicing requires devices to frequently transition between slices with different security policies (e.g., from mMTC to URLLC during emergency events [31]), yet existing PKI research do not provide mechanisms for agile policy updates without certificate reissuance. Our framework addresses this gap by decoupling policy from identity, achieving superior scalability while maintaining backward compatibility with standard X.509 infrastructure and offloading complex policy checks.

Revocation Mechanisms: Revocation is a major bottleneck for PKI scalability. Traditional CRLs grow linearly with revocations, leading to excessive bandwidth use in IoT networks [25]. While OCSP reduces client-side storage, it introduces latency and privacy concerns [8] due to real-time issuer queries. Certificate Transparency [22] and Merkle tree-based schemes [21] improve logging and provide logarithmic proof sizes, but still increase with global revocation counts. Our framework addresses both revocation frequency and data size.

Post-quantum PKI: The transition to PQC poses challenges for IoT due to increased signature sizes [17], such as 2–5 KB for lattice-based signatures [5]. Hybrid approached can double certificate size [13], and hash-based signatures are complex to manage. Our solution focuses on policy externalization to reclaim certificate space, minimize transmission frequency, and reduce the overall revocation count to facilitate PQ.

To the best of our knowledge, no prior work addresses the convergent challenges of certificate bloat, policy agility, revocation scalability, and quantum readiness in a single backward-compatible framework. Our contribution lies in fundamentally restructuring PKI to separate identity from policy, enabling simultaneous optimization across all dimensions.

4 Problem Statement

In the context of 5G SDN, *agility* is defined not only as speed, but as the capability to modify security structure instantaneously whenever conditions change [38]. 5G devices frequently transition between network slices with different security requirements (e.g., migrating from a general mMTC slice to a high-priority URLCC slice to handle an emergency event [31]). More broadly, policy updates are triggered through routine lifecycle changes such as onboarding new device types or decommissioning aging sensors, protocol permissions updates (e.g., enabling HTTP or MQTT), network slice migrations, regulatory or compliance-driven policy changes, and security-driven updates for new vulnerabilities. At IoT scale, even a modest per-device update rate translates to thousands of policy changes daily across the fleet, making agile policy management a continuous operational necessity rather than an exceptional event.

However, the current PKI infrastructure relies on “Static Trust”. By embedding policies directly into the X.509 certificate extensions, the trust model becomes rigid [20]. A simple policy update, such as modifying allowed protocols or slice permissions, invalidates the cryptographic signature of the certificate. This forces a complete revocation and reissuance cycle for every affected device, creating a structural bottleneck that makes true agility impossible. Along with this problem, there are several others that can be summarized as follows:

Problem P1 (Policy Redundancy): For N identical devices, embedding policies in each certificate leads to significant redundancy: Redundant Data $= N \times P_{\text{policy}}$. At massive IoT scale, this creates hundreds of megabytes of duplicate policy data during certificate distribution and every authentication handshake [24]. While negligible for single servers, this overhead becomes problematic in IoT, as redundant data cannot be cached or updated independently, causing bandwidth exhaustion and cellular channel congestion.

Problem P2 (Immutable Policy Coupling): The tight coupling between policies and certificates creates a fundamental rigidity. Policies are cryptographically bound to certificates: $C_i = \text{Sign}_{\text{CA}}(\text{Identity}_i \| \text{PubKey}_i \| \mathcal{P} \| \text{Validity})$. Any policy modification invalidates the signature, requiring complete certificate reissuance for all affected devices. A single policy change (e.g., allowing HTTP for mMTC sensors) necessitates: (1) revoking N certificates, (2) generating N new certificates, (3) distributing to N devices, and (4) adding N CRL entries. For $N = 10^6$ at issuance rate $r = 100$ certs/sec: $T_{\text{reissuance}} = N/r = 2.78$ hours of continuous CA operation with potential service disruption.

Problem P3 (Linear CRL Growth): CRLs grow linearly with revocations at ≈26 bytes per entry [9]. As shown in Table 1, this results in bandwidth exhaustion and unbounded storage requirements.

Table 1. CRL Growth Impact

Revocations	CRL Size	Download (1 Mbps)
10,000	260 KB	2.1 sec
100,000	2.6 MB	21 sec
1,000,000	26 MB	3.5 min
10,000,000	260 MB	35 min

As shown in Table 1, this creates scalability issues: (1) bandwidth exhaustion as every validators downloads complete CRLs periodically, (2) revocation is not real-time, allowing compromised certificates to remain trusted by browsers until the next scheduled update, (3) unbounded storage requirements, and (4) $O(R)$ search complexity. Because policies are cryptographically fused with the identity, any routine policy update forces the revocation and reissuance of the entire certificate, triggering massive revocation cascades that overwhelm the network.

Problem P4 (Policy-Induced Revocations): With embedded policies, policy changes trigger mass revocations. Even if, for instance, 10% of devices need annual policy updates, this will correspond to a significant number of unnecessary revocations when there are millions of devices. These consume revocation infrastructure despite not being security-related.

Problem P5 (PQC Integration): As mentioned, PQ algorithms require significantly larger signatures than classical cryptography. NIST-standardized algorithms like ML-DSA (Dilithium) require 2,420 bytes for signatures compared to 256 bytes for RSA-2048 [5]. The combination of large PQC signatures with existing embedded policy overhead (300–500 bytes), along with policy-induced frequent certificate reissuance, presents a critical challenge. Not only do certificates become larger, but they also must be transmitted more frequently due to policy updates. This results in increased bandwidth consumption, making PQC adoption structurally infeasible for resource-limited 5G IoT deployments.

To address these issues effectively, a solution must not only decouple policy from identity to enable real-time updates but must also be designed to *coexist* with traditional PKI so that it can be easily adopted. The challenge is to introduce dynamic policy enforcement that can "slide in" alongside existing infrastructure, allowing legacy devices (using static certificates) and modern devices (using dynamic policies) to operate simultaneously on the same network without requiring a complete overhaul of the existing CA trust chain.

5 Threat Model

Our framework leverages the existing 3-tier CA hierarchy without new infrastructure, adopting standard PKI trust assumptions [9,10]: HSM-protected CA keys, physical and network security controls, vetted CA operators, offline root CA, and Byzantine fault tolerance (system secure if $< k$ of n CAs compromised).

The proposed framework introduces an external policy database as a new component that introduces new threat vectors (T) that must be addressed.

T1 - Database File Tampering: An attacker with filesystem access could directly modify the policy database to alter policy definitions (e.g., changing permitted DNS domains or network access rules).

T2 - SQL Injection: Maliciously crafted policy OID queries could attempt to execute arbitrary SQL commands to corrupt or exfiltrate data.

T3 - Unauthorized Policy Updates: An insider with database administrative access could modify policy definitions in an attempt to alter operational permissions. For instance, allowed protocols, permitted DNS domains, and expiration dates could be altered, granting devices unauthorized access.

T4 - Database Compromise via Malware: Malware on the CA infrastructure could modify the policy database.

T5 - Complete Database Deletion: An attacker could delete the entire policy database at all CAs simultaneously, causing denial of service (DoS) for new device connections.

T6 - Man-in-the-Middle (MitM) on Policy Retrieval: An attacker could intercept policy queries between network functions and the policy database to return falsified policies.

6 Proposed Approach

Our proposed framework addresses the converging challenges of 5G IoT PKI through a fundamental restructuring of trust management: **decoupling security policies from digital certificates**. We propose a three-tier architecture that replaces static embedded X.509 policy extensions with dynamic references managed by an external authority. Next we detail the components of the proposed framework, including system architecture, cryptographic implementation, and operational call flows for enrollment in dynamic lifecycle management.

6.1 System Architecture and Integration

As shown in Fig. 3, the proposed framework introduces two main logical entities into the 5G SBA [34]: **External Policy Management** (EPM) and **Modified Certificate Authority**. Our framework is fully compatible with existing 5G infrastructure by utilizing standard X.509 extensions [9]. The Certificate Policies extension supports OID references in X.509 certificates, allowing NFs to query the EPM through software updates only, without hardware or protocol modifications.

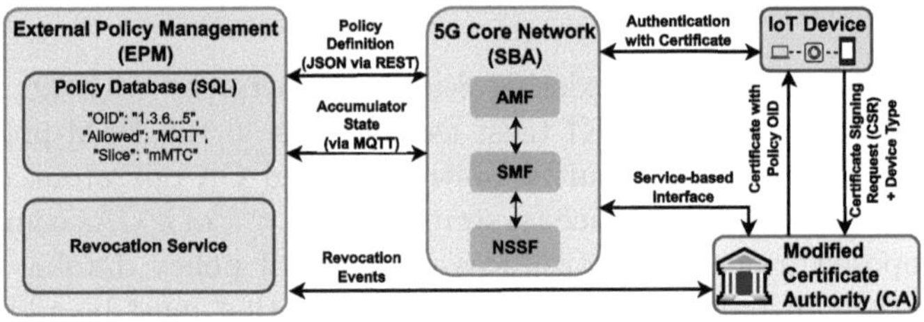

Fig. 3. Overview of the proposed framework.

Figure 4 shows the experimental deployment topology implementing our framework described above. The framework consists of one offline Root CA and three Intermediate CAs, each managing a policy database with API exposure. AMF instances validate certificates and enforce policies by querying CA policy services, with regular cross-CA hash verification to detect tampering. We now describe the details of the EPM and CA.

External Policy Management: Instead of embedding 300–500 bytes of policy data in every certificate [9], we store policies externally in a centralized database and replace embedded policies with lightweight OID references. This separation enables dynamic policy updates without invalidating certificate signatures. First, a **policy database** stores all policy definitions (e.g., allowed protocols, network access rules, and usage permissions) indexed by unique OIDs. Second, a **policy service** provides an API that NFs query to retrieve policies, with caching enabled to minimize database lookups. Third, NFs cache frequently used policies locally and enforce them during certificate validation.
Dynamic Policy Definitions: The policy service exposes an API for policy retrieval by OID, with caching mechanisms to minimize database queries. NFs

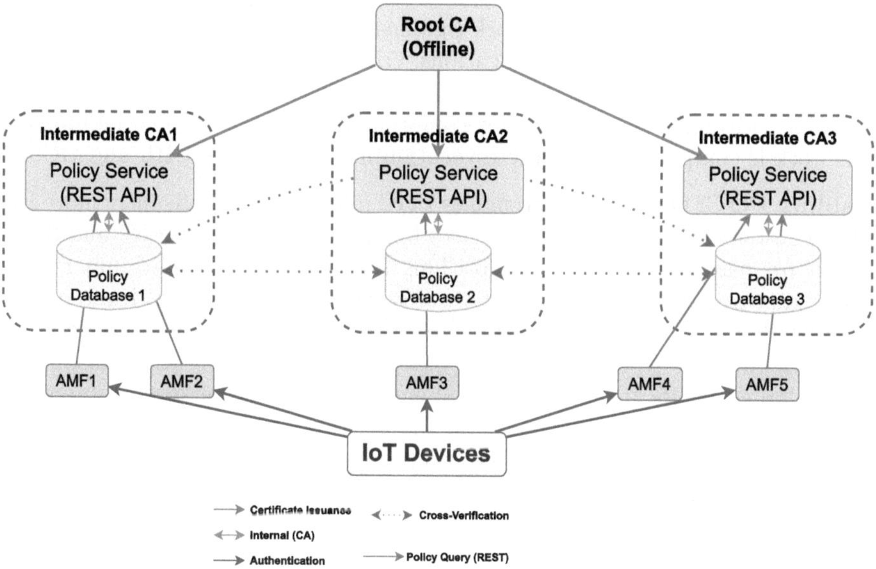

Fig. 4. EPM architecture showing policy databases co-located with CA infrastructure, AMF validation points, and device endpoints.

maintain local policy caches with configurable time-to-live (TTL) to balance freshness with query overhead.

Modified Certificate Authority: The CA issues certificates with only policy OID references instead of embedded extensions, significantly reducing certificate size. Upon receiving a Certificate Signing Request (CSR), the CA first identifies the device type by extracting it from the Organizational Unit (OU) field of the Subject Distinguished Name [9]. This device type is then linked to a pre-registered Policy OID within the EPM database. Following this, the CA generates a certificate that includes only the Certificate Policies extension with the relevant OID reference, while intentionally leaving out the five standard policy extensions: Key Usage, Extended Key Usage, Name Constraints, Policy Constraints, and Policy Mappings.

Security and Infrastructure Integration: The EPM leverages existing CA security infrastructure without requiring new mechanisms. The policy database inherits the CA's physical security, network controls, and access management. Database audit logs integrate with existing monitoring systems that already monitor certificate operations. For enhanced protection, CAs can optionally sign policy documents using the same cryptographic operations used for CRLs, allowing network functions to verify policy authenticity using existing signature verification libraries. Recovery from database compromise follows standard database backup procedures already used for certificate databases, completing in minutes to hours compared to weeks required for CA key compromise recovery.

Revocation: Our proposed framework significantly reduces revocation frequency by eliminating policy-induced revocations. OIDs identify policy types, allowing simultaneous updates for all devices under a policy when it changes. For the remaining legitimate revocations (key compromise, device decommissioning), our framework is compatible with any revocation mechanism like CRL and OCSP.

Enabling PQC: Our framework makes PQC integration significantly more feasible for resource-constrained IoT devices by optimizing both storage and transmission frequency. While PQC algorithms like CRYSTALS-Dilithium require larger signatures, our approach mitigates this overhead in two ways. First, removing embedded policies reclaims certificate space. Second, and more importantly, our design eliminates policy-induced reissuance. By restricting the transmission of these larger certificates to only initial enrollment and rare key compromises, we minimize the bandwidth impact on the network. This makes PQC feasible for 5G IoT devices despite the larger cryptographic payload.

Next, we describe the details of certificate enrollment and revocation on this new PKI architecture.

6.2 Operational Protocol 1: Certificate Enrollment and Authentication

Figure 5 illustrates the complete authentication protocol from device enrollment to policy enforcement.

Steps 1-4: Certificate Enrollment. The IoT device generates a key pair and creates a CSR containing its identity with device type in the OU field (“`iot-sensor`”). The CA receives the CSR, extracts the device type, maps it to policy OID and issues a certificate containing only this OID reference instead of embedding full policy extensions. The CA returns the signed certificate to the device.

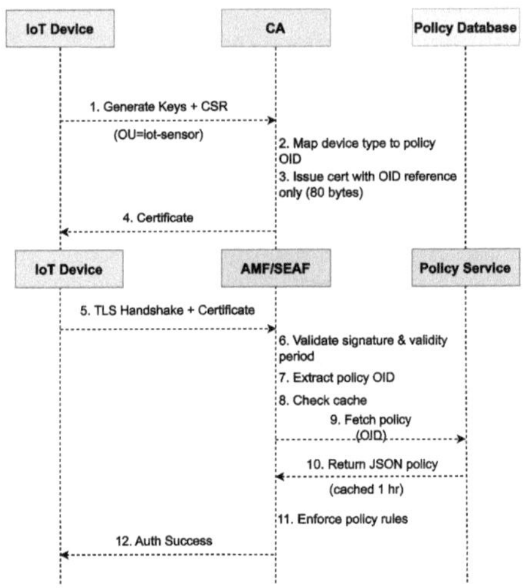

Fig. 5. Certificate Generation and Authentication Flow

Steps 5-7: Initial Authentication. When the device connects to the AMF, it presents its certificate during the TLS handshake. The AMF performs standard X.509 validation and extracts the policy OID from the Certificate Policies extension.

Steps 8-10: Policy Retrieval. The AMF checks its local cache for the policy. On a cache hit, enforcement proceeds immediately with zero external queries. On a cache miss, the AMF queries the policy service, receives the policy document, and caches it with a specific TTL. The AMF extracts the Policy OID from the Certificate Policies extension and conducts a simple API query to the CA's policy service, similar to OCSP revocation checks. No changes are needed for devices (which use standard X.509 certificates), the TLS protocol (retaining its handshake), or CA infrastructure, except for adding the policy database. Legacy network functions can still verify certificate signatures and validity, but will delay policy enforcement until they implement external policy queries.

Steps 11-12: Policy Enforcement. The AMF enforces all policy rules (key usage, permitted networks, allowed protocols, session duration) during session establishment. Authentication succeeds if all validations pass.

This workflow aligns with 3GPP specifications [1] and extends the standard certificate validation process to include external policy retrieval.

6.3 Operational Protocol 2: Revocation Check and Policy Updates

Figure 6 illustrates revocation checking and dynamic policy updates. The process of revocation protocol is explained next.

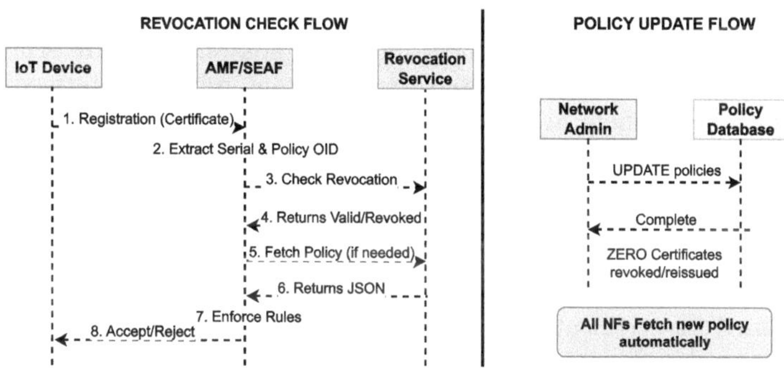

Fig. 6. Revocation Check and Policy Updates Flows.

Steps 1-2: Device initiates registration by presenting its certificate. The AMF extracts the certificate serial number and policy OID.

Steps 3-4: The AMF sends a revocation status query to check if the certificate has been revoked. The revocation service returns "valid" or "revoked" status. This can be implemented using standard mechanisms (CRL or OCSP) [9,27] or cryptographic accumulators [7], as revocation checking is independent of our policy externalization contribution.

Steps 5-7: The AMF fetches the policy (if not cached) and enforces all rules.

Step 8: Registration is accepted or rejected based on validation results.

To modify policies, administrators update the policy definition in the database. The policy update operation is extremely fast compared to traditional certificate reissuance and requires **zero certificate operations**. NFs continue using cached policies until TTL expiry. After expiry, they automatically fetch and enforce the updated policy. All N devices referencing this OID operate under the new policy without certificate modifications.

Backward Compatibility and Incremental Deployment: Our framework maintains full compatibility with existing 5G infrastructure through standard X.509 extensions and TLS protocols, enabling gradual migration without requiring infrastructure changes. Legacy NFs parse these certificates using standard X.509 libraries without modification, as the OID reference occupies the standard Certificate Policies extension field; they simply defer policy enforcement until updated.

7 Security Analysis

The introduction of the EPM framework creates new potential attack vectors (T1-T6 defined in Sect. 5). This section formally analyzes the security properties of our architecture and demonstrates how our framework mitigates these threats while preserving traditional PKI guarantees.

Assumptions: We adopt assumptions of standard PKI [9]: policy databases are co-located within intermediate CA facilities, inheriting existing physical security (HSMs, access controls) used for certificate databases; signature schemes are EUF-CMA secure, and SHA-256 is collision-resistant; multiple intermediate CAs operate with a threshold agreement model where fewer than the threshold are compromised simultaneously; all CA-to-NF communications use mutual TLS; cross-CA verification runs periodically to detect inconsistencies.

A1. Database Co-location: Policy databases reside within intermediate CA facilities, inheriting existing physical security, HSM protection, and network controls used for certificate databases and OCSP responders.

A2. Cryptographic Security: Signature schemes (RSA-2048/ECDSA/ML-DSA) are EUF-CMA secure; SHA-256 is collision-resistant.

A3. Byzantine Tolerance: Framework has n intermediate CAs with threshold k. Fewer than k CAs are compromised simultaneously.

A4. Network Security: All CA-to-NF communications use mutual TLS (deployment requirement). Policy signature verification provides defense-in-depth.

Formal Security Properties: We analyze the security of the proposed framework under threats $T_1 - T_6$ and assumptions $A_1 - A_4$.

1. Certificate Integrity. Certificate signatures are cryptographically equivalent to those in traditional PKI:

$$Sig_{CA}^{trad} = Sign(SK_{CA}, H(Cert||Policy_{embedded}))$$

$$Sig_{CA}^{ours} = Sign(SK_{CA}, H(Cert||OID_{ref}))$$

Both constructions reduce security to the unforgeability of the underlying signature scheme. Therefore, forging either signature requires breaking the signature primitive, which contradicts **A2**. As a result, database-level attacks (**T1, T4**) may alter stored policies but cannot forge certificates or enable device impersonation.

2. Policy Integrity. A policy P is valid only if signed by at least k CAs. Let PK_i denote the public key of CA i, Sig_i the signature from CA i, and $Verify(\cdot)$ the signature verification function (returns 1 if valid, 0 otherwise):

$$Valid(P) \iff |\{i : Verify(PK_i, H(P), Sig_i) = 1\}| \geq k$$

where $|\cdot|$ denotes the counts of the set of CAs that produced valid signatures.

An attacker controlling $m < k$ CAs cannot inject a malicious policy P_{mal}. Such an attacker can produce at most $m < k$ valid signatures, which is insufficient to satisfy the threshold. Any tampering is detected because the computed hash $H(P)$ must match the stored hash h_{stored}, and honest CAs refuse to sign unauthorized policies. Under **A3**, this prevents database tampering (**T1**), unauthorized administrative modification (**T3**), and malware-drive policy manipulation (**T4**), since all require at least k valid CA signatures. However, an attacker controlling all k CAs could sign arbitrary malicious policies, though this requires simultaneously compromising all intermediate CAs (each with independent physical security and HSM-protected keys), representing a catastrophic PKI failure equivalent to root CA compromise.

3. Tamper Detection Bound. Unauthorized modifications are detected within bounded time T_{detect}:

$$T_{detect} \leq \Delta + T_{verify} = 6 \text{ min (worst case)}$$

$$\mathbb{E}[T_{detect}] = \Delta/2 + T_{verify} \approx 3.5 \text{ min (expected)}$$

where Δ is the verification interval and T_{verify} is verification execution time. The timing bounds referenced in this section (detection time, recovery time) are derived from the experimental measurements detailed in Section ??."

Detection occurs via two mechanisms: (1) per-query hash and signature verification, and (2) periodic cross-CA hash comparison. Let DB_i denote the database at CA i. A compromised authority is identified as one whose database disagrees with the majority:

$$CA_{comp} = \{i : |\{j : H(DB_i) = H(DB_j)\}| < \lfloor n/2 \rfloor + 1\}$$

For $n = 3$, at least two matching hashes constitute consensus. As a result, attacks that modify database contents (**T1, T4**) are detected before widespread policy enforcement.

4. SQL Injection Prevention: Parameterized queries treat OID input as literal data rather than executable code:

```
SELECT * FROM policies WHERE policy_oid = ?
```

where ? is a placeholder parameter that gets replaced with the actual OID value through secure binding at execution time. Under standard database semantics,

parameter binding prevents query-structure modification, eliminating SQL injection attacks (**T2**) without measurable performance overhead.
5. Service Continuity under Database Deletion. Complete deletion of all policy databases does not immediately disrupt service. Recovery time $T_{recovery}$ satisfies:

$$T_{recovery} \leq \max(T_{cache}, T_{restore}) = 1 \text{ hour}$$

where cached policies remain unstable for T_{cache} (NF cache time-to-live, typically on the order of hours) and restoration from backup requires at most $T_{restore}$ (comparable to standard database recovery times. Therefore, even coordinated deletion attacks (**T5**) cause only temporary degradation rather than persistent denial of service.
6. MITM Resistance. A network attacker cannot inject a malicious policy P_{mal} because network functions accept a policy only if

$$\sum_{i=1}^{k} Verify(PK_i, H(P_{mal}), Sig_i) \geq k$$

Without access to CA private keys, an attacker cannot produce valid signatures, so the sum evaluates to zero and the policy is rejected. As a result, interception attacks on policy retrieval (**T6**) fail even if transport security is compromised, providing defense-in-depth beyond assumption **A4**.
Comparison to Traditional PKI Recovery: If a CA is compromised, traditional PKI requires revocation, certificate re-issuance, and distribution of revocation lists. This process typically takes weeks. In contrast, our approach allows to detect compromise within approximately 3.5 min, and restores the database using majority consensus in about one minute, and replaces the CA certificate in roughly five minutes. Therefore, total recovery time of the framework remains under ten minutes with no certificate reissuance.

8 Performance Evaluation and Discussion

In this section, we present the experimental analysis of the proposed framework and discuss its implications for real-world deployment.

8.1 Experimental Analysis

We evaluate the proposed framework along three critical metrics: *(1) certificate size and transmission overhead, (2) authentication latency, and (3) policy update efficiency.* Experiments compare traditional PKI against our modified architecture using identical implementations to ensure fair comparison. All experiments were conducted in a simulated 5G environment with Python-based CA, AMF, and IoT device components deployed across three Dell Precision Towers (i9 and i7, 64 GB RAM, 1TB NVMe SSD each) representing CA infrastructure and network functions.

The implementation uses Python 3.x with cryptographic libraries for X.509 operations, SQLite for policy storage, liboqs for PQC ML-DSA (CRYSTALS-Dilithium2), and pycryptodome for accumulator operations on Ubuntu 20.04 LTS.

Policy definitions are stored in an SQLite database as structured JSON documents containing security rules traditionally embedded in the certificates.

Network functions retrieve policies through a REST API with HTTP caching, while each maintains a small in-memory cache with a one-hour default lifetime. To evaluate revocation mechanisms, we implemented both traditional certificate revocation lists and constant-size cryptographic accumulators [7,33], which are proposed to be used for more efficient certificate revocation purposes.

Listing 1.1 shows the **certificate construction process**.

```
# Extract device type from CSR
device_type = csr.subject.get_attributes_for_oid(
   NameOID.ORGANIZATIONAL_UNIT_NAME)[0].value
# Map to policy OID
policy_oid = policy_mapping[device_type]
# e.g., "iot-sensor" -> "1.3.6.1.4.1.99999.1.2.3"
# Build certificate with OID reference only
cert = CertificateBuilder()
    .subject_name(csr.subject)
    .public_key(csr.public_key())
    .add_extension(
        CertificatePolicies([
            PolicyInformation(
                ObjectIdentifier(policy_oid),
                ["https://policy.5g.network/policy/"
                 + policy_oid])]}))
    .sign(ca_key, hashes.SHA256())
```

Listing 1.1. CA Certificate Construction with Policy OID Reference

Figure 4 in Sect. 6.1 shows the experimental network topology deployed on a 1 Gbps LAN. We use RSA-2048, ECDSA P-256, or CRYSTALS-Dilithium2 (via liboqs) certificates. All signatures use SHA-256. Policy cache TTL: 1 h. Certificate validity: 365 days (devices), 10 years (CAs). We implemented two revocation approaches for comparison: 1) CRLs, and 2) accumulators.

Experiment 1: Certificate Size and Transmission Overhead. We compare certificate sizes between traditional embedded-policy certificates and our OID-reference certificates across three cryptographic algorithms: RSA-2048, ECDSA P-256, and CRYSTALS-Dilithium2, as shown in Table 2.

The fixed 416-byte savings from policy externalization reclaim space to offset PQC overhead and enable instant policy updates without certificate reissuance, regardless of the signature algorithm used. This represents a 26.8% reduction for RSA-2048, 30.6% for ECDSA P-256, and 11.2% for Dilithium2, making quantum-resistant cryptography more viable for resource-constrained IoT devices.

Table 2. Certificate Size Comparison Across Cryptographic Algorithms

Algorithm	RSA-2048		ECDSA P-256		ML-DSA	
	Traditional	Ours	Traditional	Ours	Traditional	Ours
Base Certificate (B)	800	800	800	800	800	800
Policy Extensions (B)	496	80	496	80	496	80
Signature (B)	256	256	64	64	2,420	2,420
Total Size (B)	**1,552**	**1,136**	**1,360**	**944**	**3,716**	**3,300**
Reduction (%)	**26.8%**		**30.6%**		**11.2%**	

Experiment 2: Authentication Latency. We measure end-to-end authentication latency from TLS handshake initiation to policy enforcement completion.

As shown in Table 3, our framework achieves a 40.5% increase in authentication speed, mainly due to enhanced policy processing. By externalizing policies, NFs can retrieve pre-structured JSON documents (0.45 ms) instead of dealing with complex ASN.1-encoded certificate extensions (0.89 ms), resulting in a 40.5% reduction in policy processing time. Additionally, the accumulator-based revocation check offers significant speed improvements, being 13.75 times faster than traditional CRLs. The accumulator maintains constant verification time regardless of revocation count, while CRL lookup scales linearly. For 100,000 revocations, accumulator verification remains at 0.12 ms while CRL lookup grows to 782.45 ms, yielding a 6,520× speedup. Core security operations such as signature verification and validity checks remain unchanged, ensuring cryptographic integrity is preserved while delivering substantial performance gains.

Table 3. Authentication Latency Breakdown

Operation	Traditional (ms)	Ours (ms)
Signature Verification	2.34	2.31
Validity Period Check	0.08	0.07
Revocation Check	1.65 (CRL)	0.12 (Accum.)
Policy Processing	0.89 (parse)	0.45 (fetch)
Total Latency	**4.96**	**2.95**
Improvement	**40.5% faster**	

Experiment 3: Policy Update Scalability. A policy update modifies security constraints for devices, such as allowing a new protocol (HTTP), changing permitted network ranges, or migrating devices between slices. In traditional PKI, this requires certificate reissuance for all affected devices, whereas in our approach, only a database modification is needed.

Table 4 compares traditional PKI policy updates against our database-only approach. Traditional times are calculated from our measured CA issuance rate (18.6 certs/sec: 1,000 certificates in 53.8 s) plus deployment overhead. Deployment overhead includes network distribution, device installation, service restart, and CRL

Table 4. Policy Update Time: Traditional vs. Ours

Devices	Traditional	Ours	Speedup
1,000	2.3 min	9.7 ms	14,319×
10,000	23.2 min	9.7 ms	143,505×
100,000	3.9 h	9.7 ms	1.4M×
1,000,000	38.6 h	9.7 ms	14.3M×

updates. We estimate the complete process takes 2.6 times as long as certificate signing alone, consistent with industry reports of 2-5× overhead [16].

For example, while the CA can sign 1,000 certificates in 53.8 s, the complete policy update, including deployment, takes approximately 2.3 min. Modified times represent a single database UPDATE operation (9.7 ms, median of 1,000 trials).

These estimates are conservative, whereas the real-world deployments experience additional delays from network congestion, device failures, geographic distribution, and coordinated rollout requirements, making actual traditional PKI policy updates significantly slower.

Our approach updates policy once in the database, enabling instant, zero-downtime policy changes across millions of devices.

9 Conclusion

In this paper, we presented a novel framework that fundamentally restructures trust management in 5/6G-PKI by decoupling security policy from digital identity. By replacing embedded certificate extensions with lightweight OID references to an External Policy Authority, we achieved a 36% reduction in baseline certificate size, enabled policy updates in under 1 millisecond regardless of deployment scale, and eliminated policy-induced certificate revocations. The framework maintains full backward compatibility with existing X.509 standards and TLS protocols, enabling incremental deployment. Performance evaluations demonstrate 40.5% faster authentication latency and policy update operations that complete 14.3 million times faster for one million devices compared to traditional PKI. By reclaiming certificate space through policy externalization and reducing transmission frequency, our framework makes PQC adoption viable for resource-constrained IoT devices. This fundamental restructuring of trust management provides a practical foundation for meeting the security and scalability demands of current 5G and future 6G networks.

Acknowledgment. This research was funded by the US NSF under the grant No. 2147196.

References

1. 3GPP: System architecture for the 5g system (5gs). (). TS 23.501 Technical Specification 3rd Generation Partnership Project (3GPP) (2019), version 15.4.0
2. 3GPP, B.: Security architecture and procedures for 5g system (2020)
3. 3rd Generation Partnership Project (3GPP): Release 17 description; summary of rel-17 work items. Technical Report (TR) 21.917, 3GPP (Jan 2023). https://portal.3gpp.org/desktopmodules/Specifications/SpecificationDetails.aspx?specificationId=3937

4. 3rd Generation Partnership Project (3GPP): Network domain security (nds); authentication framework (af). Technical Specification (TS) 33.310, 3GPP (Sep 2025). https://portal.3gpp.org/desktopmodules/Specifications/SpecificationDetails.aspx?specificationId=2293
5. Alagic, G., et al.: Status report on the third round of the nist post-quantum cryptography standardization process (2022). https://csrc.nist.gov/publications/detail/nistir/8413/final (2023)
6. Barker, E., Barker, W.: Recommendation for Key Management, Part 2: Best Practices for Key Management Organization. Tech. rep, National Institute of Standards and Technology (2018)
7. Benaloh, J., De Mare, M.: One-way accumulators: a decentralized alternative to digital signatures. In: Workshop on the Theory and Application of of Cryptographic Techniques, pp. 274–285. Springer (1993)
8. Berbecaru, D.G., Lioy, A.: An evaluation of x. 509 certificate revocation and related privacy issues in the web PKI ecosystem. IEEE Access **11**, 79156–79175 (2023)
9. Boeyen, S., Santesson, S., Polk, T., Housley, R., Farrell, S., Cooper, D.: Internet X.509 Public Key Infrastructure Certificate and Certificate Revocation List (CRL) Profile. RFC 5280 (May 2008). https://doi.org/10.17487/RFC5280, https://www.rfc-editor.org/info/rfc5280
10. CA/Browser Forum: Baseline Requirements for the Issuance and Management of Publicly-Trusted Certificates. https://cabforum.org/working-groups/server/baseline-requirements/requirements/ (2025). Accessed 13 Oct 2025
11. Chen, X., Ng, D.W.K., Yu, W., Larsson, E.G., Al-Dhahir, N., Schober, R.: Massive access for 5G and beyond. IEEE J. Sel. Areas Commun. **39**(3), 615–637 (2020)
12. Cooper, D., Santesson, S., Farrell, S., Boeyen, S., Housley, R., Polk, W.: Internet x. 509 public key infrastructure certificate and certificate revocation list (crl) profile. Tech. Rep. (2008)
13. Cybersecurity and Infrastructure Security Agency, National Security Agency, National Institute of Standards and Technology: Quantum-readiness: Migration to post-quantum cryptography. Tech. rep., U.S. Department of Homeland Security (August 2023). https://www.cisa.gov/sites/default/files/2023-08/Quantum%20Readiness_Final_CLEAR_508c%20%283%29.pdf. Accessed 20 Jan 2026
14. De Alwis, C., Porambage, P., Dev, K., Gadekallu, T.R., Liyanage, M.: A survey on network slicing security: attacks, challenges, solutions and research directions. IEEE Commun. Surv. Tutorials **26**(1), 534–570 (2023)
15. Forsby, F., Furuhed, M., Papadimitratos, P., Raza, S.: Lightweight x. 509 digital certificates for the internet of things. In: International Conference on Interoperability in IoT, pp. 123–133. Springer (2017)
16. Gebreamlak, L.M.: PKI: the key to Solving the Internet of Things security problem, Naval Postgraduate School (2020). Ph.D. thesis
17. Hanna, Y., Bozhko, J., Tonyali, S., Harrilal-Parchment, R., Cebe, M., Akkaya, K.: A comprehensive and realistic performance evaluation of post-quantum security for consumer iot devices. Internet of Things **33**, 101650 (2025)
18. Hanna, Y., Pineda, D., Veksler, M., Paudel, M., Akkaya, K., Anastasova, M., Azarderakhsh, R.: (2024) Integrating post-quantum tls into the control plane of 5G networks
19. Joseph, D., et al.: Transitioning organizations to post-quantum cryptography. Nature **605**(7909), 237–243 (2022)
20. Khan, S., et al.: A survey on x. 509 public-key infrastructure, certificate revocation, and their modern implementation on blockchain and ledger technologies. IEEE Communications Surveys & Tutorials **25**(4), 2529–2568 (2023)

21. Larisch, J., Choffnes, D., Levin, D., Maggs, B.M., Mislove, A., Wilson, C.: Crlite: a scalable system for pushing all TLS revocations to all browsers. In: 2017 IEEE Symposium on Security and Privacy (SP), pp. 539–556 IEEE (2017)
22. Laurie, B., Langley, A., Kasper, E.: Certificate transparency. RFC 6962, RFC Editor (Jun 2013https://doi.org/10.17487/RFC6962, https://www.rfc-editor.org/rfc/rfc6962.txt, standard for public, append-only certificate logs
23. Luo, X., Xu, Z., Xue, K., Jiang, Q., Li, R., Wei, D.: Scalacert: Scalability-oriented PKI with redactable consortium blockchain enabled " on-cert" certificate revocation. In: 2022 IEEE 42nd International Conference on Distributed Computing Systems (ICDCS), pp. 1236–1246. IEEE (2022)
24. Malik, M., Kamaldeep, Dutta, M., Granjal, J.: L-ECQV: Lightweight ECQV implicit certificates for authentication in the internet of things. IEEE Access **11**, 35517–35540 (2023). https://doi.org/10.1109/ACCESS.2023.3261666
25. Mazzocca, C., Acar, A., Uluagac, S., Montanari, R.: {EVOKE}: Efficient revocation of verifiable credentials in {IoT} networks. In: 33rd USENIX Security Symposium (USENIX Security 24), pp. 1279–1295 (2024)
26. Mukhopadhyay, S.C., Suryadevara, N.K.: Internet of things: Challenges and opportunities. Internet of things: Challenges and opportunities, pp. 1–17 (2014)
27. Myers, M., Ankney, R., Malpani, A., Galperin, S., Adams, C.: X. 509 internet public key infrastructure online certificate status protocol-ocsp. Tech. Rep. (1999)
28. National Institute of Standards & Technology: Nist announces first four quantum-resistant cryptographic algorithms (Julu 5, 2022). https://www.nist.gov/news-events/news/2022/07/nist-announces-first-four-quantum-resistant-cryptographic-algorithms
29. Park, J.H., et al.: A comprehensive survey on core technologies and services for 5G security: Taxonomies, issues, and solutions. Hum.-Centric Comput. Inf. Sci. **11**(3), 1–22 (2021)
30. Paudel, M., Veksler, M., Akkaya, K.: Lightweight identity-based re-authentication for supporting post-quantum security in 5G. In: Workshop on Security and Privacy of Next-Generation Networks (FutureG), NDSS Symposium (2026). https://doi.org/10.14722/futureg.2026.23079
31. Rafique, W., Barai, J.R., Fapojuwo, A.O., Krishnamurthy, D.: A survey on beyond 5G network slicing for smart cities applications. IEEE Commun. Surv. Tutorials **27**(1), 595–628 (2024)
32. Raza, S., Shafagh, H., Hewage, K., Hummen, R., Voigt, T.: Lithe: lightweight secure CoAP for the internet of things. IEEE Sens. J. **13**(10), 3711–3720 (2013)
33. Ren, Y., Liu, X., Wu, Q., Wang, L., Zhang, W.: Cryptographic accumulator and its application: a survey. Secur. Commun. Netw. **2022**(1), 5429195 (2022)
34. Rommer, S., Hedman, P., Olsson, M., Frid, L., Sultana, S., Mulligan, C.: 5G core networks: powering digitalization, Academic Press (2019)
35. Rupprecht, D., Dabrowski, A., Holz, T., Weippl, E., Pöpper, C.: On security research towards future mobile network generations. IEEE Commun. Surv. Tutorials **20**(3), 2518–2542 (2018)
36. Series, M.: Minimum requirements related to technical performance for IMT-2020 radio interface (s). Report **2410**, 2410–2017 (2017)
37. Shahab, M.B., Abbas, R., Shirvanimoghaddam, M., Johnson, S.J.: Grant-free non-orthogonal multiple access for iot: A survey. IEEE Commun. Surv. Tutorials **22**(3), 1805–1838 (2020)

38. Singh, V.P., Singh, M.P., Hegde, S., Gupta, M.: Security in 5G network slices: concerns and opportunities. IEEE Access **12**, 52727–52743 (2024)
39. Wichary, T., Mongay Batalla, J., Mavromoustakis, C.X., Żurek, J., Mastorakis, G.: Network slicing security controls and assurance for verticals. Electronics **11**(2), 222 (2022)

Cryptographic Agility for Applications: An Assessment Framework and Principled API Design

Navaneeth Rameshan(✉) and Gregoire Messmer

IBM Research, Zurich, Switzerland
vme@zurich.ibm.com, gregoire.messmer@ibm.com

Abstract. The impending post-quantum cryptographic transition requires replacing algorithms across entire software portfolios, yet no systematic method exists for decomposing *cryptographic agility* into assessable dimensions. The term conflates distinct capabilities, including algorithm replacement, policy-driven selection, and implementation substitution, and the absence of a structured decomposition impedes both assessment and principled API design.

We make four contributions. First, we introduce a component-based assessment framework that characterizes application-level cryptographic agility along seven orthogonal dimensions, capturing non-hierarchical profiles that linear maturity models cannot represent. Second, we derive thirteen API design principles from five foundational architectural properties. Third, we demonstrate their realization through concrete Protocol Buffers API patterns. Fourth, we evaluate six representative systems (PKCS#11, OpenSSL 3.0, JCA, Google Tink, AWS KMS, and HashiCorp Vault Transit), revealing three pervasive gaps: most achieve only partial operation decoupling (uniform signatures, but algorithm-specific parameters still leak through) and none reaches intent-based key creation, making algorithm migration a per-site code-change problem; none provides policy-driven algorithm selection, so organizations govern *who* may use cryptography but not *which* algorithms; and most lack the ability to transform existing keys to new algorithms. These gaps are independent and individually sufficient to prevent agile migration, explaining why post-quantum transition remains a code-change problem despite decades of API progress.

Keywords: Cryptographic agility · Post-quantum cryptography · API design · Assessment framework · Key management

1 Introduction

The standardization of post-quantum cryptographic algorithms by the National Institute of Standards and Technology (NIST) in 2024 has initiated what may constitute the most extensive cryptographic transition in the history of deployed

D. Loebenberger and M. Stöttinger (Eds.): MAgiCS 2026, CCIS 3002, pp. 165–185, 2026.
https://doi.org/10.1007/978-3-032-28946-9_9

systems. FIPS 203 (ML-KEM) [5], FIPS 204 (ML-DSA) [6], and FIPS 205 (SLH-DSA) [7] establish new cryptographic primitives for key encapsulation and digital signatures, which must eventually replace RSA and elliptic curve cryptography across billions of devices and applications. With the deprecation of classical algorithms anticipated between 2030 and 2035 [14], addressing the underlying architectural challenges is urgent.

The challenge presented by this transition is not merely algorithmic in nature. Post-quantum cryptographic primitives exhibit fundamentally different characteristics from their classical counterparts: ML-DSA-65 public keys occupy 1,952 bytes compared to 32 bytes for Ed25519, and ML-KEM-768 ciphertexts require 1,088 bytes versus 32 bytes for an X25519 key share. These substantial differences in artifact sizes propagate through protocol designs, storage systems, and network assumptions. However, the more fundamental challenge is architectural. In most deployed systems, cryptographic algorithm choices are embedded directly within application source code [12,13], rendering algorithm migration a software development project that potentially affects thousands of files across hundreds of applications. Experience from prior cryptographic transitions suggests that such migrations require multi-year timelines, which are incompatible with security-driven deprecation schedules.

Cryptographic agility, broadly defined as the ability to change cryptographic algorithms without proportional code modifications [4], is frequently proposed as the solution to this challenge. However, the term is subject to multiple interpretations in the literature and in practice [20], and is context-dependent [16]. In protocols, agility refers to the ability to update cipher suites while maintaining interoperability, while in computing systems, agility requires the ability to adopt new cryptographic algorithms and prevent the use of weak algorithms with minimal disruption to the running system.

The absence of a systematic decomposition impedes assessment, API design, and cross-system comparison alike. We argue that meaningful progress requires a framework that decomposes agility into independently assessable dimensions, identifies the architectural properties that each dimension requires, and derives concrete design principles for cryptographic APIs that realize those properties.

This paper makes four contributions: (1) a component-based assessment framework characterizing cryptographic agility along seven orthogonal dimensions, comprising three coupling dimensions, an orthogonally-applied decoupling mechanism, a governance dimension, and two agility enablers, thereby capturing non-hierarchical profiles that linear maturity models cannot represent; (2) thirteen design principles derived from five foundational properties, with a many-to-many mapping to framework components; (3) concrete Protocol Buffers API patterns realizing these principles; and (4) evaluation of six deployed systems revealing three pervasive and independent gaps: most achieve only partial operation decoupling and none reaches intent-based key creation, none provides policy-driven algorithm selection, and most lack algorithm transformation capability.

2 Background and Motivation

Cryptographic APIs have evolved through three generations, each achieving partial agility while preserving specific forms of coupling. First-generation APIs coupled operations to algorithms: OpenSSL's `RSA_public_encrypt()` and `AES_cbc_encrypt()` require changes at every call site when algorithms change. Second-generation systems (JCA [1], OpenSSL EVP [2], Tink [3]) introduced operation-level abstraction through uniform interfaces (`Cipher`, `EVP_DigestSign*()`, `Aead`), but all couple key creation to algorithms: JCA requires `KeyPairGenerator.getInstance("RSA")`, EVP requires algorithm identifiers at key generation. Third-generation cloud KMS services (AWS KMS, GCP KMS, HashiCorp Vault) add governance through IAM and audit logs, but algorithm coupling persists: all require explicit algorithm specification at key creation, and none support expressing cryptographic intent independently of algorithm selection or changing algorithms after key creation. Each generation removes some coupling while preserving others, motivating the systematic framework we present next.

3 The Cryptographic Agility Assessment Framework

We present a component-based assessment framework (Fig. 1) for cryptographic APIs that characterizes cryptographic agility along orthogonal dimensions rather than a single linear hierarchy. The framework distinguishes between *decoupling*, which creates the conditions under which agility becomes possible, and *agility enablers*, which deliver actual migration capability. This distinction resolves a critical conflation in the literature: a system may be highly decoupled yet unable to migrate existing keys to new algorithms.

3.1 Framework Architecture

The framework comprises seven components organized into two assessment tiers.

Tier 1: Decoupling Assessment. Five components measure how *enabled* for agility a system is. Three *coupling dimensions* measure what application code knows about specific values: C1 (operation coupling, measuring algorithm awareness in cryptographic operations), C2 (creation coupling, measuring algorithm awareness in key creation), and C3 (provider coupling, measuring awareness of where cryptography executes in code). C1 and C2 address algorithm coupling in different API surfaces, while C3 addresses provider coupling. C4 and C5, described below, are not coupling dimensions but rather cross-cutting concerns that apply to them. The *decoupling mechanism* (C4) measures how coupled values are externalized, and applies orthogonally to each coupling dimension. The *authority dimension* (C5) measures who controls the decoupling mechanism. Each component admits a spectrum from minimal to maximal decoupling, denoted C$n.x$ where n identifies the component and $x \in \{0, 1, 2, 3, 4\}$ the level.

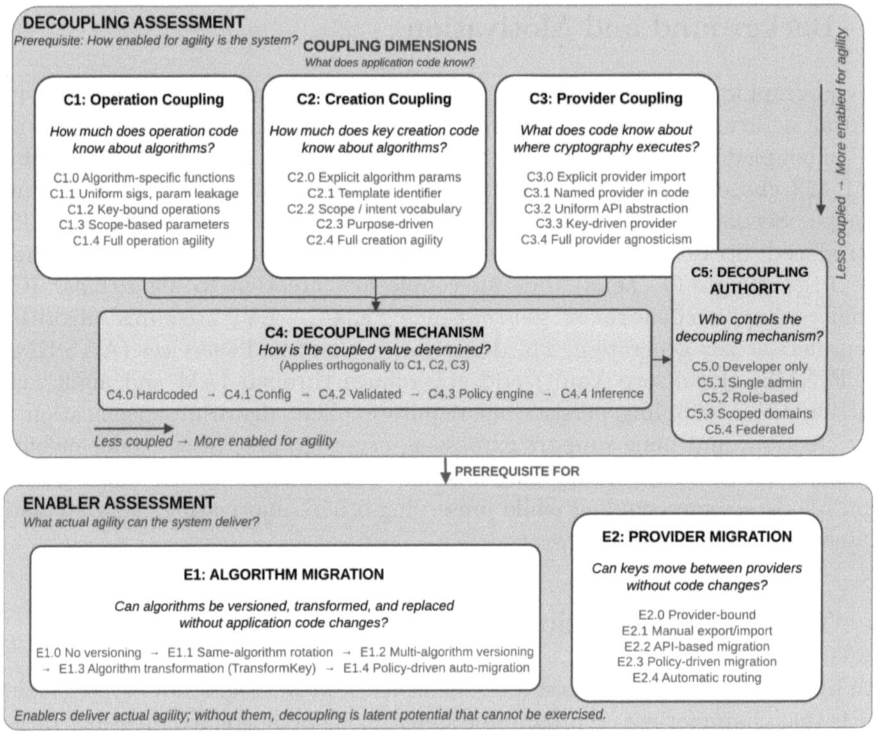

Fig. 1. The Cryptographic Agility Assessment Framework: seven orthogonal components organized into coupling dimensions (C1–C3), decoupling mechanism (C4), decoupling authority (C5), and agility enablers (E1, E2).

Tier 2: Enabler Assessment. Two components (E1, E2) measure what *actual agility* the system can deliver. E1 (algorithm migration) captures the ability to version, transform, and replace algorithms. E2 (provider migration) captures the ability to move keys between providers. These are orthogonal to decoupling but synergistic with it: high decoupling without enablers produces latent potential that cannot be exercised, while enablers without decoupling produce ecosystem-locked agility that cannot be generalized.

Architectural Vocabulary. The framework's higher levels rely on four architectural abstractions whose relationships are worth making explicit. A *scope* is a named intent category grouping algorithms with compatible operational interfaces (e.g., AUTHENTICATED_ENCRYPTION). A *template* is an immutable configuration specifying a concrete algorithm and all its parameters (e.g., `aes-256-gcm`). For consistency with CBOMs [10], they could follow the variants patterns defined by the CycloneDX Cryptographic Registry [11]. A *policy* maps scopes to permitted templates, encoding governance rules such as "use only FIPS-approved algorithms with 256-bit security". A *provider* is an execution backend (software library, HSM, cloud KMS) that implements the cryptographic operations.

3.2 Coupling Dimensions

C1: Operation Coupling. This dimension measures the degree to which cryptographic operation call sites are coupled to specific algorithms. The levels are distinguished by *what category of information* leaks through the operation's parameters. At C1.0, every algorithm requires its own function: `RSA_sign()`, `ECDSA_sign()`, and `ML_DSA_sign()` are distinct entry points, so changing an algorithm requires modifying every invocation. C1.1 introduces a uniform function signature, but all algorithm-specific details leak through parameters: both system-generatable values (IV size, IV etc.) and user-supplied operational parameters (additional authenticated data, domain-separation context etc.) are exposed. For instance, PKCS#11 [9]'s `C_Sign()` accepts a `CK_MECHANISM` structure that encodes algorithm identity, meaning call sites still carry implicit algorithm knowledge. At C1.2, operations dispatch on key identity, removing algorithm identity from the call site, but user-supplied operational parameters (such as AAD or context) may still be algorithm-specific and leak. For example, a signing API may dispatch on key identity and accept an optional `context` field; an application signing with EdDSA provides context bytes, but substituting ECDSA, which does not accept context, would silently discard that input or fail, requiring a code change to remove the field. C1.3 constrains operational parameters to be *scope-consistent*: identical across all algorithms in a scope. Applications can provide inputs such as additional authenticated data or domain-separation context, but because every algorithm in the scope accepts the same parameter structure, substitution within a scope does not break application code. This is the level at which true algorithm substitutability is achieved. C1.4 represents full operation agility: the system generates all algorithm-specific values (IVs, nonces, salts) internally, and application code provides nothing beyond user data. A fundamental *agility–flexibility tradeoff* governs this spectrum: C1.4 achieves maximum agility by removing user choice, but applications requiring deterministic IVs, domain-separation context, or AAD cannot operate at this level. C1.3 strikes a deliberate balance, preserving substitutability through parameter consistency within a scope while allowing the flexibility that real-world applications demand.

C2: Creation Coupling. This dimension measures the abstraction level at which application code expresses key creation requests. At C2.0, the application specifies the algorithm and its parameters directly: `algorithm="RSA", key_size=2048`. Any change to the algorithm requires modifying every key creation call site, which is precisely the problem that makes migration intractable at scale. C2.1 introduces a layer of indirection through *template identifiers*. A template is a named, immutable configuration that fully specifies an algorithm and all its parameters (key size, mode, padding scheme); the application requests `template="rsa-2048-oaep-sha256"` rather than enumerating these values individually. While this simplifies key creation, the template name still encodes algorithm identity, so migration still requires code changes. The qualitative shift occurs at C2.2, where applications express cryptographic intent through a scope vocabulary: `scope=AUTHENTICATED_ENCRYPTION`. At this level, the application declares *what* it needs without specifying *how* it should be accomplished, and the system (via policy or default configuration) selects an appropriate algorithm. C2.3 raises abstraction to purpose-driven requests (`purpose="sign audit logs"`), and C2.4 represents full abstraction where the system infers everything from context.

The critical design challenge at C2.2 is *scope boundary design*. Scopes must group algorithms with compatible operational parameters so that substitution does not break application code. An overly broad scope (e.g., grouping AES-GCM and RSA-OAEP, which have incompatible interfaces) creates substitution hazards; an overly narrow scope (e.g., `AES_256_GCM_SCOPE`) eliminates the abstraction benefit. Our recommendation is to derive scopes from cryptographic primitives (AEAD, digital signature, KEM) and subdivide where operational parameters diverge, for example separating standard signatures from context-bearing signatures. Performance and artifact differences are treated as filter properties, not scope boundaries.

C3: Provider Coupling. This dimension measures the degree to which application code is coupled to a specific cryptographic implementation or execution environment. At C3.0, the provider is an explicit compile-time dependency: `import cryptography.hazmat` binds the application to a particular library. Changing providers requires modifying import statements and adapting to a different API surface. C3.1 introduces named provider selection within a uniform framework: JCA's `Signature.getInstance("RSA", "BC")` selects the Bouncy Castle provider by name, meaning the application knows *which* provider to use but interacts through a standard interface. At C3.2, the application interacts with a uniform API abstraction where the same interface functions identically regardless of whether the backend is a software library, a hardware security module, or a cloud service. C3.3 extends this to key-driven provider selection: the provider is determined by where the key resides, so applications that reference a key stored in an HSM automatically route operations to that HSM without explicit provider specification. C3.4 represents full provider agnosticism, where the system manages all provider routing decisions transparently.

3.3 Decoupling Mechanism and Authority

C4: Decoupling Mechanism. *How is the coupled value determined?* C4 measures how coupled values are externalized, and applies independently to each coupling dimension (C1, C2, C3).

At C4.0, values are hardcoded in source code, so any change requires code modification, compilation, testing, and redeployment. C4.1 externalizes the value to a configuration file: the application reads algorithm names, template identifiers, or provider names from configuration rather than embedding them in code. This permits algorithm changes without code changes, but the configuration is unconstrained, meaning an administrator can specify an invalid or insecure algorithm without detection. C4.2 adds schema-based validation that rejects invalid configurations at load time, preventing semantically incorrect selections (e.g., specifying a signing algorithm for an encryption scope). The qualitative shift to C4.3 introduces a policy engine: rather than direct value lookup, the system applies rules-based mapping with semantic validation, conditional logic, and audit trails. A policy can express constraints such as "for production environments, use only FIPS-approved algorithms with 256-bit security" and enforce them automatically. C4.4 represents full contextual inference, where the system determines appropriate values from the operational context without explicit configuration.

The orthogonal application of C4 is the framework's key structural innovation. A system at C1.1 may apply C4.0 to C1 (algorithm parameters hardcoded in operations), C4.3 to C2 (key creation governed by policy), and C4.1 to C3 (provider from configuration), each independently assessed. However, C4 is applicable to a coupling dimension only when that dimension retains a coupled value: at C1.2+, operations carry no algorithm identity, so C4 on C1 is structurally inapplicable, because the coupling has been eliminated rather than externalized.

C5: Decoupling Authority. *Who controls the decoupling mechanism?* At C5.0, the developer is the sole authority: all cryptographic decisions are made in source code, and no external actor can influence them. C5.1 introduces a single administrator who can modify configuration or policy, but without role differentiation, so that one person controls everything. At C5.2, role-based authority enables different actors to control different aspects: a security architect may define approved algorithms, a compliance officer may enforce FIPS requirements, and a developer may select from the approved set. C5.3 introduces scoped governance domains, where different organizational contexts (e.g., production vs. development, financial vs. healthcare) can have independent policies managed by different authorities. C5.4 represents federated governance with policy inheritance and composition, enabling hierarchical organizations to define enterprise-wide baselines that business units extend.

C5 is meaningful only when C4 $\geq$ C4.1. Without externalized values, there is nothing to govern. Crucially, C5.2 (role-based *access* authority) is distinct from C5.3+ (authority over *cryptographic selection*); this distinction is examined in the system evaluations of Sect. 6.

3.4 Agility Enablers

While decoupling determines how *enabled* for agility a system is, enablers determine whether actual agility can be *achieved*. Without enablers, even a perfectly decoupled system cannot migrate keys to new algorithms or move them between providers.

E1: Algorithm Migration. *Can algorithms be versioned, transformed, and replaced without application code changes?*

At E1.0, no versioning capability exists: adopting a new algorithm requires creating an entirely new key and updating all references to it, a manual process that scales poorly across large deployments. E1.1 introduces same-algorithm rotation, where new key material is generated under the same algorithm and the key identifier is preserved. This addresses key hygiene and limits the exposure window of compromised material, but it cannot change the underlying algorithm. At E1.2, the system supports multi-algorithm versioning with automatic selection: a single key identity can encompass versions using different algorithms (e.g., version 1 with ECDSA, version 2 with ML-DSA-65), and the system automatically uses the latest version for new operations while retaining the ability to verify or decrypt with older versions. E1.3 provides explicit algorithm transformation through an operation such as `TransformKey()`, which migrates a key's active algorithm via a separate operation that can be access controlled. E1.4 represents policy-driven automatic migration, where the system monitors policy changes and triggers algorithm transformations without manual intervention.

The distinction between E1.1 and E1.3 is critical for the post-quantum transition: same-algorithm rotation cannot transform an RSA-2048 key into an ML-DSA-65 key, whereas algorithm transformation (E1.3) enables precisely this cross-algorithm migration.

E2: Provider Migration. *Can keys and operations move between providers without application code changes?*

At E2.0, keys are permanently bound to the provider that created them: a key generated in an HSM cannot be moved to a cloud KMS, and a key in AWS KMS cannot be transferred to Azure Key Vault. E2.1 introduces manual export and import capabilities, where an administrator can extract key material from one provider and load it into another through an out-of-band process. At E2.2, the system provides an explicit API for provider migration, specifically `MigrateKey(key_name, target_provider)`, that handles the transfer, re-wrapping, and metadata update in a single coordinated operation. E2.3 extends this to policy-driven migration, where organizational policies can trigger automatic key migration (e.g., moving all software-backed keys to a different provider when a compliance requirement changes). E2.4 represents fully automatic provider routing, where the system dynamically selects providers based on operational context such as latency, availability, or cost.

Critically, provider migration is constrained by legitimate security requirements: HSM-bound keys are non-exportable by design, and the optimal E2 level depends on the security model rather than on maximizing flexibility.

3.5 Constraints and Post-quantum Implications

Six structural constraints govern valid component combinations. Externalization (C4.1+) applied to operations requires at least C1.1 (one cannot externalize what is not parameterized), and applied to providers requires at least C3.1 (the provider must be selectable). Policy-based selection (C4.3+) requires a scope vocabulary through which policies express constraints. Governance (C5.2+) requires externalization on at least one dimension, since without externalized values there is nothing to govern. Algorithm transformation (E1.3+) is most effective with policy-driven selection (C4.3+), and provider migration (E2.2+) is constrained by the security model: HSM non-extractability is a feature, not a limitation. These constraints are structural rather than hierarchical. A system can achieve high C3 decoupling with low C2, as PKCS#11 demonstrates, which distinguishes our framework from linear maturity models.

The framework directly quantifies post-quantum readiness: at C2.0/C4.0/E1.0, ECDSA-to-ML-DSA migration requires code changes at every key creation site; at C2.2/C4.3/E1.3, policy triggers transformation of existing keys, reducing multi-year migration projects to operational procedures. Hybrid schemes (e.g., Ed25519+ML-DSA-65) are accommodated at the template layer with compatible parameters.

4 API Design Principles for Cryptographic Agility

The assessment framework of Sect. 3 characterizes where a system stands. This section addresses what API design provisions are required to advance along those dimensions. We derive thirteen principles by analyzing the functional requirements that each framework component imposes on API surfaces, identifying five foundational architectural properties, and codifying the resulting obligations as design principles. The relationship between components and principles is many-to-many, mediated by the foundational properties from which both emerge.

4.1 Five Foundational Properties

We identify five architectural properties that underpin cryptographic agility. **Abstraction** separates interface from implementation at multiple boundaries: algorithm-agnostic operations, intent-based key creation, and provider abstraction, each decoupling different concerns. **Stability** ensures that application interfaces remain consistent despite underlying changes: operation signatures, scope semantics, and API contracts persist when algorithms, mappings, or providers change. **Temporal Flexibility** enables decisions to be made or modified at times other than code authorship: algorithm selection at configuration, policy modification at deployment, and provider selection during operations. **Separation** distributes control among actors with appropriate authority, so that security teams govern policies without code access, developers invoke operations without policy authority, and operations teams select providers without changing algorithms. **Extensibility** accommodates unknowns at design time, ensuring that new post-quantum algorithms, security properties, and compliance requirements can be integrated without API modifications.

4.2 The Thirteen Design Principles

The five properties above establish what an agile API must *be*; the principles below specify what it must *do*. Each principle addresses a concrete obligation that at least one framework component imposes: for example, C1.2 requires algorithm-agnostic operations (Abstraction), which yields P1; C2.2 requires an intent vocabulary (Abstraction + Stability), which yields P3 and P4; C5.3 requires actor separation (Separation), which yields P7. Because components impose overlapping obligations, the resulting mapping is many-to-many.

We present thirteen principles organized by the foundational property they primarily provide, classified into two categories:
Core Principles are necessary conditions for cryptographic agility. Violating any core principle creates a structural barrier to algorithm or provider substitution that cannot be overcome by strengthening other dimensions. Some core principles include an *applicability threshold* (e.g., "C3.2+") indicating the component level at which the principle becomes architecturally actionable; these thresholds are not markers of optionality but rather prerequisites for the principle's realization. The framework treats all seven dimensions as essential for comprehensive agility, and the core principles collectively address all of them.
Supportive Principles improve system quality and adoption but are not prerequisites for agility itself.

Core Principles P1: Operation Independence (*Abstraction*). *Cryptographic operations must be independent of algorithms.* Operation signatures must be defined by cryptographic goals and must contain no algorithm-specific parameters, enabling C1.2+ decoupling; otherwise, changing algorithms requires modifying every call site.

P2: Temporal Decoupling (*Temporal Flexibility*). *Decisions made at different times must be changeable independently.* It must be possible to change deployment-time decisions (such as algorithm selection) without modifying code-authorship-time decisions (such as which operations to invoke), because cryptographic agility fundamentally requires changing algorithms *after* code is written.

P3: Intent-Based Specification (*Abstraction*). *Applications must express cryptographic intent, not cryptographic implementation.* Applications should specify what they need (e.g., authenticated encryption) and any required properties (e.g., quantum safety), with the system selecting an appropriate algorithm. This enables C2.2+ creation decoupling, because without an intent vocabulary, key creation remains coupled to specific algorithms.

P4: Operational Parameter Consistency (*Stability*). *All algorithms satisfying the same intent must require identical operational parameters.* This is a correctness requirement for scope design: if algorithms within a scope require different parameters, substitution causes runtime failures.

P5: Key Abstraction (*Stability*). *Keys must be referenced by stable identifiers, not by material or algorithm.* Key identifiers must remain valid across algorithm rotations, provider migrations, and policy changes, because identifiers that encode algorithm identity (e.g., `ecdsa-key-001`) force all references to change when the algorithm changes.

P6: Key Evolution (*Temporal Flexibility*). *Keys must be able to evolve without breaking existing data.* It must be possible to rotate keys to new algorithms without changing their identifiers, while maintaining version history for continued access to data encrypted or signed under previous versions.

P7: Separation of Concerns (*Separation*) [*actionable at C5.3+*]. *Those who use cryptographic services must be distinct from those who govern cryptographic policy.* This separation enables independent evolution of application logic and security governance.

P8: Algorithm–Implementation Separation (*Separation*) [*actionable at C3.2+*]. *Algorithm specifications must be structurally separate from implementation capabilities.* The choice of algorithm must be independent of the choice of provider. Because algorithm specifications and provider configurations have different lifecycles (algorithms change infrequently while provider routing may change operationally), they must be managed independently to prevent entanglement.

P9: Implementation Portability (*Abstraction*) [*actionable at C3.2+, E2.1+*]. *Cryptographic implementations must be substitutable without application code changes.* This enables organizations to switch providers in response to security, compliance, or operational requirements.

P10: Policy-Engine Independence (*Extensibility*) [*actionable at C4.3+*]. *The policy engine implementation must be pluggable.* The API should reference policies by name without mandating a specific syntax, language, or storage mechanism for the policy itself.

Supportive Principles P11: Language Independence (*Abstraction*). *APIs should use language-neutral specifications to maximize cross-platform adoption.* Formats such as Protocol Buffers or OpenAPI enable this, although language-specific APIs like JCA demonstrate that full algorithm agility is achievable within a single language ecosystem.

P12: Property Taxonomy (*Extensibility*). *Algorithm and provider properties should be categorized by purpose.* Distinguishing filtering, informational, and implementation properties improves the usability of intent-based specification by giving applications a structured vocabulary for expressing preferences.

P13: Discoverable Extensibility (*Extensibility*). *New algorithms and providers should be addable and discoverable at runtime.* This ensures that the system can accommodate post-quantum and future algorithms as they are standardized without requiring changes to the API definition itself.

The ten core principles collectively address all seven framework dimensions: P1–P6 address algorithm coupling (C1, C2), decoupling mechanism (C4), and algorithm migration (E1); P7 and P10 address governance (C5) and policy infrastructure (C4.3+); P8–P9 address provider coupling (C3) and provider migration (E2). The applicability thresholds (e.g., P8 at C3.2+) indicate when a principle becomes architecturally actionable.

5 API Design Patterns: Principle Realization

This section bridges the gap between abstract principles and concrete implementation by demonstrating how each design principle from Sect. 4 manifests in API surface design. The binding chain runs: application $\xrightarrow{\text{requests}}$ scope $\xrightarrow{\text{policy selects}}$ template $\xrightarrow{\text{dispatches to}}$ provider. Agility arises because each link can be changed independently: policy can remap scopes to different templates (algorithm agility), and templates can be served by different providers (provider agility), all without modifying application code. We present Protocol Buffers patterns that realize these principles; the patterns generalize to other interface definition languages and provide reproducible guidance for practitioners.

5.1 Algorithm-Agnostic Operations (P1)

Principle P1 requires operations containing no algorithm parameters:

```
message SignRequest {
  string key_name = 1;
  bytes input = 2;
  oneof signature_context {
    NoSignatureContext no_context = 3;
    ContextBearingSignatureContext context = 4;
  }
}
```

The key identified by `key_name` carries a persistent algorithm association established at creation; `Sign(key_name, input)` is identical regardless of algorithm. The `signature_context` oneof is defined by *scope*, not by algorithm family. Algorithms within the standard signature scope (ECDSA, RSA-PSS) require no context, while algorithms within the context-bearing signature scope (EdDSA, ML-DSA, SLH-DSA) all accept a domain-separation context byte string with identical semantics. Because the context type is scope-level, transforming a key from EdDSA to ML-DSA requires no application code change: both use `ContextBearingSignatureContext`. This is the mechanism by which P4 (parameter consistency within a scope) is realized. P1 prohibits algorithm-specific *parameters*, not scope-level context; the oneof distinguishes scopes with different operational requirements, not algorithms within a scope. Every response includes `OperationMetadata` (key version, template, algorithm parameters) that must be stored with ciphertext for correct decryption after key transformation.

5.2 Intent-Based Key Creation and Policy (P3, P4, P10)

Principles P3, P4, and P10 determine how applications express cryptographic intent:

```
message CreateKeyRequest {
  string name = 1;
  string policy = 2; // Named reference: "production-fips"
  ScopeSpecification scope_spec = 3;
}
message ScopeSpecification {
  CryptoScope scope = 1; // e.g., SIGNATURE_SCOPE_STANDARD
  map<string, string> required_properties = 2;
}
```

Applications request `scope=SIGNATURE_SCOPE_STANDARD` rather than `algorithm=ed25519`, expressing intent (P3). The scope ensures parameter consistency (P4), and the `policy` field names an external policy as a string rather than a structured document, enabling pluggable policy engines (P10). Performance and artifact-size differences are treated as filter properties, not scope boundaries. Filter properties like {`quantum_safe: true`} narrow template selection to post-quantum algorithms.[1]

5.3 Provider Portability and Key Evolution (P8–P9, P5, P6)

Principles P8–P9 require algorithm specifications and provider configurations managed independently; P5 and P6 require stable key identifiers across algorithm changes:

```
message TemplateInfo { string template_id = 1; repeated CryptoScope
    scopes = 2; }
message ProviderInfo { string provider_id = 1; ProviderType type = 2; }
message RotateKeyRequest { string key_name = 1; }
message TransformKeyRequest {
  string key_name = 1;
  ScopeSpecification new_scope_spec = 2;
}
message MigrateKeyRequest { string key_name = 1; string target_provider =
     2; }
```

The `TemplateInfo` type answers "what algorithm?" while `ProviderInfo` answers "where is it implemented?" Keys bind to both independently. The pattern distinguishes **rotation** (`RotateKey`: new material, same algorithm) from **transformation** (`TransformKey`: new algorithm, same identity, e.g.,

[1] The `ScopeSpecification` listing is simplified for presentation. The implementation uses a `oneof` with per-primitive typed specifications (e.g., `SignatureScopeSpec`, `AeadScopeSpec`) and typed security properties rather than a flat map, providing compile-time safety.

ECDSA → ML-DSA-65) from **migration** (`MigrateKey`: new provider, same algorithm). Key names remain stable across all three operations and version history maintains accessibility of historical data.

5.4 Temporal Decoupling and Separation of Concerns (P2, P7)

Principles P2 and P7 require that decisions made at different times are independently changeable and that application logic is structurally separated from security governance. The API enforces both through service-level and operation-level separation:

```
// Three structurally separate gRPC services (P7):
service CryptoService { rpc Sign(...); rpc Encrypt(...); ... }
service AlgorithmDiscoveryService { rpc ListTemplates(...); ... }
service ProviderService { rpc RegisterProviderInstance(...); ... }

// Governance separated from usage within CryptoService (P7):
message TransformKeyRequest { string name = 1; // Change algorithm
  ScopeSpecification scope_spec = 2; }
message UpdateKeyPolicyRequest { string name = 1; // Change governance
  string new_policy = 2; }
message MigrateKeyRequest { string name = 1; // Change provider
  string target_instance_id = 2;
  MigrationStrategy strategy = 3; }
```

The three-service architecture enforces P7 structurally, not merely by convention: an application granted access to `CryptoService` cannot modify provider configurations or algorithm registrations, because those operations belong to separate services with independent access control. Within `CryptoService`, `TransformKey` (algorithm change), `UpdateKeyPolicy` (governance change), and `MigrateKey` (provider change) are distinct RPCs with different field structures, enabling IAM policies that grant application teams transform access without policy-modification privileges.

P2 manifests through three temporal layers, each with its own API surface. At **code authorship**, developers write `Sign(key_name, input)` with no algorithm knowledge. At **deployment**, `CreateKey(scope_spec, policy)` binds intent to a policy-selected algorithm. At **runtime**, `UpdateKeyPolicy(name, new_policy)` changes which algorithms are permitted, without modifying application code or re-creating keys. Each layer can evolve independently because none encodes decisions belonging to another: application code contains no algorithm identifiers, key creation no provider choices, and policy changes need no redeployment.

6 Evaluation: System Assessment Against the Framework

We apply the assessment framework to six representative cryptographic systems, spanning the three API generations identified in Sect. 2: libraries (PKCS#11,

OpenSSL 3.0), frameworks (JCA, Tink), and managed services (AWS KMS, HashiCorp Vault Transit). For each system, we assigned component positions by examining the public API surface, official documentation, and source code where available. The assessment criteria are the level definitions from Sect. 3: each system is placed at the highest level whose conditions it fully satisfies for each component dimension. We evaluate systems standalone capabilities without interpretation for what consumers of those systems can abstract in order to have a consistent and objective comparison. Table 1 summarizes the results.

Table 1. System assessment: qualitative agility profiles. †Value read from configuration rather than hardcoded (C4.1). *Operations* (C1): Uniform sig (C1.1) = shared function signature but algorithm-specific parameters leak through; Key-dispatch (C1.2) = dispatch on key metadata with no algorithm parameters; Fully managed (C1.4) = system handles all parameters including nonces/IVs. *Key Creation* (C2): Raw params (C2.0) = explicit algorithm and parameters; Named tmpl (C2.1) = named template identifiers. *Provider* (C3): Hardcoded (C3.0) = compile-time dependency; Named (C3.1) = named provider selection within uniform framework; Uniform API (C3.2) = provider-agnostic interface; Key-driven (C3.3) = provider determined by where key resides. ‡Enterprise only (managed keys). *Governance* (C5): Access ctrl (C5.2) = role-based authority over who may use which operations. *Algo. Migr.* (E1): Same-algo (E1.1) = same-algorithm key rotation; Multi-algo (E1.2) = multi-algorithm versioning with automatic selection. *Prov. Migr.* (E2): Manual exp. (E2.1) = manual export/import via wrap/unwrap.

System	Operations	Key Creation	Provider	Governance	Algo. Migr.	Prov. Migr.
PKCS#11	Uniform sig	Raw params	Uniform API	None	None	Manual exp.
OpenSSL 3.0	Uniform sig	Raw params	Named†	None	None	None
JCA	Uniform sig	Raw params	Named	None	None	None
Google Tink	Fully managed	Named tmpl	Hardcoded	None	Multi-algo	None
AWS KMS	Uniform sig	Named tmpl	Uniform API†	Access ctrl	Same-algo	Manual exp.
Vault Transit	Key-dispatch	Named tmpl	Key-driven‡	Access ctrl	Same-algo	Manual exp.

6.1 System-by-System Assessment

PKCS#11. Uniform function signatures (`C_Sign()`, `C_Encrypt()`) decouple operations from algorithms at the API level, but the `CK_MECHANISM` parameter still encodes algorithm identity, placing operations at C1.1. Key creation requires explicit mechanism specification (C2.0). The slot/token abstraction provides a uniform interface across HSM vendors (C3.2), but the slot identifier is a programmatic parameter to `C_OpenSession()` with no built-in configuration mechanism. All three coupling dimensions are hardcoded in application code (C4 at 0 on C1, C2, and C3). No governance layer exists (C5.0). Migration is limited to manual `C_WrapKey`/`C_UnwrapKey` sequences (E2.1), and there is no key versioning capability (E1.0).

OpenSSL 3.0. The EVP layer provides uniform function signatures (`EVP_DigestSign*()`, `EVP_EncryptUpdate()`), but algorithm-specific values leak through `OSSL_PARAMS`: AES-CCM requires `msglen` before encryption, and tag-length parameters differ across AEAD modes. Swapping AES-GCM for AES-CCM requires adjusting these parameters, placing operations at C1.1 rather than C1.2. The provider architecture introduced in version 3.0 supports named backend selection (C3.1), with the provider name typically loaded from `openssl.cnf` (C4 at 1 on C3). Key creation remains algorithm-explicit (C2.0), with algorithm identifiers hardcoded in source (C4 at 0 on C1 and C2). As a library rather than a service, OpenSSL provides no governance (C5.0), no key versioning (E1.0), and no provider migration capability (E2.0).

Java Cryptography Architecture (JCA). Engine classes (`Cipher`, `Signature`) provide uniform operation interfaces, but algorithm names appear as string parameters (`Cipher.getInstance("AES/GCM/NoPadding")`), placing operations at C1.1. The provider model supports named provider selection (`getInstance(alg, "BC")`), corresponding to C3.1. Key creation is a two-step process: key generation selects the algorithm family, then algorithm-specific parameters are supplied. This constitutes C2.0 rather than C2.1. Unlike OpenSSL's `openssl.cnf`, JCA provides no built-in configuration mechanism for algorithm or provider selection; all three coupling dimensions are hardcoded in application source (C4 at 0 on C1, C2, and C3). No governance or migration capabilities exist (C5.0, E1.0, E2.0).

Google Tink. Primitive interfaces (`Aead`, `PublicKeySign`) represent cryptographic intent rather than algorithms, achieving C1.4 (no operational parameters beyond user data). Key creation, however, uses algorithm-specific template names (`AES128_GCM`, `ECDSA_P256_SHA256`) rather than intent-based scopes, placing it at C2.1 (named templates) rather than C2.2. Keyset management provides multi-algorithm versioning with automatic selection (E1.2): a single keyset can contain versions under different algorithms, and Tink automatically uses the primary version for new operations while retaining backward compatibility with older versions. Despite these strengths, algorithm and provider selections are hardcoded in keyset configuration (C4.0 on C2 and C3; C4 on C1 is inapplicable since operations carry no algorithm identity). No external policy mechanism exists to change algorithms without modifying the keyset itself, no governance layer is provided (C5.0), and provider portability is deliberately excluded (C3.0, E2.0). Tink thus achieves agility through *restrictiveness* (C1.4) and *versioning* (E1.2) rather than externalized decoupling, delivering ecosystem-internal agility.

AWS KMS. Operations use uniform function signatures, but algorithm identity leaks through required parameters: the `Sign` API requires a `SigningAlgorithm` argument (e.g., `ECDSA_SHA_256`), placing operations at C1.1. Key creation uses named key specifications (`KeySpec=ECC_NIST_P256`) rather than raw algorithm-plus-parameter sets, corresponding to C2.1, with algorithm selections hardcoded (C4 at 0 on C1 and C2). AWS KMS supports multiple key store types (default HSMs, custom key stores backed by CloudHSM, and external key stores) with an identical API surface regardless of backing store. The key store is selected at configuration time rather than in application code, placing provider abstraction at C3.2 (C4 at 1 on C3). Key material can be imported via `ImportKeyMaterial` and external key stores allow material to reside outside AWS (E2.1).

AWS KMS provides role-based access authority through IAM (C5.2): distinct roles receive distinct permissions for key creation, usage, and management. However, IAM governs *who* may create keys with *which* algorithms, not *which algorithms satisfy which intents.* IAM can express "Service X may create RSA_2048 keys" (access control) but cannot express "for signing intent, use ML-DSA-65" (cryptographic selection policy). This distinction places AWS KMS at C5.2 (role-based access authority) rather than C5.3+ (authority over cryptographic algorithm selection). Key rotation is supported within the same algorithm (E1.1), but cross-algorithm transformation is unavailable, precluding E1.3.

HashiCorp Vault Transit. The `/transit/sign/` and `/transit/encrypt/` endpoints dispatch on key configuration with no algorithm parameters (C1.2). Key creation uses named type identifiers (`type="ecdsa-p256"`, `"aes256-gcm96"`), corresponding to C2.1, with type values hardcoded in requests (C4 at 0 on C2). Enterprise Vault supports managed keys backed by PKCS#11 HSMs or cloud KMS services; the Transit API surface is identical regardless of backend, and operations route to the HSM hosting the key without explicit provider specification (C3.3). Vault policies provide role-based access control (C5.2) but do not govern algorithm selection. Key rotation is same-algorithm only (E1.1). Keys can be exported (when `exportable=true`), imported via `/transit/keys/:name/import`, and transferred between Vault instances using `byok-export` (E2.1).

6.2 Synthesis and Gap Analysis

Three patterns emerge from this evaluation:

Pattern 1: Operation Decoupling is Partial; Creation Decoupling Absent. All six systems achieve C1 at position 1 or higher, but four of six remain at C1.1, where algorithm identity and system-generatable parameters (mechanism identifiers, IV size, tag length) still leak through uniform signatures. Changing algorithms across parameter boundaries (e.g., AES-GCM to AES-CCM, which requires different tag-length handling) requires modifying call sites. Only Tink (C1.4) avoids this leakage fully, at the expense of flexibility; Vault (C1.2) avoids it partially. Meanwhile, no evaluated system achieves C2.2 (intent-based key creation): all six require algorithm-specific identifiers at key creation, making algorithm migration a per-site code-change problem.

Pattern 2: Access Authority Exists; Cryptographic Governance Does Not. AWS KMS and Vault both reach C5.2 (role-based access authority) through IAM and ACL policies respectively, but no evaluated system achieves C5.3+. Organizations routinely conflate access authority (*who may use which keys*) with cryptographic governance (*which algorithms satisfy which intents*), and the C5 dimension makes this conflation precise. An organization with sophisticated IAM may believe it has policy-driven cryptography while algorithm selection remains hardcoded (C4 at 0 on C2). Bridging this gap requires both externalized selection (C4.3+) and an intent vocabulary (C2.2+).

Pattern 3: Enablers are the Missing Dimension. The most striking gap lies in the enabler components. No system reaches E1.3 (algorithm transformation); only Tink achieves E1.2 (multi-algorithm versioning), and only AWS KMS and Vault provide E1.1 (same-algorithm rotation). Provider migration is uniformly weak (E2 at 0 or 1). Consequently, even where systems are reasonably decoupled, they cannot act on it: existing keys cannot be transformed to new algorithms, and encrypted data cannot be re-encrypted under stronger primitives.

The Orthogonal Advantage. The component-based framework reveals profiles that a linear model would obscure. Tink achieves high coupling decoupling (C1 at 4, C2 at 1) and strong algorithm migration (E1 at 2) without any externalized decoupling mechanism (C4 at 0 throughout). PKCS#11 and JCA both achieve C2 at 0 but differ sharply on C3 (2 vs. 1). These non-hierarchical profiles demonstrate that cryptographic agility comprises genuinely independent dimensions, achievable through different architectural strategies.

6.3 Threats to Validity

The framework's dimensions were derived from deployed-system analysis rather than formal specification, and alternative decompositions are possible. System assessments relied on public APIs and source code, so undocumented capabilities may shift individual scores, though cross-cutting patterns (e.g., the universal absence of C5.3+) are robust to minor changes. Six systems spanning three API generations were evaluated; broader coverage may reveal additional dimensions.

7 Related Work

Application-Level Agility in APIs. Tink [3], SecAlgo [18], EverCrypt [21], and eUCRITE [15] abstract over algorithm identity by exposing primitive-level interfaces (e.g., AEAD, digital signature), so that call sites need not change when the underlying algorithm is replaced. Among these, only Tink supports key rotation and only SecAlgo allows selecting the cryptographic library. Abstraction does not only benefit agility but also security as it limits API misuse [8].

Frameworks for systems agility. ELCA [22] introduces a centralized cryptographic configuration service, and Cho et al. [17] propose a software-defined cryptography layer. Both target microservice architectures with policy-driven algorithm selection. In both cases the provider API is opaque and our work complements theirs by defining the agility requirements and design principles that such providers must satisfy.

Assessment Frameworks. Existing frameworks define maturity levels and risk metrics for organizational crypto-agility [19,23–25] but specify limited requirements for agile cryptographic APIs. Our component-based model fills this gap at the API level.

8 Conclusion

We introduced a component-based framework that characterizes cryptographic agility along seven orthogonal dimensions and derived thirteen API design principles realized through Protocol Buffers patterns. Evaluation of six systems reveals three pervasive gaps: most achieve only partial operation decoupling—uniform signatures but algorithm-specific parameters still leak (C1.1)—and none reaches intent-based key creation (C2.2), making migration a per-site code-change problem. None provides policy-driven algorithm selection or algorithm transformation, so organizations govern *who* may use cryptography but not *which algorithms satisfy which intents*, and temporal separation of code-authorship, deployment, and governance decisions remains the unrealized foundation for reducing multi-year migrations to operational procedures.

References

1. Sun Microsystems. Java Cryptography Architecture (1997)
2. OpenSSL Project. EVP Cryptographic Functions. https://www.openssl.org/. Accessed 30 Mar 2026
3. Duong, T., Nguyen, Q.: Tink cryptographic library. Google (2018). https://github.com/tink-crypto. Accessed 30 Mar 2026
4. Housley, R.: Cryptographic algorithm agility guidelines. RFC 7696 (2015). https://doi.org/10.17487/RFC7696
5. NIST. FIPS 203: ML-KEM standard (2024). https://doi.org/10.6028/NIST.FIPS.203
6. NIST. FIPS 204: ML-DSA standard (2024). https://doi.org/10.6028/NIST.FIPS.204
7. NIST. FIPS 205: SLH-DSA standard (2024). https://doi.org/10.6028/NIST.FIPS.205
8. Green, M., Smith, M.: Developers are not the enemy! IEEE Secur. Priv. (2016). https://doi.org/10.1109/MSP.2016.111
9. PKCS #11 Cryptographic Token Interface Current Mechanisms Specification Version 3.0. Edited by Chris Zimman and Dieter Bong. OASIS Standard (2020). https://docs.oasis-open.org/pkcs11/pkcs11-curr/v3.0/os/pkcs11-curr-v3.0-os.html. Accessed Mar 30 2026
10. CycloneDX. CBOM Standard v1.6 (2023)
11. CycloneDX v1.7. Cryptographic Registry. https://cyclonedx.org/registry/cryptography/. Accessed Mar 30 2026
12. Lazar, D., Chen, H., Wang, X., Zeldovich, N.: Why does cryptographic software fail? A case study and open problems. In: Proceedings of the 5th ACM/IEEE Asia-Pacific Workshop on Systems (APSys) (2014). https://doi.org/10.1145/2637166.2637237

13. Acar, Y., Backes, M., Fahl, S., Kim, D., Mazurek, M.L., Stransky, C.: Comparing the usability of cryptographic APIs. In: Proceedings of the IEEE Symposium on Security and Privacy (S&P) (2017). https://doi.org/10.1109/sp.2017.52
14. NIST. SP 1800-38: Migration to Post-Quantum Cryptography (Draft) (2024). https://csrc.nist.gov/pubs/sp/1800/38/iprd-(1). Accessed Mar 30 2026
15. Zeier, A., Wiesmaier, A., Heinemann, A.: eUCRITE 1.0 API—usable cryptographic interface. Version 1.0 (2020). https://cspub.h-da.io/eucrite/. Accessed 6 Feb 2026
16. Barker, E., et al.: Considerations for achieving crypto agility: strategies and practices: national institute of standards and technology, Gaithersburg, MD (2025). https://doi.org/10.6028/NIST.CSWP.39
17. Cho, J., Lee, C., Kim, E., Lee, J., Cho, B.: Software-defined cryptography: a design feature of cryptographic agility. https://arxiv.org/abs/2404.01808. Accessed 30 Mar 2026
18. Kane, C., Lin, B., Chand, S., Stoller, S.D., Liu, Y.A.: High-level cryptographic abstractions. In: Proceedings of the 14th ACM SIGSAC Workshop on Programming Languages and Analysis for Security, pp. 31–43. (2019). https://doi.org/10.1145/3338504.3357343
19. Ma, C., Colon, L., Dera, J., Rashidi, B., Garg, V.: CARAF: crypto agility risk assessment framework. J. Cybersecur. (2021). https://doi.org/10.1093/cybsec/tyab013
20. Näther, C., Herzinger, D., Steghöfer, J.-P., Gazdag, S.-L., Hirsch, E., Loebenberger, D.: Toward a common understanding of cryptographic agility – a systematic review (2025). https://arxiv.org/abs/2411.08781. Accessed 30 Mar 2026
21. Protzenko, J., et al.: EverCrypt: a fast, verified, cross-platform cryptographic provider. In: 2020 IEEE Symposium on Security and Privacy (SP), pp 983–1002 (2020). https://doi.org/10.1109/SP40000.2020.00114
22. Sikeridis, D., et al.: ELCA: introducing enterprise-level cryptographic agility for a post-quantum era software-defined cryptography: a design feature of cryptographic agility (2023). https://arxiv.org/abs/2404.01808. Accessed 6 Feb 2026
23. FS-ISAC Post-Quantum Cryptography Working Group. Building Cryptographic Agility in the Financial Sector: Effective, Efficient Change in a Post Quantum World. Financial Services Information Sharing and Analysis Center (FS-ISAC) (2024). https://www.fsisac.com/hubfs/Knowledge/PQC/BuildingCryptographicAgilityInTheFinancialSector.pdf. Accessed 6 Feb 2026
24. Alliance for Telecommunications Industry Solutions. Strategic Framework for Crypto Agility and Quantum Risk Assessment. ATIS-I-0000098 (2024). https://atis.org/resources/strategic-framework-for-crypto-agility-and-quantum-risk-assessment/. Accessed 6 Feb 2026
25. Hohm, J., Heinemann, A., Wiesmaier, A.: Towards a maturity model for crypto-agility assessment. In: Jourdan, G.-V., Mounier, L., Adams, C., Sèdes, F., Garcia-Alfaro, J. (eds.) Foundations and Practice of Security, pp. 104–119. Springer, Cham (2023). https://doi.org/10.1007/978-3-031-30122-3_7

Post-quantum Blockchains with Agility in Mind

Manuel B. Santos(✉), Danno Ferrin, Ron Kahat, and Michael Lodder

Tectonic Labs, Miami, Florida, USA
manuel.batalha.santos@gmail.com, {danno,ron,mikelodder}@tectonic.xyz

Abstract. Blockchains intend to provide long-term integrity guarantees through cryptographic primitives that may become vulnerable over time due to algorithmic advances or paradigm shifts such as quantum computation. While cryptographic agility, the ability to transition between algorithms without disrupting operation, is recognized as essential, existing blockchain systems lack comprehensive support for such transitions. We address this gap by designing an Ethereum virtual machine (EVM) compatible blockchain that introduces support for cryptographic agility from genesis.

We first propose a flexibility framework that characterizes how algorithm choice can be distributed across blockchain components. We then present two technical contributions aligned with this framework: (1) cryptographically agile transactions (CATX), a new transaction format that decouples body and signature to enable user-selected signature schemes; and (2) a consensus-layer key registration mechanism that allows validators to migrate between signature schemes as operational upgrades without hard forks. We exemplify the agility of our design with ECDSA, Falcon-512, and ML-DSA signatures by conducting experimental evaluations over 30,000 blocks and 11 million transactions, showing that the CATX format introduces no measurable overhead.

Keywords: Cryptographic agility · Post-quantum cryptography · Blockchain

1 Introduction

Blockchains provide decentralized trust through cryptographic verification rather than reliance on trusted third parties. Unlike centralized systems where data can be modified, blockchains are designed to be persistent and immutable, providing long-term integrity guarantees. Their security relies on multiple building blocks, including the consensus layer, execution layer, transaction mechanisms, and peer-to-peer communication protocols. These components are built on cryptographic primitives such as hash functions (e.g., SHA-256 [1], Keccak [2]) and digital signature schemes, making them foundational to blockchain integrity [38].

Historical precedent shows that cryptographic primitives can become vulnerable due to algorithmic advances (e.g., MD5 [60], SHA-1 [56]), implementation

D. Loebenberger and M. Stöttinger (Eds.): MAgiCS 2026, CCIS 3002, pp. 186–208, 2026.
https://doi.org/10.1007/978-3-032-28946-9_10

flaws, or paradigm shifts such as quantum computation [53]. Given the long-term lifespan of blockchains, systems must be able to transition cryptographic primitives without disrupting operation. This ability, referred to in NIST CSWP 39 as cryptographic agility [13], is essential for sustaining security over time. However, the properties that make blockchains valuable also create challenges when cryptographic primitives must be updated, replaced, or deprecated, making cryptographic agility a fundamental design feature.

The most immediate threat to blockchain cryptography comes from quantum computers. Current systems rely heavily on elliptic curve signature schemes such as ECDSA [3] and EdDSA [14], which are vulnerable to cryptographically relevant quantum computers via Shor's algorithm [53]. Despite this risk, migration to post-quantum cryptography remains slow. A survey of over 14,000 blockchain users found that although quantum threats are widely acknowledged, 58.8% stated that post-quantum security is "not important" when choosing chains or applications [5]. This perception gap, combined with coordination challenges, deployment processes that risk network forks, and long-term backward compatibility requirements for legacy accounts, significantly delays transition efforts.

These challenges help explain why major blockchain systems such as Bitcoin [48] and Ethereum [22] currently lack cryptographic agility, and why platforms with partial agility support, including Hedera [11] and Cosmos [42], still struggle with comprehensive post-quantum transitions. Existing analysis, such as NIST CSWP 39 [13], also lack an overview of current approaches and best practices to achieve crypto agility in decentralized systems. This paper addresses these gaps by designing a blockchain with cryptographic agility as a foundational principle from genesis, enabling secure cryptographic transitions as threats evolve while preserving the persistence and immutability that define blockchains.

1.1 Our Contribution

We propose an Ethereum virtual machine (EVM)-based blockchain that addresses cryptographic agility needs in different layers of the protocol stack to allow future migrations and post-quantum support. More specifically, we present the following contributions.

- *Flexibility framework* (Sect. 3). We propose a framework that specifies how cryptographic algorithm choice can be addressed. We identify three flexibility types (singular, negotiated, selected), and map each blockchain layer to the appropriate type based on its coordination constraints.
- *Cryptographically agile transactions* (Sect. 4). We design CATX, a new transaction format that decouples transaction body from signature into independent components with explicit type identifiers. This enables users to select their signature algorithm without protocol changes, following the selected flexibility type.
- *Consensus key agility* (Sect. 5). We introduce a mechanism to migrate the consensus-specific signature scheme as an operational upgrade via consensus-layer transactions, with activation gated by voting power $> 2/3$.

- *Experimental evaluation* (Sect. 6). We evaluate the performance impact of post-quantum cryptography across the protocol stack, measuring transaction throughput under various signature schemes. We identify block size, not computation, as the limiting factor for larger post-quantum signatures.

1.2 Related Work

The blockchain industry has recognized the quantum threat for over a decade, prompting various high-profile projects to adopt distinct approaches to post-quantum security. We examine existing efforts, dividing them into chains requiring migration and post-quantum-native solutions.

Chains Requiring Migration. Solana introduced the Winternitz vault in January 2025 [59], a sophisticated construction based on the Winternitz one-time signature [20]. The vault mechanism employs programmatic address derivation to compress signatures, achieving post-quantum security while mitigating blockspace overhead. However, this opt-in, application-layer solution creates a fragmented security landscape where only proactive users gain protection while the majority remain vulnerable. Moreover, vaults must be instantiated through standard transactions that themselves rely on quantum-vulnerable elliptic curve (EC)-based signatures, leaving the bootstrapping process exposed.

Algorand
pioneered post-quantum implementations among major blockchains, introducing State Proofs in 2022, consisting of post-quantum secure certificates signed by validator supermajorities using Falcon signatures [9,37]. While State Proofs represent a significant achievement, other aspects of Algorand continue to rely on quantum-vulnerable cryptography: transaction signatures use EC cryptography, and the consensus mechanism depends on a classical verifiable random function [10]. Since Algorand launched without post-quantum security from genesis, its transition process faces the coordination and migration difficulties inherent to protocol-wide cryptographic upgrades.

Bitcoin's migration discourse centers on several community proposals under active discussion. The prominent draft by Lopp [45] outlines a phased approach: Phase A would prohibit transactions to legacy quantum-vulnerable address types (P2PK, P2PKH) three years after BIP-360 [15] implementation, forcing new UTXOs (unspent transaction output) into quantum-resistant formats (P2QRH). Phase B would invalidate transactions from legacy addresses after a fixed period, freezing unmigrated funds. However, these approaches have met with skepticism within the community. The viability of such migrations depends heavily on the BIP-32 wallet standard [16], creating problems for non-conforming wallets such as paper wallets.

Ethereum has adopted a comprehensive research approach through multiple initiatives [32,34]. For user-level transaction signing, post-quantum migration remains under heavy research without concrete implementation plans. While account abstraction (EIP-4337) [29] has been proposed as a potential enabling technology [33], theoretical proposals involving STARK proofs face significant practical challenges including substantial computational overhead and unclear migration paths. At the consensus layer, Ethereum researchers investigate quantum-resistant alternatives for BLS signatures in Proof-of-Stake [27]. Despite this theoretical sophistication, Ethereum's approach faces enormous coordination challenges affecting every layer of the protocol stack, requiring consensus among globally distributed stakeholders.

Baldimtsi et al. [12] presents a migration strategy for EdDSA-based chains with backward compatibility. However, this approach lacks the cryptographic agility necessary for future transitions beyond the initial post-quantum migration, as it relies on proving knowledge of the seed used in EdDSA key derivation.

Post-Quantum Chains and Solutions. Several academic works propose blockchain transition schemes. Sato et al. [52] proposes a scheme inspired by long-term signature schemes, but assumes availability of a secure timestamping service and a trusted public key infrastructure (PKI), requiring decentralization of the PKI system with critical practical consequences and added governance issues. Meng and Chen [47] work further develops and formalizes the transition scheme, but does not take into account API and data format details in blockchain implementations, presenting transitions only at a conceptual level addressing hash and signature schemes rather than specific blockchain subsystems. Fukuda and Matsuo [35] highlights migration issues but only mentions generic migration paths.

Among existing chains, Quantum Resistant Ledger (QRL) [58] uses XMSS signatures [21] for post-quantum security, implementing a cap on the number of signatures generated and an address format that allows for different signature schemes. However, QRL is not an EVM-based chain, limiting its compatibility with the broader Ethereum ecosystem. QANplatform [50] incorporates ML-DSA [55] signatures for cross-chain signing, but this addresses only a narrow aspect of post-quantum security rather than the comprehensive stack-wide problems. The platform lacks cryptographic agility in its design, focusing on a single post-quantum primitive without migration mechanisms. The Quantus design [54] addresses post-quantum security in both peer-to-peer (P2P) node communication and transaction layers. However, Quantus follows a Proof-of-Work consensus mechanism, whereas our approach uses Proof-of-Stake, creating fundamental architectural differences in how consensus and security are achieved. Neptune Cash [57] implements post-quantum cryptography, but lacks modularity and does not incorporate cryptographic agility or migration strategies in its design, making future transitions difficult.

2 Preliminaries

2.1 Definitions

Definition 1 (Digital Signatures). *A digital signature scheme is a tuple of algorithms* $(\mathsf{KeyGen}, \mathsf{Sign}, \mathsf{Verify})$ *defined as follows:*

- $(\mathsf{pk}, \mathsf{sk}) \leftarrow \mathsf{KeyGen}()$*: generates a public/private key pair.*
- $\sigma \leftarrow \mathsf{Sign}(\mathsf{sk}, m)$*: produces a signature* σ *on message* m*.*
- $\{0, 1\} \leftarrow \mathsf{Verify}(\mathsf{pk}, \sigma, m)$*: returns 1 if the signature is valid, 0 otherwise.*

A signature scheme is correct if $\mathsf{Verify}(\mathsf{pk}, \mathsf{Sign}(\mathsf{sk}, m), m) = 1$ *for all messages* m *and corresponding keypairs* $(\mathsf{pk}, \mathsf{sk})$*, and secure if it satisfies EUF-CMA (existential unforgeability under chosen-message attack) [46].*

The elliptic curve digital signature algorithm (ECDSA) [3] is a digital signature scheme based on elliptic curves. In Ethereum [61], ECDSA is instantiated over the secp256k1 curve, and a signature on a message m consists of three components: $(\mathtt{r}, \mathtt{s}, \mathtt{v})$, where $\mathtt{r}$ and s are 32-byte integers and $\mathtt{v}$ is a recovery parameter. The recovery parameter $\mathtt{v}$ encodes information about the parity of the public key y-coordinate. Therefore, given $(\mathtt{r}, \mathtt{s}, \mathtt{v})$ and m, the public key can be uniquely determined without explicitly transmitting it. This property is exploited in Ethereum during transaction validation [61, Appendix F].

2.2 EVM-Based Blockchains

Blockchains are decentralized systems for maintaining a shared, append-only ledger among a set of untrusted parties. Instead of relying on a central authority, a blockchain uses cryptographic techniques, such as hash functions and digital signatures, and distributed consensus to ensure that all parties agree on the order and contents of recorded transactions.

Ethereum virtual machine (EVM)-based blockchains [22] organize their protocol stack into distinct layers, each responsible for a specific functionality. Next, we describe the four primary layers of blockchain systems.

Transactions. Transactions are the units of state change in a blockchain. In Ethereum, transactions use recursive length prefix (RLP) encoding [61, Appendix B] as the canonical serialization format, providing deterministic encoding. Since EIP-2718 [28], Ethereum transactions follow a typed envelope format:

$$\mathtt{Tx} = \mathtt{type} \mathbin{\|} \mathsf{RLP}(\mathtt{payload}),$$

where type is a single-byte identifier distinguishing transaction formats (e.g., 0x02 for EIP-1559 fee market transactions). This typed structure enables protocol evolution by allowing new transaction formats and we redesign it to accommodate different signature schemes (cf. Sect. 4).

Execution Layer. The execution layer (EL) consists of nodes, called clients, which verify and execute transactions and update the network's global state. This involves executing smart contract bytecode in a virtual machine. A specific category of operations in EVM bytecode are precompiled contracts, which offer efficient implementations of computationally intensive cryptographic functions that would otherwise be prohibitively expensive to execute.

Consensus Layer. The consensus layer (CL) secures the integrity of block finalization, ensuring all honest nodes agree on the canonical chain of blocks. Byzantine fault tolerant (BFT) [19,43] consensus protocols enable agreement even when some validators behave maliciously.

In weighted BFT systems such as Tendermint [19], each validator has an associated voting power and a block is finalized when validators representing more than 2/3 of voting power sign commit messages for that block. The consensus proceeds in rounds consisting of three phases: *Propose* (proposer broadcasts a candidate block), *Prevote* (validators vote for the proposal), and *Precommit* (validators commit upon seeing sufficient prevotes). We use this structure to allow for cryptographic agility in the validator's signature scheme used (cf. Sect. 5).

P2P Communication Layer. The peer-to-peer (P2P) layer enables nodes to discover each other and exchange messages without centralized coordination. This layer consists of two main components: a discovery protocol that maintains a distributed hash table (DHT) for peer discovery, and a transport protocol that establishes secure communication channels.

In Ethereum's execution layer, the Discv4 protocol [31] enables peer discovery via UDP gossip. Discovery packets are authenticated using ECDSA signatures with public key recovery, binding messages to node identities. The RLPx transport protocol [30] then establishes encrypted sessions between discovered peers using ECIES [36] for key agreement.

3 Cryptographic Flexibility in Blockchains

Cryptographic agility (CA) is a design principle that enables systems to adapt their cryptographic algorithms over time without disrupting their live functioning [13]. In this section, we introduce some principles established by NIST Cybersecurity White Paper (CSWP) 39 [13] to enable effective cryptographic agility and highlight the unique challenges blockchains face in adopting them. We then present a flexibility framework that characterizes how algorithm choice can be distributed across blockchain participants, providing a lens through which to analyze the design space for cryptographic transitions.

3.1 Challenges

NIST CSWP 39 [13] establishes a set of principles that enable effective cryptographic agility. Among others, it stresses the need for: algorithm identification through ciphersuite negotiation and naming conventions; modularity that separates cryptographic algorithms from application logic, enabling algorithms to be treated as interchangeable components; policy and mechanism separation that allows cryptographic policies to be stored in configuration files rather than hard-wired in source code; and mechanisms for preserving interoperability during transitions. Additionally, systems must handle the deployment of algorithm transitions, which can take years when new infrastructure is required, and manage cryptographic keys associated with deprecated algorithms through proper key expiration and revocation procedures.

While the NIST principles provide a foundation for cryptographic agility in traditional systems, each concept faces unique challenges when applied to blockchain environments. More specifically, ciphersuite negotiation, which works effectively in point-to-point protocols like TLS [51], becomes impractical among an unbounded number of distributed nodes. Modularity is limited when protocols depend on algorithm-specific properties rather than using cryptography as a black box. For instance, KZG [41] commitments are tied to specific data types, and BLS [18] signatures are chosen specifically for their aggregation properties, making drop-in replacements non-trivial. Moreover, preserving interoperability presents asymmetric challenges between blockchain entities, as different participants face different coordination constraints (discussed in Sect. 3.2). Key lifecycle management is particularly problematic in blockchains, where addresses serve as long-lived identities tied to deprecated algorithms, making key expiration and revocation difficult to implement without disrupting user accounts. Finally, deploying algorithm transitions in consensus scenarios is more complex than in centralized systems. Indeed, not all nodes upgrade simultaneously, making it difficult to determine which nodes are honest, potentially leading to forks and increased vulnerability to 51% attacks during transition periods.

3.2 Flexibility Framework

The challenges outlined in Sect. 3.1 demonstrate that blockchain systems cannot adopt traditional cryptographic agility principles wholesale. Instead, cryptographic agility in blockchains is best understood as a design space where different components require different degrees of flexibility based on their coordination constraints, which we unfold next.

Coordination Constraints. Different blockchain participants face different pressures when cryptographic algorithms change. Node operators actively manage staking collateral and operations, enabling them to coordinate quickly: when consensus-critical vulnerabilities emerge, the economic cost of non-compliance (missed rewards, slashing, chain splits) creates strong incentives for rapid, synchronized upgrades. The patching of CVE-2018-17144 within days [17] exemplifies this dynamic. For these stakeholders, hard transitions at defined upgrade points are operationally feasible. However, even for node operators, hardware adoption can present significant barriers. Many hardware security modules

(HSM) lack support for certain post-quantum algorithms (e.g., Falcon [49]), and operational constraints such as long HSM purchasing and refresh cycles can slow down cryptographic migration. This makes it necessary to support multiple signature schemes to accommodate different business and hardware timelines, even among participants who are otherwise willing to coordinate.

End users, by contrast, interact with the chain sporadically and cannot be expected to upgrade in lockstep. Also, they lack a comparable pressure to migrate since their funds may remain accessible under legacy schemes and the quantum threat may feel distant [5]. Ideally, a user who returns after some period of time should not discover that their funds are inaccessible because they failed to migrate during a specific time frame. Therefore, for user-facing components, the system should support multiple algorithms simultaneously, allowing gradual adoption without forcing coordinated action. This trade-off is supported by the selected flexibility type (Sect. 3.2) below, which shifts the burden of multi-algorithm support to validators.

These asymmetries, between those who operate the network and those who use it, determine which flexibility strategies are feasible for each layer.

Flexibility Types. We characterize cryptographic agility along a flexibility spectrum that captures how algorithm choice is distributed across participants. This spectrum ranges from enforcement of a single algorithm to full user-side choice, with a negotiated type in between:

- *Singular.* Exactly one algorithm is permitted system-wide at any point in time. All participants must use the same algorithm, which simplifies verification logic but creates a single point of cryptographic failure: if that algorithm is broken, the entire system is compromised. This model suits components where all parties can coordinate upgrades synchronously.
- *Negotiated.* Both communicating parties select an algorithm from the intersection of their individually supported sets. This approach is standard in point-to-point protocols but difficult to generalize to decentralized systems where transactions must be validated by an unbounded set of nodes without prior negotiation.
- *Selected.* One party unilaterally chooses an algorithm from a protocol-defined allowed set. This shifts flexibility to the edge where users can adopt new algorithms at their own pace. The tradeoff is that verifiers must maintain implementations of all supported algorithms.

Mapping Blockchain Components. Based on the flexibility framework and the coordination constraints, we propose the following positioning for our design.

Transactions: Selected. Since transactions originate from users who cannot be forced to upgrade synchronously, legacy wallets must remain functional while users adopt post-quantum signatures at their own pace. We therefore adopt a selected model where senders choose their signature algorithm from an allowed set, and all nodes processing transactions (EL clients) must support verification of every algorithm in that set. The CATX transaction format (Sect. 4) enables this by encoding algorithm identifiers directly in the transaction structure, decoupling signature schemes from transaction semantics. User migration from legacy to post-quantum schemes proceeds through wallet creation and fund transfer: a user generates a new keypair under the target scheme (e.g., ML-DSA-44), derives a new address from that keypair, and transfers funds from their legacy address via a standard transaction. This approach requires no protocol-level coordination but it changes the user's on-chain address.

Execution Layer: Selected. On-chain cryptographic operations exposed via precompiled contracts follow the same selected model as transactions. Smart contracts invoke signature-specific precompiles, and the execution layer must support all algorithms in the allowed set. This enables contracts to adopt new cryptographic primitives without requiring protocol upgrades for each addition.

Consensus Layer: Singular. Consensus requires all validators to agree on block validity using identical verification logic. Supporting multiple signature algorithms would complicate fork-choice rules and increase the attack surface during transitions. We therefore adopt a singular model where all validators use the same algorithm (Falcon-512 [49] in our implementation). Section 5 details a migration mechanism for transitioning between singular algorithms without requiring a hard-fork and based on consensus.

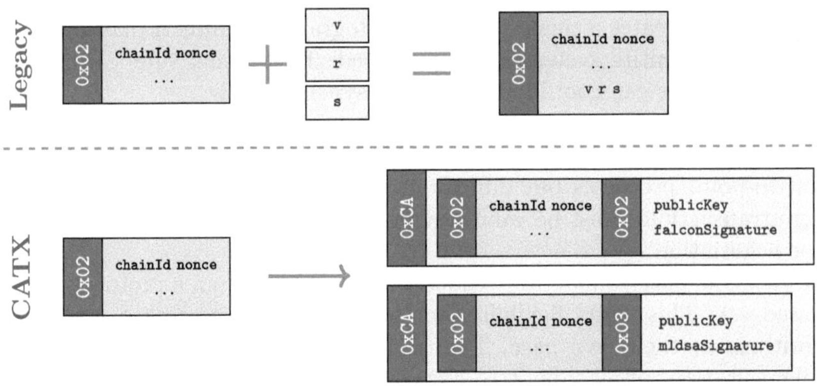

Fig. 1. Legacy transactions (top) embed ECDSA signature fields directly into the body. CATX (bottom) wraps body and signature as separate typed components within a `0xCA` envelope, enabling different signature schemes.

P2P Communication: Singular. The peer-to-peer layer establishes secure channels between nodes. Because P2P participants are node operators who can coordinate upgrades, a transition to new algorithms is feasible.

4 CATX

In this section, we propose a new transaction format as traditional Ethereum transaction formats have a fundamental barrier to cryptographic agility through their deep integration of ECDSA signatures into the transaction structure [23]. The signature components, specifically the recovery parameter `v` and the signature values `r` and `s` (cf. Sect. 2), are directly embedded within the RLP-encoded transaction payload along with its body data (e.g., `chainId`, `nonce`) as exemplified below with EIP-1559 [23] (Type `0x02`):

$$\text{Tx} = \texttt{0x02} \parallel \mathsf{RLP}\begin{pmatrix} \texttt{chainId, nonce, maxTip, maxFee, gasLimit,} \\ \texttt{destination, amount, data, accessList, v, r, s} \end{pmatrix}.$$

This design creates several limitations that prevent cryptographic agility. First, the transaction format assumes a public key recovery mechanism. This represents a concrete case of the modularity challenge identified in Sect. 3.1: the transaction protocol is not designed to use cryptographic primitives in a black box manner, but rather depends on specific properties of ECDSA (namely, public key recovery) that are baked into the transaction structure itself.

Second, the signature structure is hardcoded into the transaction serialization format, violating the modularity principle discussed before. Unlike point-to-point protocols such as TLS, where cryptographic algorithms can be negotiated at runtime through ciphersuite selection, blockchain transactions must be validated by an unbounded set of distributed nodes without prior negotiation. This distributed validation requirement, as discussed in Sect. 3.1, makes runtime algorithm negotiation impractical and necessitates that the cryptographic algorithm be encoded directly in the transaction format.

CATX Design. To address the above issues, we present cryptographically agile transactions (CATX), which introduces transaction type `0xCA` that achieves cryptographic modularity. As shown in Fig. 1, CATX design maintains the same core transaction items and base signing object as traditional Ethereum transactions, but package it into a self-contained blob. The core crypto agile innovation lies in separating the transaction body from its signature, enabling independent evolution of transaction semantics and cryptographic primitives. CATX structure can be described as follows:

$$\texttt{Tx} = \texttt{0xCA} \parallel \texttt{bodyType} \parallel \mathsf{RLP}(\texttt{bodyData}) \parallel \texttt{sigType} \parallel \mathsf{RLP}(\texttt{sigData}).$$

This design choice creates four independent components: body type (`bodyType`), body data (`bodyData`), signature type (`sigType`) and signature data (`sigData`).

The body type identifies the transaction body format, allowing for multiple transaction body formats and each identified by a unique body type value (e.g., `0x02` for fee market EIP-1559 transactions). The body data contains the transaction semantics (e.g., chain ID, nonce, gas parameters). This body type registry allows new transaction formats to be added without affecting signature handling. The signature type identifies the cryptographic signature algorithm, enabling pluggable cryptographic schemes. This follows the crypto agility norm of algorithm identification [13], where an identifier is used for an implementation to tell the verification peer which algorithm is being used. For our experiments, we set the following algorithm identities: `0x01` for ECDSA-secp256k1, `0x02` for FALCON-512 and `0x03` for ML-DSA-44. Finally, the signature data contains the algorithm-specific signature material. For ECDSA, the signature data contains the standard three parameters (`v`, `r`, `s`). Post-quantum signatures might have support for extractable public key from a signature. Depending on the signature type supported, specified by `sigType`, the verification precompile input pattern accepts two variants: (`pubKey` || `signature` || `digest`) or (`extractableSignature` || `digest`).

Message Digest. Post-quantum signature algorithms typically support signing messages of arbitrary length [55]. At first glance, it may therefore seem natural to sign the transaction data directly. However, for consistency with the ECDSA-based design, we instead adopt a message-digest approach, since ECDSA only accepts 32-byte inputs. Concretely, under CATX the signed message is

$$\texttt{digest} = \mathsf{Keccak256}\,(\texttt{bodyType} \parallel \mathsf{RLP}(\texttt{bodyData}))\,.$$

This design choice offers two main advantages. First, it preserves compatibility with the existing ECDSA workflow, improving interoperability with current tooling, and enabling signatures to be treated as a black box. Second, in the presence of large transactions, signing the full message can significantly impact certain signing environments (e.g., key management systems), whereas a fixed-size digest avoids these limitations.

Address Derivation. For externally owned accounts (EOAs) that do not rely on ECDSA and instead use post-quantum signature schemes, a mechanism is required to map a public key to an address. To support multiple signature schemes while preserving cryptographic agility and enabling smooth migration, address derivation follows a structure similar to that used for ECDSA-based accounts. To separate concerns across different signature types, a signature identifier (`sigType`) is appended to the public key prior to hashing. Concretely, addresses are derived by

$$\texttt{address} = \mathsf{Keccak256}\,(\texttt{sigType} \parallel \texttt{pubKey})\,.$$

4.1 Precompiles in Execution Layer

Beyond EOAs, Ethereum supports a growing number of smart contract wallets that rely on EVM execution logic for authentication. Account abstraction proposals such as ERC-4337 [29] enable smart contracts to define custom signature verification logic, opening a potential path for post-quantum cryptography:

contracts could implement post-quantum signature verification directly in EVM bytecode.

However, the EVM is highly inefficient for the low-level arithmetic required by post-quantum signature schemes. Benchmarks show that pure-EVM verification of Falcon-512 signatures consumes approximately 6.6 million gas, while ML-DSA-44 verification requires approximately 13.5 million gas [62,63].

To address this limitation, we expose post-quantum signature verification as precompiled contracts. The precompile interface follows the pattern established by existing Ethereum cryptographic precompiles (e.g., `ecrecover` at address `0x01` [61]), accepting the public key, signature, and message as inputs:

$$\mathsf{Verify}(\texttt{pubKey}, \texttt{signature}, \texttt{message}). \tag{1}$$

The argument ordering differs from ECDSA's `ecrecover` for two reasons. First, post-quantum schemes do not necessarily support public key recovery from signatures, making the public key a required input. Second, NIST post-quantum algorithms support signing arbitrary-length messages directly [55], so the message appears last in the argument list to allow variable-length inputs. For consistency with ECDSA workflows, many implementations still sign over a hash digest, but the precompile interface accommodates both patterns.

To conform with the algorithm identification principle for crypto agility, the precompile addresses align with the CATX signature type identifiers: `0xCA00xx`, where `xx` corresponds to the signature type (e.g., `0xCA0001` for ECDSA, `0xCA0002` for Falcon-512, `0xCA0003` for ML-DSA-44). A new ECDSA precompile is also provided at `0xCA0001` with the unified argument layout, enabling smart contracts to handle all signature types through a consistent interface. This design supports the *selected* flexibility type: smart contract wallets can verify any supported signature algorithm, allowing users to choose their preferred scheme.

5 Cryptographic Agile Consensus

Consensus layers usually enforce a single and fixed cryptographic signature scheme set at genesis, with all nodes validating at startup to ensure configuration consistency [61]. This approach mirrors the singular flexibility type discussed in Sect. 3.2. However, embedding the scheme in the genesis configuration means that changing the consensus signature algorithm requires a hard fork, creating a significant barrier to cryptographic migration. This migration barrier is particularly concerning at the consensus layer, where a cryptographic compromise does not merely affect individual users, but undermines the entire chain's history.

In this section, we present an extension to Tendermint-based consensus [19] that enables scheme changes via on-chain governance while maintaining consensus safety. The key insight is that transitions between schemes can be coordinated through consensus-layer transactions, allowing the network to migrate to new algorithms as operational upgrades without requiring a hard fork.

5.1 Architecture

The core contribution of this design is the introduction of key registration transactions, which is a new consensus layer transaction type that enables validators to register new cryptographic keys for upcoming upgrades. Unlike EVM execution layer transactions, key registrations are processed entirely within the consensus layer. The proposer includes valid key registration transactions in the block's consensus data, and all validators process them as part of block finalization.

Figure 2 illustrates how key registrations reside in the consensus portion of the block. Validators learn all nodes' consensus keys by deterministically executing the chain state with no additional P2P gossip layer required. The supported consensus signing schemes can include different post-quantum schemes such as Falcon [49], ML-DSA [55], and SLH-DSA [4], although only one scheme is active at any given height as explained below.

Consensus Data	**Execution Data**
`height`	`ExecutionPayload`
`round`	(EVM transactions)
`proposer`	
`validatorSet`	
`keyRegistrations` ←	
`commitSignatures`	

Fig. 2. Block structure with key registrations as consensus layer data, separate from EVM execution data.

5.2 Upgrade Mechanism

The upgrade process involves four phases coordinated through on-chain state. To support this process, the consensus layer maintains two new data structures that track pending upgrades and validator readiness.

Data Structures. The consensus layer maintains a `ConsensusParams` record in chain state to track the cryptographic configuration and coordinate upgrades across all nodes. This record stores the currently active signing scheme, ensuring all validators use the same algorithm for block signatures, and a minimum upgrade delay that enforces a safety window between proposal and activation.

When governance proposes a scheme change, a `PendingSchemeUpgrade` is added to `ConsensusParams`. It stores the target activation height, the new scheme identifier, and a readiness threshold (representing $> 2/3$ of voting power [19]). This record allows all nodes to know that an upgrade is scheduled and track how many validators have prepared for the transition.

Validators signal their readiness by submitting a `KeyRegistrationTx`, which contains the validator's address, their new public key for the target scheme, the upgrade height, and a signature computed with their current consensus key over:

$$\mathsf{Sign}\,(\texttt{oldKey}, \texttt{"KEY\_REGISTRATION"} \parallel \texttt{address} \parallel \texttt{scheme} \parallel \texttt{height} \parallel \texttt{newKey})\,.$$

Signing with the current key proves that the legitimate validator (not an impersonator) is authorizing the transition to the new key.

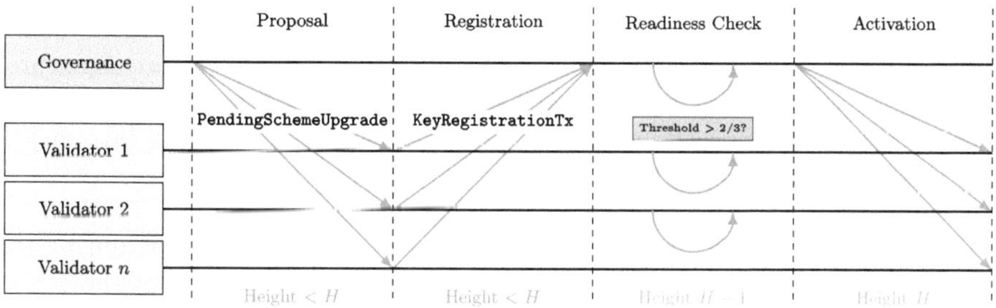

Fig. 3. Consensus layer upgrade mechanism. Governance proposes a scheme change at future height H. Validators register new keys via `KeyRegistrationTx`. At height $H-1$, the protocol checks if sufficient voting power has registered. At height H, the scheme activates and unregistered validators are excluded.

Upgrade Mechanism. The upgrade mechanism is described in Fig. 3 and it is based on the following steps. *(1) Proposal:* Governance proposes a scheme change at a future block height H, setting the `PendingSchemeUpgrade` in consensus state. External coordination is expected before this proposal, particularly for validators using hardware security modules that may require lead time to provision new key material. *(2) Registration:* Each validator generates a new keypair for the target scheme and submits a `KeyRegistrationTx` signed with their current key. *(3) Readiness check:* At height $H-1$, the protocol verifies that sufficient voting power (exceeding the 2/3 threshold) has registered new keys. If the threshold is not met, the upgrade is cancelled. Importantly, the chain continues operating under the current scheme rather than halting. *(4) Activation:* At height H, the consensus signing scheme switches to the new algorithm. Validators who failed to register are excluded from the active validator set; they must restake and follow standard procedures to rejoin.

5.3 Extension

Let us extend the upgrade mechanism to handle edge cases and catastrophic scenarios: emergency migration mode and validator lifecycle management.

Emergency Migration Mode. The upgrade mechanism presented before assumes the current signature scheme remains secure throughout the migration window. However, that assumption might not hold. In that case, signatures can be forged, allowing an attacker to register arbitrary new keys and hijack the whole consensus upgrade mechanism.

To mitigate this issue, we introduce a dual-key system where each validator maintains two independent keys: a primary key for normal consensus, and a recovery key used for emergency migration. The recovery key should rely on a different security assumption than the primary key. Since the recovery key is only used sporadically, we can use a more conservative signature scheme (e.g., SLH-DSA [4]). Then, when governance declares an emergency upgrade the authentication mechanism switches: `KeyRegistrationTx` transactions require signatures from recovery keys instead of primary keys. This design effectively prevents an attacker from hijacking the consensus upgrade mechanism under a broken primary signature scheme.

Validator Lifecycle During Upgrades. The validator set is not static during the upgrade window as validators may join or exist. We need to address both scenarios during a normal and emergency upgrade.

When a new validator joins during a normal pending upgrade, they must provide keys for both the current scheme and the pending scheme. Requiring both keys at onboarding ensures new validators can participate immediately while surviving the upgrade, and their pending key is automatically registered in `ConsensusParams.pending_keys`.

When a validator exits during a normal pending upgrade, their registration state must be deleted and readiness recalculated dynamically. If this exit causes readiness to drop below the 2/3 threshold, the upgrade is automatically cancelled to preserve chain liveness. This dynamic recalculation ensures that the upgrade only proceeds if the current validator set has sufficient readiness, not just the validator set that existed at proposal time.

During emergency upgrades, since primary signatures cannot be trusted for identity verification, validators cannot join and must wait until the emergency upgrade completes.

5.4 Security Considerations

The mechanism addresses several security threats. Insufficient readiness cancels the upgrade rather than halting the chain, preserving liveness. Replay attacks are prevented by including the upgrade height in the signed registration data. Duplicate keys are rejected during validation to prevent voting power inflation. Downgrade attacks intend to make verifiers accept an weaker consensus signing scheme. Assuming honest governance, such attacks reduce to replaying previously issued upgrade artifacts (e.g., a stale `PendingSchemeUpgrade`), which is mitigated because scheme activation is derived deterministically from finalized consensus state at each height and upgrade-specific authentication is bound to the intended activation height (so replays fail). Additionally, upgrade cancellation preserves the currently active scheme rather than reverting, preventing downgrade via propose/cancel behavior.

Additionally, historical verification must be preserved after scheme changes. Old keys must be retained in chain state to verify old blocks since the deterministic replay of chain state ensures this data remains available.

6 Experimental Evaluation

We developed a Layer-1 implementation with CATX integrated as described above. It combines `malachite` BFT consensus engine [24] with Ethereum's `reth` execution client [7]. It provides EVM compatibility with CATX supporting ECDSA, Falcon-512, and ML-DSA-44. All experiments and benchmarks were run in a local 3 node network on an Apple M3 Max with 36 GiB of memory. We also measured SLH-DSA [4] variants (SHAKE-128f and SHAKE-128 s), but report them only in microbenchmarks. In end-to-end experiments, SHAKE-128f began to degrade around 200 TPS and failed at 300 TPS, while SHAKE-128 s sustained only about 16 TPS and proved impractical to benchmark locally due to its 8,576× higher signing cost compared to ECDSA.

In this section, we evaluate the impact of post-quantum signatures on the blockchain performance. Our evaluation spans over 30,000 blocks and 11 million transactions under sustained load, enabling analysis of steady-state behavior. Under these conditions, throughput is limited by three resources: (1) *CPU*, when verification time approaches the 12 s slot limit [61]; (2) *gas*, when the block gas limit is reached; and (3) *block size*, when the block size cap is hit. Identifying the active bottleneck is essential to explain performance differences across signature schemes. We begin with microbenchmarks of the cryptographic primitives to isolate the effects of computation, transaction size, and network propagation on overall performance.

6.1 Signatures Microbenchmarks

We start by establishing a computational baseline through isolated benchmarks. Table 1 reports key generation, signing, and verification times for ECDSA and post-quantum schemes Falcon-512, ML-DSA-44 and SLH-DSA for SHAKE-128f and SHAKE-128 s variants.

We observe that for both Falcon-512 and ML-DSA-44 schemes, signature verification – the dominant cryptographic operation executed by the validating nodes – is faster than ECDSA [40]. These measurements indicate that post-quantum verification does not introduce a computational bottleneck for these two schemes. On the other hand, both SLH-DSA variants exceed the verification latency between 7× and 23×.

Signing costs are higher for all post-quantum schemes, where the SLH-DSA variant optimized for size being the most affected (8,576×). However, signing

Table 1. Public key and signature sizes (bytes) and median cryptographic operation performance (μs) using Rust crate `criterion` [6] with 100 samples and 5-second measurement periods. Values in parentheses are relative to ECDSA.

Scheme	Sizes (B)			Latency μs		
	Public Key	Signature	Total	Key Gen.	Sign	Verify
ECDSA	33	65	98	31	45	51
Falcon-512	897	666	1,563 (16.0×)	4,035	119 (2.6×)	**18 (0.4×)**
ML-DSA-44	1,312	2,420	3,732 (38.1×)	37	165 (3.7×)	**40 (0.8×)**
SLH-DSA-128f	32	17,088	17,120 (175×)	808	19,185 (426×)	1,154 (23×)
SLH-DSA-128 s	32	7,856	7,888 (80.5×)	49,985	385,903 (8,576×)	371 (7.3×)

occurs off-chain and, therefore, does not affect consensus throughput. In addition, key generation is a one-time account initialization cost, which is amortized over its lifetime without affecting performance.

In contrast, signature and public key sizes differ by more than two orders of magnitude across schemes and have a direct effect on transaction size and block utilization. Table 1 summarizes these size differences as well.

6.2 Gas Computation

As mentioned before, gas costs have an impact on blockchain throughput. These are computed from three components: (1) intrinsic gas, a base cost of 21,000 gas per transaction; (2) data gas, charged at 4 gas per zero byte [61] and 16 gas per non-zero byte [8] in transaction data; and (3) execution gas, for operations like signature verification via precompiles.

For signature verification, ECDSA uses a fixed 3,000 gas precompile cost [61], while post-quantum schemes use base costs plus per-message length charges: Falcon-512 requires 1,300 gas base plus 12 gas per 32-byte word of message data, and ML-DSA-44 requires 2,800 gas base plus 12 gas per word. These execution gas parameters are derived by scaling proportionally to measured signature verification times, using ECDSA as the reference.

6.3 CATX Impact

We next evaluate CATX transactions (cf. Sect. 4) under sustained load to quantify end-to-end throughput.

We first investigate the transaction sizes and the gas threshold at which blocks become constrained by the 8 MB block size rather than by the gas or CPU limit, reported in Table 2.

We observe that ECDSA transactions remain far below the data-limited regime under any realistic gas configuration. Falcon-512 approaches data saturation only at approximately twice the current Ethereum gas limits (45 M [25]). In contrast, ML-DSA-44 becomes data-limited within the range of existing

Table 2. Transaction sizes and gas at 8 MB block size limit. B: billion; M: million.

Type	TX size	Data-limited at	Practical impact
Legacy[a]	121 B	1.456 B gas	Never data-limited
Falcon-512	1,622 B	108.6 M gas	~2× current Ethereum config.
ML-DSA-44	3,790 B	46.5 M gas	Below 60 M target

[a] The results for CATX ECDSA and legacy transactions are reported to be equivalent.

Ethereum target parameters (60 M [26]), indicating that block size, not gas or CPU, becomes the constraint.

Next, we present the resulting throughput measurements in Table 3, allowing us to identify the dominant bottleneck for each transaction type. The CATX transaction format introduces no measurable overhead: ECDSA achieves the same throughput as legacy EIP 1559 transactions, with both ultimately limited by the slot time. Falcon-512 maintains high throughput despite significantly larger signatures, operating near the transition between gas- and size-limited regimes. In contrast, ML-DSA-44 exhibits lower throughput because blocks reach the 8 MB size limit before exhausting the available gas.

Table 3. Transactions per second (TPS), gas and block size consumption, and the primary performance bottleneck for legacy `0x02` and CATX transaction types.

Type	Peak TPS	Sustained TPS	Gas%	Size%	Bottleneck
Legacy	4,021	3,963	19%	1%	CPU
ECDSA	4,032	3,964	22%	2%	CPU
Falcon-512	3,730	3,212	78%	72%	Mixed
ML-DSA-44	2,210	1,880	46%	**100%**	**Block size**

This behavior arises from the fact that overall transactions per second (TPS) is directly determined by transactions per block (TPB) and blocks per second (BPS): TPS = TPB×BPS. At the extreme, although ML-DSA-44 accommodates more transactions per block due to larger block sizes, the slower block production rate dominates, yielding lower net TPS. Figure 4 highlights the negative correlation between block size and block production rate across all evaluated signature schemes. Hence, faster cryptographic verification does not translate into higher system throughput once block propagation becomes the limiting factor.

For completeness, exploratory end-to-end runs with SLH-DSA showed that SHAKE-128f reached only around 200 TPS, whereas SHAKE-128 s was not practical to benchmark because signing is 8,576× slower than ECDSA.

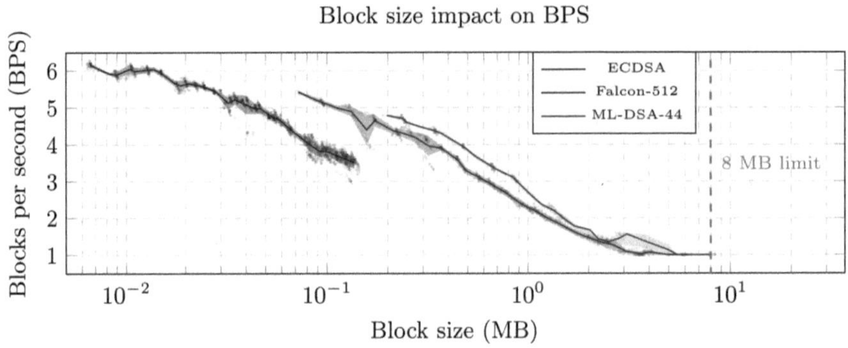

Fig. 4. Block size impact on BPS. Error bands show ±1 standard deviation. Based on observation from a live blockchain node (aggregated into 15-s windows), showing BPS behavior when each scheme dominates block production (ECDSA: 2,294 windows; Falcon-512: 1,104 windows; ML-DSA-44: 493 windows).

7 Conclusion

This work takes a concrete step towards cryptographically agile blockchain infrastructure by showing that cryptographic scheme changes, specifically transitions to post-quantum algorithms, can be introduced as operational upgrades without requiring hard forks, while preserving EVM compatibility and operational continuity. Our evaluation reveals an important shift in system bottlenecks (cf. Sect. 6): although post-quantum signatures such as Falcon-512 verify up to 2.83× faster than ECDSA and sustain 3,200 TPS (≈80% of baseline), and ML-DSA-44 reaches 1,900 TPS (≈47%), throughput becomes constrained not by computation but by block size and network bandwidth. These results highlight that future post-quantum blockchain designs must optimize for bandwidth efficiency as much as cryptographic performance.

This bandwidth pressure extends beyond the transaction layer into the P2P communication layer, where existing protocols impose tight size constraints that post-quantum schemes cannot satisfy through simple algorithm substitution. Discovery protocols such as Discv4 [31] rely on UDP gossip packets constrained to 1280 bytes (the IPv6 minimum MTU) [39], while Ethereum Node Records (ENRs) [44] are limited to 300 bytes. Since post-quantum signature schemes require transmitting both signatures and public keys, unlike ECDSA which supports public key recovery, they would exceed these limits, making a direct transition infeasible without protocol redesign. Exploring alternative authentication mechanisms for discovery protocols that preserve post-quantum security while respecting existing packet size constraints remains an important direction for future work.

Acknowledgments. We thank our reviewers for their helpful feedback and Léo Ducas for valuable comments.

References

1. Secure hash standard (2015). https://doi.org/10.6028/nist.fips.180-4
2. SHA-3 standard:: permutation-based hash and extendable-output functions (2015). https://doi.org/10.6028/nist.fips.202
3. Digital Signature Standard (DSS) (2023). https://doi.org/10.6028/nist.fips.186-5
4. Stateless hash-based digital signature standard (2024). https://doi.org/10.6028/nist.fips.205
5. The great quantum disconnect: Why web3 knows about quantum, but doesn't care (yet) (2025). https://www.tectonic.xyz/blog/the-great-quantum-disconnect. Accessed 01 Feb 2026
6. criterion: A statistics-driven micro-benchmarking library for rust. https://docs.rs/criterion/latest/criterion/ (2026). online documentation. Accessed 05 Feb 2026
7. Reth: Ethereum full node implementation. https://github.com/paradigmxyz/reth (2026). online documentation. Accessed 13 Feb 2026
8. Akhunov, A., Sasson, E.B., Brand, T., Guthmann, L., Levy, A.: EIP-2028: transaction data gas cost reduction (2019). https://eips.ethereum.org/EIPS/eip-2028
9. Algorand: State proofs overview. Algorand Developer Portal (2024). https://developer.algorand.org/docs/get-details/stateproofs/
10. Algorand Foundation: Post-quantum technology (2024). https://algorand.co/technology/post-quantum
11. Baird, L., Harmon, M., Madsen, P.: Hedera: a public hashgraph network & governing council (2020). https://files.hedera.com/hh_whitepaper_v2.2-20230918.pdf
12. Baldimtsi, F., Chalkias, K., Roy, A.: Post-quantum readiness in EdDSA chains. Cryptology ePrint Archive, Paper 2025/1368 (2025). https://eprint.iacr.org/2025/1368
13. Barker, E., et al.: Considerations for Achieving Crypto Agility: Strategies and Practices (2025). https://doi.org/10.6028/nist.cswp.39
14. Bernstein, D.J., Duif, N., Lange, T., Schwabe, P., Yang, B.Y.: High-speed high-security signatures **2**(2), 77–89 (2012). https://doi.org/10.1007/s13389-012-0027-1
15. Bitcoin Community: Bip-360: Pay to tapscript hash (p2tsh). Bitcoin Improvement Proposal (Draft). https://bip360.org/bip360.html
16. Bitcoin Core Developers: BIP 32: Hierarchical Deterministic Wallets. Bitcoin Improvement Proposal (2012). https://github.com/bitcoin/bips/blob/master/bip-0032.mediawiki. Accessed 09 Feb 2026
17. Bitcoin Core Developers: Disclosure of cve-2018-17144 and bitcoin core 0.16.3 patch (2018). https://bitcoincore.org/en/2018/09/20/notice/. Accessed 05 Feb 2026
18. Boneh, D., Lynn, B., Shacham, H.: Short Signatures from the Weil Pairing, p. 514–532. Springer, Heidelberg (2001). https://doi.org/10.1007/3-540-45682-1_30
19. Buchman, E., Kwon, J., Milosevic, Z.: The latest gossip on BFT consensus (2018). https://doi.org/10.48550/ARXIV.1807.04938, https://arxiv.org/abs/1807.04938
20. Buchmann, J., Dahmen, E., Ereth, S., Hülsing, A., Rückert, M.: On the security of the Winternitz one-time signature scheme, pp. 363–378 (2011). https://doi.org/10.1007/978-3-642-21969-6_23
21. Buchmann, J.A., Dahmen, E., Hülsing, A.: XMSS - A practical forward secure signature scheme based on minimal security assumptions, pp. 117–129 (2011). https://doi.org/10.1007/978-3-642-25405-5_8
22. Buterin, V.: Ethereum: a next-generation smart contract and decentralized application platform (2013). https://ethereum.org/en/whitepaper/

23. Buterin, V., Conner, E., Dudley, R., Slipper, M., Norden, I., Bakhta, A.: Eip-1559: fee market change for eth 1.0 chain (2019). https://eips.ethereum.org/EIPS/eip-1559. Accessed 05 Feb 2026
24. Circle Internet Financial, LLC.: Malachite: Flexible bft consensus engine in rust. https://github.com/circlefin/malachite (2026). online documentation. Accessed 13 Feb 2026
25. CoinDesk: Ethereum block gas limit reaches 45 million units (2025). https://www.coindesk.com/tech/2025/07/21/ethereum-validators-signal-intention-of-upping-gas-limit-to-45m/. Accessed 05 Feb 2026
26. Cointelegraph : Ethereum block gas limit raised to 60 million units (2025). https://cointelegraph.com/news/ethereum-validators-push-gas-limit-60m-scaling. Accessed 05 Feb 2026
27. Drake, J., et al.: Hash-based multi-signatures for post-quantum ethereum. Cryptology ePrint Archive, Paper 2025/055 (2025). https://eprint.iacr.org/2025/055
28. Ethereum Community: Eip-2718: Typed transaction envelope (2019). https://eips.ethereum.org/EIPS/eip-2718. Accessed 05 Feb 2026
29. Ethereum Community: Eip-4337: Account abstraction using alt mempool. Ethereum Improvement Proposal (2023). https://eips.ethereum.org/EIPS/eip-4337
30. Ethereum DevP2P: Rlpx transport protocol (2016). https://github.com/ethereum/devp2p/blob/master/rlpx.md. Accessed 05 Feb 2026
31. Ethereum DevP2P: Node discovery protocol v4 (discv4) (2019). https://github.com/ethereum/devp2p/blob/master/discv4.md. Accessed 05 Feb 2026
32. Ethereum Foundation Privacy & Scaling Explorations: Post-quantum cryptography and ethereum (2025). https://pse.dev/projects/post-quantum-cryptography
33. Ethereum Research: Poqeth: Efficient post-quantum signature verification on ethereum (2024). https://ethresear.ch/t/poqeth-efficient-post-quantum-signature-verification-on-ethereum/21554
34. Ethereum Research: Tasklist for post-quantum eth (2024). https://ethresear.ch/t/tasklist-for-post-quantum-eth/21296
35. Fukuda, K., Matsuo, S.: Post-quantum blockchain: Transition landscape amidst evolving complexity. Cryptology ePrint Archive, Paper 2025/1626 (2025). https://eprint.iacr.org/2025/1626
36. Gayoso Martínez, V., Hernandez Encinas, L., Sánchez Ávila, C.: A survey of the elliptic curve integrated encryption scheme. J. Comput. Sci. Eng. **2**, 7–13 (2010)
37. Gentry, C., Peikert, C., Vaikuntanathan, V.: Trapdoors for hard lattices and new cryptographic constructions. In: STOC 2008. pp. 197–206. ACM (2008). https://eprint.iacr.org/2007/432
38. Giechaskiel, I., Cremers, C.J.F., Rasmussen, K.B.: On bitcoin security in the presence of broken cryptographic primitives, pp. 201–222 (2016). https://doi.org/10.1007/978-3-319-45741-3_11
39. Internet Engineering Task Force: Internet protocol, version 6 (ipv6) specification. RFC 8200 (2017). https://www.rfc-editor.org/rfc/rfc8200.html. Accessed 05 Feb 2026
40. Juaristi, P., Agudo, I., Rios, R., Ricci, L.: Benchmarking Post-quantum Cryptography in Ethereum-Based Blockchains, pp. 340–353. Springer, Cham (2025). https://doi.org/10.1007/978-3-031-82349-7_23
41. Kate, A., Zaverucha, G.M., Goldberg, I.: Constant-Size Commitments to Polynomials and Their Applications, pp. 177–194. Springer, Heidelberg (2010). https://doi.org/10.1007/978-3-642-17373-8_11

42. Kwon, J., Buchman, E.: Cosmos: A network of distributed ledgers (2016). https://github.com/cosmos/cosmos/blob/master/WHITEPAPER.md
43. Lamport, L., Shostak, R., Pease, M.: The byzantine generals problem. ACM Trans. Program. Lang. Syst. (TOPLAS) **4**(3), 382–401 (1982)
44. Lange, F.: Eip-868: Node discovery v4 enr extension (2018). https://eips.ethereum.org/EIPS/eip-868. Accessed 05 Feb 2026
45. Lopp, J., Papathanasiou, C.: Post quantum migration and legacy signature sunset. Bitcoin Improvement Proposal (Draft) (2025). https://qbip.org/
46. Menezes, A.J., van Oorschot, P.C., Vanstone, S.A.: Handbook of Applied Cryptography. CRC Press, Boca Raton (1996)
47. Meng, L., Chen, L.: A blockchain-based long-term time-stamping scheme, pp. 3–24 (2022). https://doi.org/10.1007/978-3-031-17140-6_1
48. Nakamoto, S.: Bitcoin: A peer-to-peer electronic cash system (2008). https://bitcoin.org/bitcoin.pdf
49. Prest, T., et al.: FALCON. Technical report, National Institute of Standards and Technology (2020). https://csrc.nist.gov/projects/post-quantum-cryptography/post-quantum-cryptography-standardization/round-3-submissions
50. QANplatform: QANplatform: A Quantum-Resistant Hybrid Blockchain Platform (2026). https://qanplatform.com/. Accessed 04 Feb 2026
51. Rescorla, E.: The transport layer security (tls) protocol version 1.3. RFC 8446, Internet Engineering Task Force (2018). https://www.rfc-editor.org/rfc/rfc8446
52. Sato, M., Matsuo, S.: Long-term public blockchain: resilience against compromise of underlying cryptography. In: 2017 26th International Conference on Computer Communication and Networks (ICCCN), pp. 1–8. IEEE (2017). https://doi.org/10.1109/icccn.2017.8038516
53. Shor, P.W.: Algorithms for quantum computation: Discrete logarithms and factoring, pp. 124–134 (1994). https://doi.org/10.1109/SFCS.1994.365700
54. Smith, C.: Quantus network whitepaper, version 0.3.1 (2026). https://github.com/Quantus-Network/whitepaper. Accessed 05 Feb 2026
55. of Standards, N.I., (NIST), T., Dang, T., et al.: Module-lattice-based digital signature standard (2024-08-13 04:08:00 2024). https://doi.org/10.6028/NIST.FIPS.204, https://tsapps.nist.gov/publication/get_pdf.cfm?pub_id=958463
56. Stevens, M., Bursztein, E., Karpman, P., Albertini, A., Markov, Y.: The first collision for full SHA-1, pp. 570–596 (2017). https://doi.org/10.1007/978-3-319-63688-7_19
57. Szepieniec, A., Værge, T.: Neptune white paper (2025). https://neptune.cash/whitepaper. Accessed 05 Feb 2026
58. The QRL Foundation: Qrl: The quantum resistant ledger whitepaper (2018). https://github.com/theQRL/Whitepaper
59. The Quantum Insider: Solana takes a step toward pqc era with quantum-resistant vault (2025). https://thequantuminsider.com/2025/01/04/solana-takes-a-step-toward-pqc-era-with-quantum-resistant-vault/
60. Wang, X., Yu, H.: How to break MD5 and other hash functions, pp. 19–35 (2005). https://doi.org/10.1007/11426639_2
61. Wood, G.: Ethereum: A secure decentralised generalised transaction ledger (yellow paper) (2014). https://ethereum.github.io/yellowpaper/paper.pdf. appendix B: Recursive Length Prefix (RLP)
62. ZKNoxHQ: Ethdilithium: Dilithium signature for ethereum (2025). https://github.com/ZKNoxHQ/ETHDILITHIUM. Accessed 05 Feb 2026
63. ZKNoxHQ: Ethfalcon: Falcon signature for ethereum (2025). https://github.com/ZKNoxHQ/ETHFALCON. Accessed 05 Feb 2026

Poster Abstract

Post-quantum Discovery as a Governance Capability: Evidence-Based Cryptographic Visibility and Exposure Prioritisation in a Critical Service Provider

Jelena Zelenovic(✉), Leila Taghizadeh, Edoardo Pena-Gonzalez, Jaime Gómez García, and Bart Preneel

COSIC, KU Leuven, Kasteelpark Arenberg 10 Box 2452, 3001 Leuven, Belgium
jelena.zelenovic@student.kuleuven.be

Abstract. Post-Quantum Cryptography (PQC) readiness is increasingly constrained not by algorithm availability, but by cryptographic visibility, dependency complexity, and fragmented governance. This paper presents an anonymised case study of a large European critical service provider that initiated PQC readiness through a discovery-first strategy, utilizing tool-supported cryptographic inventorying to establish an evidence-based baseline prior to migration planning. The discovery phase revealed systemic challenges, including distributed cryptographic ownership, uneven evidence quality across legacy and modern environments, and high dependency on third-party cryptographic roadmaps. To operationalise these findings, the organisation introduced a structured exposure register that enabled prioritisation based on asset criticality, confidentiality longevity, and migration feasibility. We argue that PQC discovery should be understood as a governance capability that stabilises organisational knowledge and converts cryptographic uncertainty into measurable accountability, supporting risk based decision-making and ecosystem coordination. The results contribute actionable lessons for institutions pursuing crypto-agility and resilience under post-quantum "harvest-now, decrypt-later" threat models.

Keywords: Post-quantum cryptography · governance · crypto-agility · resilience

1 Contributions

The contributions of this paper are threefold:

The first three authors contributed equally to this work as co-first authors. The authors write in a personal and academic capacity. The opinions expressed are solely their own and do not reflect the views or positions of their employers.

D. Loebenberger and M. Stöttinger (Eds.): MAgiCS 2026, CCIS 3002, pp. 211–212, 2026.
https://doi.org/10.1007/978-3-032-28946-9

- We propose a discovery-first methodology to establish cryptographic visibility across heterogeneous and distributed technology estates, positioning discovery as a measurable, repeatable, and auditable governance capability rather than a one-time technical inventory exercise.
- We introduce a structured exposure register model that enables risk-based asset prioritization across multiple dimensions, including systemic criticality, confidentiality longevity, long-term integrity and authentication assurance, and migration feasibility. While confidentiality durability is a primary driver in many post-quantum cryptography (PQC) transition scenarios, we explicitly account for systems characterized by extended operational lifecycles with predominant integrity and authentication requirements. This includes, for example, embedded and field-deployed upgrade or firmware validation mechanisms that may remain operational for 15–20 years or longer, in contexts where post-deployment cryptographic modification is technically constrained or operationally infeasible.
- We present empirical observations from a large-scale real-world case study, demonstrating that ownership fragmentation, variable evidence confidence levels, and supplier dependency chains represent primary structural barriers to PQC migration and broader crypto-agility adoption.

Acknowledgements. This work was supported by the Flemish Government through the Cybersecurity Research Program with grant number: VOEWICS02.

Disclosure of Interests. The authors have no competing interests to declare that are relevant to the content of this article.

Author Index

D. Loebenberger and M. Stöttinger (Eds.): MAgiCS 2026, CCIS 3002, p. 213, 2026.
https://doi.org/10.1007/978-3-032-28946-9

FSC
www.fsc.org

MIX
Papier aus verantwortungsvollen Quellen
Paper from responsible sources
FSC® C105338

If you have any concerns about our products,
you can contact us on
ProductSafety@springernature.com

In case Publisher is established outside the EU,
the EU authorized representative is:
Springer Nature Customer Service Center GmbH
Europaplatz 3, 69115 Heidelberg, Germany

Printed by Libri Plureos GmbH
in Hamburg, Germany